M000102820

The Political Optimist

The Restoration of Common Consent

Keith R. Kelsch

Vision Impact Publishing
St. George, Utah
http://www.visionimpactpublishing.com

To those willing to taste the waters of truth and stem the tide of a hypocritical world, now is the time of great knowledge, the kind that is not set to destroy but rather to quench the thirst of those ready to understand. This book will not help those who look to control others or to seek riches of great honor. Instead, this book will help those willing to correct our misguided thinking about leadership and how we should organize and self-govern ourselves.

Samuel Louis Dael

The Political Optimist

The Restoration of Common Consent

Printed in the United States of America

Second Edition

ISBN 978-0-9827313-5-2

About the Author

Keith R. Kelsch

For over thirty years Keith has worked in higher and secondary education, community non-profits, and business development. Keith is a powerful presenter for improving genuine optimism through greater consent in business, community and in government. A former actor in Hollywood with a Bachelor of Arts from California State University Northridge, Keith later obtained his Master of Arts from Humboldt State University in the teaching of writing. He completed his PhD in American Studies from George Wythe University and teaches at Dixie State University. He is a licensed general contractor at www.kelschconstruction. com and co-founder of www.localcommonwealth.org, along with his wife Malissa A Kelsch. You can see Keith on his weekly podcast at www.thegenuineoptimist.com, where his focus is on removing political gridlock in corporate and community cultures using the principles of common consent.

Appreciation

The completion of a challenge is like putting a long journey to bed, and like Ulysses said at the end of his journey, "I am part of all that I have met." This book is no exception.

To Malissa, for carrying so much weight through extremely difficult times. There is no other person who truly made this book possible.

To my children, Kaden, Kyler, and Makinzie, thanks for letting me write this book at a great cost.

To my father, collaborator and captain, Ronald Louis Kelsch, and my mother, Dori Kelsch, for her encouragement. I was given the best parents.

To Naomi Wolf and Jeannette de Beauvoir for their experienced advice at the start and at the finish. Both helped to get rid of the heavy academic. And to John Allen and Randy Thompson, first readers and tough critics, thanks for your help.

And to the many students, friends and family who told me to change the world, let this book measure up.

Cover design Richard Isom of Vive Studios

If you pretend to be good, the world takes you very seriously. If you pretend to be bad, it doesn't. Such is the astounding stupidity of optimism.

Oscar Wilde

Table of Contents

The Restoration of Common Consent 2

Appreciation 4

About the Author 4

Cover design Richard Isom of Vive Studios 4

Introduction 8

Section I The Politics of Optimism

Our Denial of Fear 12

Political Fear 12

Our Mortal Fear 16

The Real Meaning of Fear 20

Final Undressing 25

The Staged Optimist 30

Seeing the Political Ones 30

The Real Art of Acting 34

The Use of Deflection 39

All Energy, No Spark 47

Definition Par Excellence 51

The Intimidating Optimist 56

Defining Intimidation 56

The Enjambment 64

Standing in Dissent 72

The Optimism of No 80

Intimidation in Hierarchies 83

The Irrational Optimist 86

The Stubborn Mind 86

The Magic of Irresponsibility 93

Momentum of Enthusiasm 96

Faith vs. Magic 100

More Clarity 104

Section II The Genuine Optimist

Our Responsible Faith 114

A Step Forward 114

Understanding Faith 118

The Believing Optimist 124

This is Work 124

Like Chuck 126

Linear Verses Relational 134

The Encouraging Optimist..**140**
What is Encouragement?.. *140*
The Rough Edges.. *140*
Smooth Edges... *145*
Dissolving the Left-Right Paradigm............................. *151*
The Principled Optimist...**158**
The Progression of Optimism..................................... *158*
The Principle of the Tree of Life *166*
The Conservation of Responsibility.............................. *173*

Section III
Restoration of Common Consent

Personal Responsibility..**180**
Political Idolatry.. *180*
A Vision from Our Own Minds................................... *188*
The Discussion Gap *192*
The Enemy to Personal Responsibility......................... *196*
Cutting out the Middleman.. *200*
Sowers of Discord Everywhere *202*
Social Responsibility **206**
Community... *206*
Iron Bubble.. *212*
The Scale of No Return... *215*
The Collective and the Individual............................... *221*
Social Justice vs. Social Contract *225*
The Optimism of Common Consent..............................**230**
Sugar and Water.. *230*
The Insidious Whole of Big Institutions *234*
Restoring Natural Leadership *237*
Round Tables, Long Halls, and Open Forums.............. *239*
The Restoration of Common Consent........................... *243*
Looking at the Numbers Realistically *247*
The Ideal of Common Consent *250*
Last Word.. *253*
Index **260**

Introduction

A political optimist imposes confidence from an elitist distance. They are outside consultants telling you how to handle an inside crisis. They look and sound close, but in truth, their heart is far from you. They charge the air with their capital success without any attempt to understand your concerned mind. In a way, greater success separates the political person from the responsibility of genuine optimism.

Modern motivational self-help is to blame, in part. We emphasize political distance from any open dissent. This is because we treat disagreement with disdain, as if all dissent is negativism. We even say that a politically correct democracy without open dissent improves the workplace, the community, and the family. In truth, the silencing of discussion is politicalized optimism; it feeds on our worship for authority at the cost of losing our agency.

Today we use the distance of success to magically detach us from the burdens and disagreements others carry. This is opposite the leader who carries those burdens and openly stands to be questioned. At every turn, political optimists produce top-down, centrally controlled organizations with no access to rise against their authority. This model places leadership at a greater distance from a genuine democracy of dissent.

Written for those who struggle with political people, you will love *The Political Optimist*. It promotes the safeguards of "being real" as a counter measure to "being political." It teaches how we must stand to be corrected while still questioning authority.

If you want to know the difference between political people and genuine optimists, this book explains it all. The answer requires that we give relational thinking equal footing to the linear mind. This will undoubtedly challenge central power structures everywhere. It will also change everything we have been taught about leadership.

The solution to a political world is nothing new but something lost. *The Political Optimist* highlights our lost humanity for optimism and calls for a return to the oral traditions of common consent.

It is time we see democracy stripped of coercive controls. It is time for the best of democracy to rise in common consent and to see it scale in both modular and horizontal form. If there is one thing this book will do, it will ignite a long overdue discussion about democracy.

Section I The Politics of Optimism

...history is the career of a frightened animal who has to deaden himself against life in order to live. And it is this very deadening that takes such a toll of others' lives. *Ernest Becker – Escape From Evil*

Have you seen a pack rat? This is a person who piles up stuff that they never use or properly dispose of. It is like a political pack rat, which is a person who piles up supposedly important connections purely to advance their own status.

Compare a pack rat to a packhorse. A packhorse carries the load whereas a pack rat hoards the load. Most people are either a political pack rat, or they are a packhorse. Pack rats are political. Pack horses are not.

Political pack rats collect power and position but they never use or properly dispose of power. In other words, they never give power to those below or to the side. Because their focus is directed toward a power source above them, and often at a distance, they are hard to read. Even worse, they never carry the load like a packhorse.

Therefore, if you want to learn how to read political people and attract more pack horses into your organization, this section of the book will help you.

As in all things rebellious, some undressing will need to take place. We need a bit of bravery within each of us to say openly, "The optimist has no clothes."

To those afraid of speaking in public, we often say, "imagine the audience is naked." Why not say, "Imagine the speaker is naked."

It is just as helpful to see those in leadership undressed and naked, as it is to see the audience naked. It may be the only way to stop the destructive worship of authority over our own minds.

Learning to read political people requires that we see them naked on stage when most remain captivated by their show. When we undress the political person, we quickly see staged acts, underhanded intimidation, and irrational energy. All three attract political pack rats in great numbers.

The *Political Optimist*, as we will find, is sometimes one and sometimes all. They can destroy entire nations and collapse a thriving corporation. If there is one thing alone that will save your business and make for a better society, learning to read political people is that one thing. The second is learning how to deal with them.

When we undress the political person using a fake optimism to cover a hidden intent, we see the same underlying problem that every human confronts, namely a lot of repressed fear.

1

Our Denial of Fear

We will reexamine a word that has been all but forgotten, but should be resurrected into its rightful and dominant position in our lives. That word is an unabashed, unqualified, and resounding "NO." It is what this book is all about.

Donald G. Smith *How to Cure Yourself of Positive Thinking*

Political Fear

In the Seattle airport, a couple decided to opt out of walking through the Transportation Security Administration's naked body scanners. They refused to have their bodies scanned with what they believed to be harmful levels of radiation. In addition, they didn't like their naked images viewable on a monitor, something they considered an intrusion of their privacy. Immediately after the couple vocalized their dissent, forty others standing in line suddenly lifted their heads—as if the wicked witch from the Land of Oz was finally dead—and they decided to opt out of the intrusive scanning technology as well.

The optimism of speaking your own mind in public doesn't seem acceptable to most people because of the fear of social rejection. You can hide in a uniform of authority or you can come out from behind yourself and confront the uniform.

Most people hide, while less than five percent of the population will choose to reveal their true mind to the powers over them. This is why it's so hard to read political people; most are too eager to speak the accepted view above in order to keep others from reading their true thoughts below. A genuine optimist doesn't care about what is accepted. They expect only to have the freedom to listen and to speak. In a personal history written by my father, the following excerpt from his biography explains the problem now pervasive throughout all of society:

> A newspaper suddenly fired its ad director. The replacement was younger and typically more positive. Knowing the political play from experiences in the newspaper industry in another state, I came to the paper overqualified and did my best to imply no interest in management and preferred a low-level sales position. Most would easily feel threatened by someone having thirty years of experience. To fit into a sales job required very little politics.
>
> Then the classified manager left. I applied for his job, thinking all was politically stable. The new ad director asked in the interview, "I understand you did not want a management position?" I sensed, for the first time, my concern for political play in business. I indicated my enthusiasm for this particular company. For whatever reason, other than my expressed views, age or experience, I became the classified manager and did an outstanding job in management as well as continuing in sales. Concluded by no other reason than an increase in sales, I became popular.
>
> I received several nice raises, but the raises were too liberal for the size of the paper. They just built a new building and the artificial cleanliness they required did not match the newspapers previously known. Something seemed amiss or someone was trying to impress another? Political play was surfacing.
>
> Then they fired the new ad director and so I applied and took his position thinking he was the problem. Political play did not end and I should have seen it coming when they hired a human resource executive trainer. So polished, he fooled everyone into thinking he cared. Every manager was learning a cleaver system of employee reviews that seemed to advance everyone to some level of incompetency to justify subtle intimidation to seek employment elsewhere.
>
> Not very long after, I was out the door by my own choosing. Companies go to great lengths to achieve specified results. Companies spend millions on special advisors, consultants, and ideas thought to be more sophisticated but they design

a form of musical chairs employment by highly energized individuals who know how to downsize successfully.

I began to see how everyone moved up and eventually out. All replacements came from our sister newspapers. The next generation came in with a smaller salary. Methods became political ploys in the name of honest value. I witnessed this many times before. In every case, the business eventually closed or sold after infestation of strange human resource policies.

In the next employment interview I vocally stood up to these practices and I was hired and still found a very different system of false honesty. I finely retired from the metropolitan rat race at the age of 48 and started at the bottom again with a family manufacturing business in a small town where I grew up. Again, I worked up to the top and finely retired at sixty-five. I continued as an advisor until the business collapsed under a political system of intellectual dishonesty.

We don't live in an environment of skilled, hardworking, and honest individuals. We live in a political landscape that comes from the need to satisfy power centers and formulaic models in order to retain positions of control. We call this being political. However, in truth we should call this Political Optimism because the real skill of being political is all about falsifying optimism. You see, everyone loves an optimist because an optimist by definition is someone who says this is the best of all possible worlds. They generally appear more happy and content with life. If you want people to fall in line with your power and position of control, all you have to do is convince the majority in any room that what you have is the best of all possible worlds. If just enough agree, usually 51%, the debate is over and what we see is by default the best of all possible worlds.

Imagine taking an idea in a certain direction down the road and you come to an intersection. You are trying to find the best of all possible routes to a certain goal. In order to reach your destination you are faced with turning left or right. How do you make the decision to turn left or right? The answer is you don't make the decision by yourself. You ask a fellow driver or pedestrian. You start bringing in outside input that you do not have by yourself. One person alone may have a great idea, but alone one person cannot find the best of all possible routes to launch an idea in a business, a community or a nation.

Unfortunately, political optimists work like a virus: they can infect decisions at various intersections in life with staged acts, impressive intimidation and they can even redirect with irrational new magic, but the virus just gives a new name to "this is the way" or "I have the answer" without outside input. We accomplish nothing and produce moles that excuse themselves from hard work, honesty, and vision. When intimidation begins to set in, procedures from politically derived solutions take control. Often labeled a *policy* or a *procedure* toward a nebulous authority, they demand adherence rather than allow the ideal of a wider consent to rule.

Conventional wisdom says that if you pay more, you will obtain better teachers, managers, and CEOs. This is a fallacy. Studies actually indicate that human nature performs better through appreciation rather than higher pay. Sadly, political optimists inject sophisticated change in order to justify more control and higher pay, while honest responsibility becomes intimidated and eventually leaves the political arena. It would be wise if human resource managers could first determine whether an employee manifests political tendencies, usually measured in superficial success.

In the process of interviewing people to hire, here's a trick for finding political people. Juxtapose a sense of justice against personal responsibility when you interview candidates. Ask a management applicant to comment on whether employees respond better to appreciation, higher pay, or better controls. Those seeking more money and more power tend to be more political, and they'll offer more controls as a solution—because that's what linear minds do. This is especially evident when they emphasize their methods for control over the encouragement of ideal consent. A skilled interviewer will recognize political optimists and refuse to hire them.

Skills and experience are important, but a passion for control has become the downfall of many corporations.

Political optimists create an aura of staged trust, but when good judgment is required, the interviewer sees the political applicant talk in terms of applying intimidating force through adherence to policy and authority. Rather than allowing the voice of consent to take the lead, the intimidating optimist employs staged acts, intimidation and charismatic energy to assume leadership.

This book will change your mind about leadership. What many political opportunists reveal may appear upbeat and justified, but in truth, they are playing to the power centers above them and to the side. A power center can be a single person or a minority able to dominate a majority. In every case, they discredit the real optimism of dissent that democracies fail to embrace.

This book will reveal the difference between being *political* in optimism, which is linear and much like a pack rat, and being *genuine* in optimism, which is relational and much like a pack horse. A linear mind says, "let's vote and let the majority decide." A relational mind says, "let's discuss until we can reach a consensus." Once we understand the difference, we can solve the many political issues of our time and especially the inherent problem of idolatry toward central authority that all democratic majorities hoard in one place. To solve this problem, we must first admit to the universal influence of human fear in our models of control. From here, we can see the problem inherent in all majority-rule organizations.

Our Mortal Fear

There are two characteristics seen in all political optimists. One *manifests* power, while the other seeks the acceptance of authority through *administering* that power. People advance because their subjects support them. The controller seeks acceptance of his subjects, and the subjects in turn lust for acceptance by worshiping the controller and hoping for some benefit. The two work together in what we call "adulation engineering." This is where one person serves the whims and desires of another in order to advance and get gain. It is like befriending a very spoiled person from a wealthy family. Never at any time does anyone challenge or question real fears in this person because this could threaten any possible reward. Political optimists seek after some kind of reward, and you can see this in their need for attention, obedience, and self-gratification.

Social structures built on these rewards foster idolatry, which is the worship of people we place over us or what the majority too often follow. So why not say the truth—a bureaucracy is itself the idolatry of authority? Idolatry happens because one seeks honor with power and position, while the other seeks acceptance of the power center. Both are idolatrous, and each scratches the other's back to gain a benefit.

Keep in mind that political power adds to the need for acceptance; it never diminishes it. The higher controller has to be honored in order to advance your own position. If not this, you must be willing to stand alone and take their ridicule and become genuinely optimistic. To hide fear in the name of self-protection just to advance in power does nothing to create a better world.

By way of a personal example, I'll tell you when I first glimpsed my own fear. It happened when panic met responsibility for the first time.

I was up reading the night before, so I woke up late on this particular morning; I was eighteen and tired. Outside my window, a garbage truck began making its rounds, and the sudden realization came upon me that some day, I, too, would become garbage—that I would die.

I felt paralyzed by the thought and also by the requirement of getting up, getting out, and getting on with the day. The concepts fused into one thought, avoiding responsibility reminded me of death. Sleeping in was no longer a lovely time of diminished responsibility; the garbage trucks' noise interrupted it.

The book I'd been reading late into the night was Ernest Becker's *The Denial of Death*, a book my father had given me to read two days before. Reading this book certainly had something to do with waking up to such weighty thoughts!

For the next year, I read everything written by Ernest Becker, including *Angel in Armor*, *The Birth and Death of Meaning*, *Beyond Alienation*, *The Structure of Evil*, and finally *Escape From Evil*. If any of his books were out of print, I found them at a university library and checked them out with no intent of returning them. I was a thief for the complete written works of one man. Then something happened; the responsibility to wake up became the responsibility to know more.

Becker inspired me to study Otto Rank, because he referred to Rank throughout his writings. For twenty years, Rank was one of Sigmund Freud's closest colleagues and did more for psychology than history has been willing to recognize. This is why Becker dedicated his last book to Rank: because he told the truth about human fear.

Next on the reading list was Otto Rank's *Art and Artist*. My awakening became permanent. In this book, Rank wrote about the artist's struggle to self-create a life's value in the work created. Once success is reached, the artist too often pollutes a life of creative expression with over-the-top behavior to grab that same attention once easily obtained and now craved. Without this attention, it is as if the artist were dead. This is where many fail as artists: they become lost the moment they pervert their art to overcome their subconscious anxiety about life and death. If the word subconscious bothers you, then replace it with *the under mind*.

Because of Earnest Becker and Otto Rank, not even a garbage truck could disturb my day. By that time, life had become one long morning. As Hamlet said to his mother, I was "too much in the sun."

A few years later, while other students in my college psychology class were reading Adler, Jung, and Freud, I was reading Rank, Becker, and Shakespeare. Every night, these authors provided light to my hungry mind. From then on, I preferred relational understanding, no matter how hard to swallow, over linear conclusions. I could never master being political. I was doomed.

Shortly after this year of awakening, I started interpreting literature, movies, and human behavior through the psychology of fear inspired by Becker, Rank, and Shakespeare. I quickly set aside the vain pursuit of studying to be an actor in Hollywood: I had some minor accomplishments, but my conceit didn't allow me to continue. I was used to showing a certain level of confidence to the world, but I was so aware of feeling afraid that I couldn't keep up the façade. I was at the same time fascinated by those who were able to put on a good show despite their fear. A lifelong study of optimism was born.

We often believe that everyone can see the real fear inside, that we cannot hide this fear. Even with several years of professional training in acting, my fear was too much in the forefront of my mind for me to act as if it wasn't there. To make matters worse, I became very jealous of those who could.

Odd as this may seem, the person who is more aware of their own insecurities is not skilled in hiding them. However, the same person is often a far better employee, because they are far less political, despite seeming far less optimistic and less confident in first-impression interviews. This happens because their fear is at the surface. They get the job based on the positive referrals of others—almost never on their own. Their optimism is not quick to see, but rather it comes to the surface more slowly, and only after a lot of intimate discussion and close relation building. Because of an inherent nature to serve others, many people saw me as a better worker than most others. I was a packhorse by nature. However, this took time to see. It was never a quality you could see in a first impression. I always got the job on the recommend of others who knew me, and almost never from a blind interview.

Living a genuinely confident life doesn't *look* optimistic on the surface. Take a naively honest person, for example: it's impossible for them to put on a show when they are aware of the falseness in their own actions. It actually bothers them inside when they try to be phony in front of others; they look and behave unnatural almost all the time in public. Over time, such a person becomes either an introvert—or a crusader. They appear odd because their under mind and conscious mind are always drawing closer and closer together. Political people are always pushing their two minds apart.

Meanwhile, the public fails to recognize genuine optimism because most move with the collective by blending in with a one-sided mind, or the expected way of living. This is why the genuine optimist sees the accepted way as political and phony, or as I say in this book too linear. Moreover, because they cannot blend in, they look awkward. Because their fear rises to the surface, they do not appear optimistic. It is time we read fear better; otherwise, the greater potential for leadership will always fall to the political.

The Real Meaning of Fear

When talking about fear, most people avoid words like *deeper* and *subconscious,* even though those words sound impressive. They avoid them because the terms do not convey an honest meaning of fear that makes sense with experience.

For example, fear isn't a concrete noun—like Frisbee, fries and French toast. Instead, fear is an abstraction such as faith, freedom and friendship. You can't touch the abstract. Unlike items in the physical world that are easy to grasp, fear is the most difficult of all abstract words to get a hold of. We know this because fear affects all of all us deeply and in surprisingly different ways. It is something in the under mind that rises to the conscious mind.

Take a young girl who reaches under her bed in the dark to grab a toy and suddenly feels a large cat bite her hand. She pulls her hand out in panic and begins to cry. Is fear the palpitation of the heart? Is fear the excessive secretion of adrenalin upon being startled? Is fear the bleeding from the bite marks? The truth is that fear comes from *how we react to symbolic meaning*. We react to what events and things *mean* rather than to the events and things themselves.

The best way to understand how fear works is to see how we place a "symbol" before the mind at the time we "experience" a close encounter with life rejection or physical death. From that time forth, whenever we meet the symbol, our *psyche* or *under mind*, because it computes in a straight-line linear path, feels the terror of death or the terror of rejection in life. When Steven Spielberg produced *Jaws*, beaches around the world suffered a huge drop in tourism. The image of swimmers alone in the ocean stimulated the frightful image of a great white beneath. This is a linear conclusion without relational facts.

Why do rejection and death become so paramount? The psyche, or subconscious, has no eyes, ears, or other senses to determine the difference between the symbol and the real thing. We are dealing with the logic of intelligence and not the brain's ability to interpret the five senses.

For example, the symbol of a gun is equivalent to the experience of death. If a person is fascinated with guns, they may be covering their fear by trying to see how close they can come to death and live. We call this denial, and it's a product of linear thinking, a way to push away the under mind far away from the conscious mind. If a person honestly respects guns, they may be called upon to save a life or defend against a tyrannical state. This very important difference comes with conscious understanding, which is part of relational thinking rather than linear thinking. However, the subconscious psyche doesn't think logically until the individual begins to see their true self. Only then can people give symbols a true meaning and gain control of their full minds.

For example, sickness symbolizes death. A lack of affection symbolizes rejection. Poverty can symbolize both rejection and death. Any bit of data (or symbol) conditions one to respond as if the real thing is happening. This means the psyche does not respond to real things as much as we might think: instead, it reacts to *symbolic representations*.

We can correct the meaning of these symbols by removing the false cover and revealing the real source of our fear. Even though sickness may symbolize death, sickness itself is not death. The conscious mind corrects the strangeness of the subconscious. We can do this if we understand ourselves. If not, we're prisoners chained to the back of our minds.

Perhaps it's simplistic to use the example of a child frightened by a cat: but consider how easy it is to make symbolic connections of meaning. A boy came home late one summer night, entered the side door of the garage in the dark, and reached in to turn on the light. There by the light switch, just inside the garage door, something wet touched his hand. He lost his breath and fell to his knees. He couldn't run or scream; he was literally paralyzed for a few seconds until he could get to his feet and run around to the front door.

The next day, on a sunny afternoon, he peeked into the garage and found a grass catcher from the push mower hanging over the light switch and filled with wet grass from the day before. He imagined something completely different, and for several years after he still feared reaching into a dark room to turn on a light.

Some might argue that this is what fear is. Being afraid to walk into a dark garage to turn on the light is only a re-experience of something symbolic in the mind connected by prior events or ongoing perceptions. The dark garage doesn't scare us; the meaning of what touches us in the dark is what is terrifying.

Fear is something in the mind that promotes the discomfort we feel; it's *linear*. However, the more we know about the stuff in the back of the mind, the less we fear: it's *relational*. Not surprisingly, the latter is when we become less political as well. Fear is the significant meaning we give to what we experience, and symbolic fear happens when we come close to rejection or death. The symbols are different for every person.

When the boy reached in the garage to turn on the light, he thought that a monster was grabbing him, and monsters kill. He failed to recognize his own fear in his own head. This is what makes human character so dynamic; we all symbolize fear differently, and the taproot of all fear inevitably drinks from the twin fears of rejection in life and entropy in death.

The lifelong intensity of fear begins to change, however, with real human trauma. Consider a young man on the field of war smelling and seeing decomposing body parts. Consider the condition of a married woman suffering from breast cancer and a husband who abandons her and her three kids. Now let's ask ourselves what these situations mean *symbolically*.

Consider corporate management circumventing your best efforts at excellence by raising employees to an ever-higher level of incompetence just to avoid lawsuits attached to dismissal. Imagine the thousands of straight-line linear connections we make every day. Do we see real death, real rejection, and real failure? Perhaps we only see a psychic image of death that, to our mind, is the real thing. It doesn't matter whether we get it through loss of life, social criticism, or the political pressures placed on us; fear becomes the symbolic linear conclusion we give to life experiences.

If we could envision this kind of depth, then a psychology of fear would loom larger than any academic clinical analysis. The clinical view may even be itself a form of denial—an easy escape from the real responsibility of dealing with fear. Just look at how we favor Freud who gave us an external cause of fear rather than an internal symbolic motive illustrated by Rank. If you disagree, read Freud's *Civilization and Its Discontents* (1930) and then read Otto Rank's *The Trauma of Birth* (1929); you'll quickly see that while Freud gives us an outside social excuse for not taking responsibility, Rank reveals our essential inner responsibility to life. Freud's version is linear thinking suggesting a cause-and-effect result that fosters non-relational deductions with no internal honesty. Many college professors teach using this approach. Rank's version shows relational thinking based on psychological concepts, promoting more self-conscious human beings. This version promotes better leaders, because people must become more aware to add value. This is contrary to the political optimist, who is not aware—and seldom, if ever, adds value.

The point is that we often say that fear comes from social, genetic, and political pressures outside our own subconscious. This explanation never highlights the denial present in the political bully, who uses denial to avoid taking responsibility. He is linear in his thinking, and this keeps him from standing up to his own inner fear. The bully will create situations to show his daring so he can come out alive without facing any real responsibility.

All responsibility is relational. Denial is linear, and linear thinking is the very reason a teenager dares to spark-fly a skateboard down the metal railing of three flights of concrete stairs. He enjoys the exhilaration of coming out alive and not the actual act itself. He rejects responsibility toward good judgment in exchange for a false heroism. Relational thinking employs wisdom, clear meaning, and most importantly responsibility. Linear thinking isn't responsible: it is, at best, mere tunnel vision.

The growing number of blood-and-murder suspense thrillers, in novels and on television, provide a similar tunnel vision. They allow us to look upon decay and death—to stare them in the face—and see how close we can get to gruesome morbidity and still feel alive. This is the denial of our fear created to help us avoid taking greater responsibility in relation to others. Marketing firms live by it; movie houses profit from it; politicians spread the discord that inflames more denial; and motivational speakers and success pushers sell this lame heroism as true optimism.

If we could see genuine, non-political people in the value they add, we could see better candidates to hire, better partners to marry, and better leaders to support. If we can't see the truly genuine, we are blind and we fall prey to more central control and more executive distance with more vertical power structures.

These grotesque models of control attract the political optimist and snub the genuine human being.

In order to avoid a false show of optimism to hide our internal fear, we must realize that actual experiences with death and rejection are one thing; the significance in meaning we give them is quite another. Most people talk about the experience itself, whereas genuine optimists talk about the meaning we give those experiences. Fear is the significance in meaning we give to rejection and death.

We can come close to death through a few encounters, but too many narrow escapes can place the personality into catatonia and perhaps even schizophrenia. General neuroses of all kinds may result when the individual carries too many symbols, or when one symbol carries too many terrors. *Fear is therefore a reaction to conditioned, symbolic representations and not necessarily to things themselves.* We fear the meaning of things, produced from linear conclusions, rather than the real things themselves. Most of academia will disagree because it's lost in the sophistication of its own denial.

All political optimists are blind to their fear—and that makes them the most irresponsible among us. Not seeing these political optimists creates destruction, and we don't see them because we first can't see our own fear. When we can finally see who we are, we can see the political optimist in staged performances, doing upbeat intimidation, and promoting irrational enchantments. All of these actions are attempts to deny responsibility in ways that appear magically optimistic.

Final Undressing

We spend millions every year hearing one motivational speaker after another spew the same political optimism that shuts down public access to real motives. If we could truly sit with these speakers and talk with them in our own living rooms, we would find their true hearts, something that never happens in any kind of public venue. As long as they remain a success

figure, their motives will also remain private and inaccessible—
and we'll continue to idolize them for it.

This doesn't mean that there's no value in motivational
inspiration; it just means that without knowing true motive
behind that inspiration, it's hard to believe. Genuine optimists
have a hard time accepting what is said at a distance and
removed from personal discussion. As a result, they are labeled,
blacklisted, and pushed aside. They're told to "be political" or
they are told their attitude "sucks."

If you place both the political with the genuine in the
same room, and if you make them reach one hundred percent
agreement on one thing, you might be surprised to find how
much leadership and success dogma that the politicos teach is
wrong. The problem with human interaction is not always about
attitude. As we will see, it's mostly about freedom.

The problem is that we're dealing with political people
who have separated themselves from genuine access: there's
no real freedom to question them. It is not so much that we're
dealing with our own inadequacies—rather, we're dealing
with political personalities who refuse to confront our honest
expressions. This is why people say, "You need to be political."
It's the same as saying, "You need to hide your real mind."

In the first part of this book, we'll talk about three
types of political optimists and their inability to show belief,
encouragement, or principle. They're completely inaccessible as
human beings. Like chasing a rainbow, as you move in, they
move away. At a distance, they constantly remain aloof while
always appearing as if they are close.

Before we undress these political optimists, we must first
consider two concepts that will help us better recognize why
political people play to our perception without making a real
connection.

The first concept is that political people *do not add value*.
Secondly, political people refuse to talk about the *meaning of
things* in both public and private.

Think about both *value* and *meaning*. We fail to read political people because we don't see real value—there's no real meaning. We no longer gather and discuss things and work out differences to enable a common consensus of meaning that everyone can accept. This is the only way we can see value in a relational context. Instead, we listen to central authorities tell us what to think in a straight-line linear feed loaded with all the tools of charisma, rhetoric, magic, intimidation, and the newest control model employed.

Let's communicate it this way: Political optimists use forced mental expectations that place pressure on others and themselves to mask personal fear. We find this in just about every motivational teaching out there. It becomes abusive and turns outward onto others when used without securing the most powerful expression of optimism—the freedom of dissent. You can see this abuse when we pass our responsibility over to the person or people asserting leadership authority.

Take a manager who says to an independent-minded employee, "It's time we synergize as a team." The phrase seems harmless, until the employee ends up in a department completely outside his skills. Expressions used in an attempt to appear progressive often come from someone politically groomed to cover their real intent. In other words, a position swap takes place between two people in the company.

The positive expression "it's time we synergize as a team" can cover the real intent of the manager, which is to silence one employee because the pressure of his independent mind reminds the manager of his absence of ideal consent. The manager keeps his own position protected by diplomatically keeping any better methods from surfacing that might threaten his control. Common sense might call this political meandering. Even more confusing is that neither person wants the swap to take place. While one expresses dissent against "it's time we synergize as a team," the other goes along to get along.

The genuine optimist inevitably quits, and certain staff members—those favored by the manager in charge—advance into the vacated slots with no attempt to cross-train them. The phrase "it's time we synergize as a team" is a positive mental exertion used for subversive intents. It's a linear approach to destroying relational minds.

Because of their destructive natures, and because they don't add value, it's time that we read political people better. It's time for us to see their false optimism in three types: as the staged performer, the upbeat intimidator, and the irrational peddler of magic that attracts gullible people. We call them political optimists because they reject the freedom to dissent (which is relational in understanding), and they use in its place a potent denial of fear seen in their worship of authority (which is linear). Their idolatry toward authority escapes the natural and responsible form of democratic consent. This is most apparent in the first political type, the one we call the **staged optimist**.

When we are young we are often puzzled by the fact that each person we admire seems to have a different version of what life ought to be, what a good man is, how to live, and so on. If we are especially sensitive it seems more than puzzling, it is disheartening. What most people usually do is to follow one person's ideas and then another's depending on who looms largest on one's horizon at the time. The one with the deepest voice, the strongest appearance, the most authority and success, is usually the one who gets our momentary allegiance; and we try to pattern our ideals after him. But as life goes on we get a perspective on this and all these different versions of truth become a little pathetic. Each person thinks that he has the formula for triumphing over life's limitations and knows with authority what it means to be a man, and he usually tries to win a following for his particular patent. Today we know that people try so hard to win converts for their point of view because it is more than merely an outlook on life: it is an immortality formula. *Ernest Becker – The Denial of Death*

2

The Staged Optimist

When it comes to optimism, there is no need for a
performance. Optimism is not a show we perform. When
someone makes it a show, that person is on life's stage only
to project himself into the audience. This optimism does not
entertain, it does not teach, and the actor is not believable.

Samuel Louis Dael

Seeing the Political Ones

Staged optimists follow trends rather than the developed
insight within themselves. They pretend to have a life full of
vitality, but in no way express a vision of value. They remain
stuck with common and clichéd verbiage derived from
acceptable fashion and not responsible focus. They demonstrate
smooth language, but they keep from questions by taking upon
themselves the central entertainment fixture. While at center
stage, they deflect criticism by being obtuse just to give a poise
of confidence. In the more common vernacular, they maintain a
rock star presence. In truth, it is the same old executive distance.

My first encounter with a staged optimist came in
college while working as a host for a French-cuisine restaurant
in Westlake Village, California. It was a fine-dining restaurant
where we prepared the food table side, including fresh Caesar
salad with smoked chicken, Dover sole cooked in white wine,
and bananas foster fired in sweet liqueur. My uniform was a
freshly pressed tuxedo, polished black shoes, and manicured
hands; the clientele, for its part, was new money.

The maître d' was Richard, a twenty-eight-year-old handsome MBA graduate from the University of Spoiled Children (a name those who attended UCLA gave to their rival USC). The subsequent tension inspired conflict over sports rivalries and explained my built-in dislike for Richard.

Richard connected with new people, but he never sustained that connection over time. He was the spitting image of Frankie Avalon, the teen heartthrob and singer/actor in the sixties who co-starred in several beach movies with Annette Funicello. With dark curly hair cut short, a small frame, and a tailored uniform, Richard had the same transient energy as Frankie. Every moment was a beach party. His first impression was his best impression, which seemed to crash within a week or two of every new relationship.

The floor captain, also called the lead waiter, was just the opposite. His name was Mike and he loved food and people, and it showed in his happy, blotchy face. Personal and one-on-one, he built a kindred relationship with everybody, especially over time.

The difference between these two men surfaced not so much in the impressions they left as much as the richness in human connection that Mike had and Richard did not. Everyone gravitated toward Richard, while it took more time to know Mike.

First impressions can promote a false optimistic feeling in others. It's like the first time you meet a cotton-candy cheerleader at a high-school football rally: she's bubbly and delightful at first, but without the deepness of meaning expressed in one's quality of life, these superficial first impressions disappear in time. Eventually this same person stands naked in front of you in their raw insecurity. This is why a political optimist eventually disappears like warm breath in the cold night air. In the cotton-candy analogy, the fun and energy were there—and then they're gone.

This quick disappearance of energy does not describe real optimism, which has to comprise lasting human value. The two men I referenced above taught me this. One lived a life of show; the other lived a life of service. Richard was linear and a political pack rat for the newest groupie to follow him. Mike was relational and a packhorse always willing to carry a friend.

When I was hired to host, Richard gave me specific instructions to overbook the reservations and to keep the tables filled—with guests waiting in the hotel lobby. The reservations were booked exactly as he told, but at a loss of quality service. This was felt particularly by Mike, the floor captain. Mike didn't appreciate being slammed with multiple tables at once, and so he complained of it: "You're putting me in the weeds," he said to Richard.

After a few weeks of working with this indiscriminate management, Mike quietly approached the host station when he saw Richard leave to talk with some teenage girls dressed in miniskirts and loitering in the hotel lobby. Mike quickly grabbed a pen and added several names to the reservation book. While putting a small dot near the end of each name he told me, quietly, "This is quality control." When Richard returned, he saw the reservation book filled, and assumed the restaurant was booked for the night.

From then on, I doctored the reservations on my own, under Mike's approving eye. It was a weird feeling of autonomy that stuck with me for life, and it came from an experience that felt like a negative act against the coercive pressure of a shortsighted boss. I was nineteen and I was running the floor.

Political optimists do not allow others to run things on their own. This is why life was great at the restaurant, until Mike took a job in Hawaii and Richard moved me to a busboy position and hired a few scantily dressed girls to run the reservation book. Richard lived in the hotel and gravitated toward new and attractive people, always taking center stage everywhere he went. He captivated new friends every few weeks, and his marriage lasted only six months. It was amazing how quickly people came and went in his life. When intimate human contact caught up with him—which actually happened rather fast—life became difficult as new people started to see the hollowness inside. This is why we dislike unnatural salespeople so much: they live in the world of performance and avoid walking off-stage to show who they really are.

Within months, the restaurant closed and Richard left to open another new establishment. Before his departure, service crumbled, experienced employees left, and a better job for me opened at a German restaurant in Santa Monica. While working with some great waiters—and learning German on the side—it took a good year to realize that the "staged optimist" is difficult to spot because we too often measure people as optimistic on a first impression. Because of the energy of the staged optimist, genuine people have become a fading flower as we stumble over political liveliness as optimistic repeatedly. As long as we continue to promote the worship of a first impression, we'll never get a backstage pass to real human life.

I had a strong sense of loss when I left. I knew that I would miss my friendship with Mike: he was beautifully genuine amidst so much that was not. Mike offered me my first chance to *think* on the job. He also loved to talk about the meaning of things. He had a natural affection for discussion and inspired the best quality in others, things found only in open dialogue.

Discussion anchors the mind to all things honest and builds lasting depth needed in art, business, government, and in our religious and family ties.

Once you realize how staged optimists maintain a constant cheerleader performance on and off-stage, it becomes more painful working around them. They avoid showing any genuine emotional range. I'm not saying that they need to be gloomy—they just need a steady stream of honesty about who and what they are. If optimism includes honesty, then only in discussion with others can we see the real stuff, what we call empathy, logic, personal responsibility, patience, and friendship. Without these qualities, we lack real connectivity. Soon the staged optimist has nothing of value to show, and nothing of themselves to offer. Not showing your real stuff when people could sure use it is being politically optimistic, the way many make a living on their performance and not on any value added. In fact, most political people give the real art of acting a bad name.

The Real Art of Acting

Truly great actors use bits and pieces from their own lives to make their performances real and accessible to themselves and to others. It's not just performance *on the surface*; the real stuff eventually *rises to the surface*. This translates into something believable to the audience. Skilled actors listen to other characters, and they react from their own emotional and intellectual responses. This is what is meant by the phrase "acting is believing." Orson Wells put it best when he defined the art:

> ...acting is like sculpture, in other words it's what you take away from yourself to reveal the truth of what you are doing that makes a performance. A performance, when it deserves to be considered great or important, is always entirely made up of the actor himself, and entirely achieved by what he has left in the dressing room before he comes out in front of the camera. There is no such thing as becoming another character by putting on a lot of makeup. You may need to put on the makeup, but what you are really doing is undressing yourself. And even tarring yourself apart and presenting to the public that part of you which corresponds to what you are playing. And there is a villain in each of us, a murderer in each of us, a fascists in each of us, a saint in each of us, and the actor is the man or women who can eliminate from himself those things which interfere with that truth.[1]

Can you imagine actors today talking like that? Acting is not a false notion that you *are* the character (staged optimism) but that you *believe in* the character (genuine optimism). When you truly believe in something and are willing to show it from the depths of your own soul, you stand in the raw skin of who you really are. You are actually revealing something of yourself rather than hiding behind a façade. A genuine and believable actor has enough stability in his or her own life to make the character believable to others. This exemplifies the art of true acting, to display on stage something about you that helps others believe in a character on paper. Some call this acting against the grain. It means undressing much of your real life in order to reveal a new character. If Hollywood truly understood the real art in acting, we would not have so much personal insecurity intruding upon the actor's performance.

Unfortunately, this is exactly the case with the staged optimist as well as the many bad actors in Hollywood. They execute a strict routine without thought. They energetically telegraph their reactions and they express absolutely nothing of themselves in doing it. In the entertainment business, they're known as bad actors; in real life, they're what we call staged optimists. They are predictable and never in the moment, because they're not listening to anyone—when someone is talking to them, they're preparing their next line.

You'd actually be surprised to learn how many well-known celebrities and politicians perform like this. You can tell them apart by their lack of the real mental and emotional improvisational skills demanded of them in challenging theatrical scenes and in answering unscripted questions in the open public.

Because teleprompters have replaced the need to respond to questions on the spot, fewer and fewer people actually take questions anymore. Too many leaders cannot improvise and move into real meaning. Improvisation is an oral tradition of constant dialogue in the home, with friends, and within one's community. It's the only and best way to check against pride, idolatry for authority, and logical fallacies of all kinds. Here are ten fallacies committed by political optimists all the time. Each is defined to the right. **See Figure 2-1**.

Take any person raised in an environment where they receive challenging questions daily, and compare that person with someone who approached learning through a linear path.

Fig. 2–1 Fallacies Defined

Fallacies	Fallacy Defined
Red herring	Evasion
Slippery slope	Assumption
Circular reasoning	Restating in different words
Oversimplification	Ignorance
False analogy	Contradiction
Equivocation	Lazy defining
Ill-founded generalization	Unjustified conclusions
Non sequitur	Faulty causal connections
Ad homonym	Personal attack of a person

While the relational person born out of discussion is ready to lead others, the person on the linear book-learning path struggles with leadership and a lack of vision. What is disturbing, as we will find throughout this book, is that the majority of the population is linear and not relational. This is no fault of their own. It is just that we are mostly born into a linear society.

Those raised on conversation always try to reach a consensus. A book never questions any assumptions a reader makes in private. Therefore, what the reader concludes from reading is never tested in open discussion. Even an education based on classics that doesn't incorporate intensive discussion tends to promote more linear minds that learn from published authority. An education based on constant questioning and open discussion, where information does not become a matter of fact implied by some power center, will yield relational consensus.

Look at the education of Thomas Jefferson. As a young man in his early teens he studied under a mentor, George Wythe, along with several others. They would read great classics and show up to talk about what they read for hours. In private they kept a commonplace book of thoughts to further build on their ability to relate the content to their own mind. There was no lecture, just an open table of discussion. Who would have thought that such an education based on a discussion of classics would have produced a statesman who would later draft *The Declaration of Independence*? Do you think Henry David Thoreau wrote *On Civil Disobedience* without any adversarial challenge? Even Benjamin Franklin constantly engaged in discussion, and the famous dialogues of Socrates are derived from pure discussion. Ralph Waldo Emerson and Thomas Carlyle conversed overseas for years via written dialogue.

Just as bad actors never receive training in the use of improvisation, a poor leader lacks the experience of confrontation and taking questions in the open. Just reading a book doesn't mean we are able to question its conclusions. Once, I purchased a used copy of a groundbreaking book that won the Pulitzer Prize for general nonfiction. A previous reader had marked it up, and every written comment showed this reader's ignorance. Had others been there during the reading, they could have questioned the conclusions written in the margin. Linear minds never engage in confrontation, so they lack the relational skill found in the genuine optimism that I'm referring to in this book, the kind that lives by intimate human interaction. If we continue to believe a book is richer in content than a conversation with living human beings, we will continue to reject the agency of each other as valuable in our lives. Superiority and elitism will continue to separate those with a deep reading list from those with questions to ask.

The author and physicist Samuel Louis Dael has an incredible reach into religious studies, psychology, epistemology and philosophy. His own writings are derived from keeping a question alive through three generations of discussion in his own family and from friends. Compare that to the average scholar today who derives his or her work from countless published works and from the most recent peer-reviewed articles. Where is the open challenge from all walks of life and over a longer period of time? No wonder innovation is stifled in academia.

Camera angles, editing, loud music and hidden teleprompters with adjusted lighting all mask a lack of depth and understanding. In the political arena, the staged optimist avoids real discussion and never enters the open forum of dissent against their own authority unless it has become popular to do so, and always on safe turf of their choosing. The bigger the audience with a popular focus, the less they need to show anything real and genuine. However, when it gets intimate and when the questions are pointed at them, they avoid these real situations. "All the world's a stage" to these political optimists. The minute we take this stage away, the target is wide open, but only if we dare question their motive.

Staged optimists have learned exactly how to perform without believing in anything. This explains the rise of so many politicians who rhetorically speak like passionate leaders without the will to engage in reaching a wider democratic consent. They perform without belief. As Orson Welles said, they refuse to show that special truth to which they "subscribe their entire soul."

The staged optimist doesn't like to sit around and talk about the meaning of things. This reveals internal emptiness, which is why they live for the public stage—removed from the close proximity of prying eyes. However, with enough open and intimate talk (face-to-face if possible), and certainly over time and from many third party witnesses, they reveal their true nature. It always takes time to spot them, and herein lies the rub.

For example, a handyman arrived at my house. When he entered, he was full of energy and quick to talk up a storm. This is the best way to spot a staged optimist: they talk themselves up as the main attraction. Hired to do sheet-rock and finish work, this handyman surprised us by behaving lewdly toward my wife. He had nothing of value that he truly believed with his whole heart; he was an empty pervert and a dead giveaway as a staged optimist. It took time, private access to his empty head, and observation from others to see his hidden drive. His perverted over-confidence didn't keep him on the job. It got him fired. Back then, it took three days for me to recognize the situation. Now it's immediate.

It would be great if we could apply the same real-time scrutiny to public figures. If they could sit in our living rooms or in a local neighborhood forum, and if we could listen to their responses to questions and comments posed by our parents, our spouses, even our children, then certainly everything would surface—and be teleprompter-free! Talk-show hosts have lost this art of honest questioning, and reporters no longer have an independent voice that seeks clear answers. For this and many other reasons, people accept the idea that the outward projection of self-confidence is optimism. Without having to reveal what they truly believe, these linear minds exemplify the staged optimist.

Because we all love confidence and smiles, we're easily seduced by every new performance that comes along. Unfortunately, most of us cannot see real people until we can get them to talk about real things. This is how we find motive and meaning in human character: we engage in open discussion without a controlling figure telling us what and how to think. A relational context reveals those people who do not operate inside one.

We must prefer common consent to executive control. By not requiring consent around public expressions of meaning, staged optimists get to hide their motives behind the executive desk. We can change this by demanding more discussion and by slowing the process, allowing individual expression of dissent. It's the only way to make thoughtful reflection work. The first Lincoln Douglass Debates between Abraham Lincoln and Stephen A. Douglass were conducted in many locations. The format for each debate started with one candidate speaking for 60 minutes, then the other candidate speaking for 90 minutes, and then the first candidate was allowed a 30-minute "rejoinder." The debates were later published in their long format in the local papers for readers to follow.

Today, political people are not thoughtful, which is why we need a better model. We will soon find that common consent organized by a greater degree of social discourse will keep political optimists from exercising deflection.

The Use of Deflection

Staged optimists do not like to talk about the meaning of things. They live for the public stage, removed from any questioning. It takes skill to spot them, and this is the challenge: the only way to see them is to understand how they deflect answering questions.

Staged optimists fight against dissenting voices, while a genuine optimist listens to find additional facts. Staged optimists move the conversation to a politically corrected topic to avoid any dissent. They sometimes apply defensible indifference when the conversation gets a little too thick in real meaning, and they avoid a personally invested conviction by pulling a gag. You can see this when they deflect their lack of depth by politely walking their audience through rude laughter. We think they are smart and witty when the intent is to draw the attention back to them. The mastery of deflection keeps others from seeing one's lack of understanding.

Look at the former vice-president of the United States, Al Gore, who said (regarding the politicized alarm around global warming): "The debate is over." It's very odd that a baby boomer would say such a thing. Rather than argue global warming, which later became climate change, it's more optimistic to say, as John Stewart Mill said, "The silencing of discussion is an assumption of infallibility."[2]

Consent has to come out of agreement and not out of assumed authority. For instance, Gore advocated imposing a tax on carbon emissions—but where was the discussion that asked, "who gets the carbon tax, and what will it be used for?" He made every effort to shut down dissent on climate-change skeptics in order to shut down those who would speak against a carbon tax. We don't all have the time to dig to find a speaker's motive, so we accept the polished act without seeing that the staged performer has a hidden agenda. For instance, according to The Telegraph on November 3, 2009, "Al Gore could become the world's first carbon billionaire." It made sense for him to sell the idea of a carbon tax to help support his investments in green energy companies.[3]

Staged optimists deflect all dissenting voices that might reveal that hidden agenda. It will always be easier to spot someone shutting down dissent than it will be to follow the money, so it's a first clue.

We never know the silent intent of the staged optimist serving some power center behind the scenes. Even the best of us fall into the trap of following authority because we have learned the skill of deflecting away any responsibility to question them. When England imposed a stamp act on all manufactured products and textiles made in America before the revolution, the real motive was to limit the industrial power America was gaining over England. The use of the tax in America and not equally applied in England deflected attention away from that political truth.

So what did the colonists do in response? Did they attack the industrialists in England working behind the scenes to shut down America, or did they shut down their idolatry for a king? They went after the king. By shutting down the king, they shut down the unjust tax. Read *The Declaration of Independence* and note how it lists abuses by the King that were done to maintain central control—all to bolster the wealthy in England.

Most of the time, political optimists use deflection as part of an argument for some good, but this implied good simply means more control. The staged optimist says, "Give me all the power, the honor, and the money, and I'll show what great works I can do." We only hear brief clips of these staged optimists' speeches; and there's often no honesty in them. If these unquestioned promoters organized a small discussion where everyone had an equal opportunity to speak, we would come to know the truth faster through more open consent than what we get through mass media's subliminal narrative.

Staged optimists truly hate questions from an opponent; it's why seemingly optimistic narratives hide behind controlled presentations written for our supposed good. When these false optimists make fantastic statements such as, "we must save the earth," the statement covers their real motive, and all we see are the deflective words encouraging us to trust them. With blind trust, we remain unable to undress their theatrics.

Deflecting the issue with a fantastic statement shows how a staged optimist can avoid any confrontation that might reveal some underling motive. They hide behind optimistic statements thanks to the word associations employed. We cannot debate *must, save,* and *earth,* because ideas that are desirable deflect the mind from the truth—in this case, the desire for control over the world's natural resources.

"Everyone has a right to affordable health care" is another optimistic deflection. *Everyone, right,* and *health* again deflect us from the motive of large insurance corporations desirous of gaining control over every healthcare transaction.

At one time, we broke up monopolies. However, when they became legalized, we lost control by empowering corporate control. Free enterprise no longer survives. All that we have left is a bloated government that has lost its heart to stand against crony powers that have grown greater than its own.

It was no surprise to see President Obama employ that same rhetoric when speaking of his healthcare act when he said the debate "is and should be over."[4] This is odd, since there never was a debate. When you have one side of the political aisle vote for a bill, and the other side vote unanimously against the same bill, this isn't a debate. A lack of consensus is a direct lack of real freedom in discussion.

A classic deflection was the *fat-free diet,* which has an additional component: deflection by association. For many years, food processors had trouble preserving the shelf-life of processed foods. Ever since pasteurization and homogenization became the norm in dairy products, larger corporations sought to eliminate fat from foods in order to extend the shelf-life. A medical doctor came along at the perfect time and said, "Fat causes heart disease." This was a perfect deflection, allowing marketing campaigns to remove fats from products, increase the shelf-life, and sell the by-product to animal feed producers (or have more fats, like butter, to sell). Since then we've learned that pasteurization kills enzymes, making milk an allergic product for many people. Most recently, even heart specialists have actually stated that Omega 3 fatty acids can help heart patients. We now have the common knowledge of good fats versus bad fats. Despite this, the public mind still thinks fat equals a fat tummy.

We will not see the truth for many years because of our lust for cheap, highly processed foods. Few people understand the body's ability to convert empty calories into fatty tissue. Statistically, weight gain has increased substantially since fat-free starches have become the new staple. This isn't a conspiracy: it's the central control model of linear thinking that moves food processing away from smaller communities to larger processing plants. Improved transportation has also centralized production and empowered massive corporations, subliminal mass media, and more government control.

The problem is that the community is falling apart because it has lost all culture for local conversation. National advertisers have replaced local dialogue, and gossip is a social network post. If you are a person who follows a lot of alternative media and from many different sources, just try to strike up a conversation with those who still get their information from one or two mainstream outlets. It is fast becoming clear that we're losing touch with our neighbors. The whole world has become a virtual landscape of political optimism.

We've come to the point of no return because we think, "authority knows best" rather than allowing "free and open discussion to decide." The first is linear and centralizes all responsibility; the latter is relational and decentralizes responsibility. We no longer have to see, learn, and understand as long as a doctor in a white lab coat does it for us.

Silencing discussion and dissent, in time, becomes the linear mission of centrally controlled authority. We are fast becoming a generation that learns to hide our mind—a fundamental trait of staged optimism. Notice the traits of a Staged Optimist to the right aligned with characteristics to the left. We call each horizontal line item a *character trait*. When it comes to the character trait of idolatry, the staged optimist is driven by glory. They demand the reward of attention and their intelligence is defined by social position and not by their ideas or their value added. We will apply the same characteristics to the traits of all political optimists. A unique distinction will surface when we use the same characteristics to reveal the traits of genuine optimists. The only difference is that the word *faith* better describes the traits of genuine optimists and the word *idolatry* best fits political optimists. **See Figure 2-2**.

Fig. 2-2 Traits of the Political Optimist

Character	Traits
Idolatry	Seeks Glory
Intelligence	Glory in Position
Agency	Disobeys Truth
Motivation	Desires Honor
Reward	Demands Attention

We have talked about deflection and its use through association. Another, more classical method, is deflection through a change in meaning. The earlier use of *the right to affordable health care* is a perfect example. The word *right* is under assault. Compare it with *the right to bear arms* or *the right of free speech,* which indicate a freedom to possess, perform, or admonish. The progressive statist has changed the meaning of the term *rights* to force our responsibility onto another, and often this means a bureaucratic agency without your consent.

Bigotry and discrimination have inspired many people to get involved in civil rights, but in time, we've chosen to accept a new direction of incremental government control. Built to mask the hidden intent, these political optimists call themselves progressives to deflect from their statist agenda. Odd as it may seem, progressives are just another form of force. Through national government force, we trade our local freedom for some demanding social justice at a distance. Constitutions may guarantee civil liberties (the right to life, liberty, and privacy), but not a personal right to take from the government. Today there is more interest in demanding more personal rights than in any effort to preserve civil liberties. This has to do with the linear thinking of political optimists. Let me give an example.

Imagine a wealthy community with higher property tax revenue to support their education and imagine a poor community not having enough revenue for education. The progressive statist will seek to equalize funds between communities. With this approach both communities lose consent in how they educate. The statist mind never looks at equality of rights between individuals in a community, which is what a constitution protects, but instead the statist wants to solve the inequality between communities and even whole groups. Today in our modern era, now the statist wants global equality with absolutely no local consent.

Only in preserving civil liberties first can we promote personal and social responsibility in the community rather than government force. The key is *in the community*. This is the optimal place for a democracy of common consent to flourish and the only way to reach the greatest level of diversity the world has ever seen.

When we conserve as much social responsibility as possible at this level, then the progressive statist no longer has an excuse for taking responsibility away. When will conservatives, libertarians, and constitutionalists ever figure this out? As long as they refuse to scale the consent of one person into the common consent of community, they will never combat controlling oligarchs from usurping social control for personal gain. It is time to get away from the constitution as a "cure all." It is not a living exercise of responsibility; it only protects against the abuse of individual liberties for a short while until the new democratic idolatry rewrites it.

If conservatives would start talking of community sustainability and even use phrases like "the social community," "sovereign culture," or "common consent," this would easily rob the statists on both sides of the political aisle of their tendency to push for national socialism controlled by executive orders and federal bureaucracies. Hey, why not even take the phrase "community socialism," have it run by a micro republic of direct and unanimous consent and just watch the federal oligarchs squirm at losing their central control. Again, the relational mind that decentralizes power and widens consent needs to confront the linear mind that centralizes power and narrows access to consent.

It is truly odd that controlling statists fail to see how more rights from government do not demand any more responsibility from the individual or the community. In fact, it is just the opposite. The progressive mind pushing for centralized control never understands this. They advocate that the state take control of social responsibilities to remove their guilt for not showing any responsibility on their own. List ten political statists and compare them with a local cooperative business venture. Add up all the money, service, and value added to the community by each and you'll quickly see the selfishness of the statist and the true service of the local cooperative.

If all responsibility for social good is controlled at the national level, then laws are written without local consent. Even worse, we do this without any room to invest in our own liberty. Always remember that liberty is what adds value. Give this liberty to controllers at great distances and you'll lose your voice in the process and all invested responsibility in your community.

When civil rights become more important than personal responsibility, we foster the plan of tyrants and not the plan of the people. It is through personal responsibility that we preserve civil rights.

Changing the meaning of a term to obtain more central control and deflect away from local responsibility is a staged optimist's way of avoiding the truth. It's the fundamental cause of darkness throughout history. Darkness covered Christianity when the early saints gave power over to Roman authority. Even after a long reformation that brought us out of this darkness, Hitler, Mao, Stalin, and others of the last century saw fit to alter the right to bear arms in order to obtain complete control—all in the name of safety and protection.

When we regress into the all powerful state again (as in *gun control*) for the sake of avoiding evil, insanity, and the death of a few, we'll find ourselves in such a place of darkness that living will not be worth it. Many will seek death but won't be able to find it. If we take away liberty for life, we are already dead. And if we choose to empower controlling authority at a great distance to replace the work of a local community, we will continue to slide down the path of annihilation.

All Energy, No Spark

Talk with a staged optimist about the definition of reason, about the meaning of education, intelligence, or love. Ask them questions about vision—and you'll quickly see their lack of it. You may find that staged optimists voice opinions about physical exercise, food, and cars, and even express minor emotions about human relations, and sometimes you'll hear a trivial political talking-point used to sound informed. What you won't find is the insight that defines a deliberate life that adds value. You may find a cordial smile and great oral delivery, but not the willingness to stand in the face of rising dissent.

It is time we all study collective meritocracies. They are the positioning of a growing body to advance people of merit through adulation engineering. This is the process of honoring a power above to gain a position below. Together, this collective authority approves people for advancement in such a way to maintain a central and vertical power structure. This is how controllers dressed in staged optimism work.

While the merit of an independent mind may choose to rise on its own horizontally, a political person is always looking for the power center or central power group with which to align. This is why majority-rule organizations are so destructive. Political staging of artificial optimism never succeeds by showing an independent thought publicly, but rather it comes from the praise of a power center in an idolized and worshiped majority. We see over and over how idolatry, not faith, drives political optimists.

This is why we lack honesty in open discussion. Our expressions are controlled in a centrally manipulated collective, which requires our adoration for authority under the false impression that we are working as a team. Open disagreement is completely removed, and this is witnessed in all corporate, religious and government structures.

Plato's *Republic* is a good example. He fabricated a collective hierarchy designed to cover the collective intent of control. Socrates, on the other hand, didn't aspire to create a vertical power structure to stage collective control. He preferred open discussion in order to encourage honest meaning from each individual. Socrates never sought collective control: education came from small discussions rather than national media.

Again, always look at how we idolize authority. It's much easier to determine political corruption than by trying to follow the money.

Political conventions create a collective that's often designed to cover self-seeking motives. Each attendee, engulfed in a collective hierarchy that doesn't allow individual dissent, is left intimidated. Some people appeal to certain controlling figures to get their acceptance, while others are willing to stand to correct the collective power. Only the latter are genuinely optimistic, even though they appear the most antagonistic in the collective.

But there's a catch. Optimism through dissent must also be willing to stand correction. Just putting the dissenter in power doesn't guarantee the next dissenter the same freedom.

We cannot say, "question everything" and then not "stand to be corrected." This second half of the principle doesn't survive well from one generation to another. When anyone tries to surface a nonconforming view, collective controllers deflect the attempt by saying "We're off-subject," or "we need to get with the program." The dissenter then appears anti-optimistic. Shutting them down is not an act of responsibility.

When empowered by a majority and run by central authority, the collective organization, whether a church, a political party, or a business meeting, has its own staged optimists ready to walk away from questioning minds. As a whole, entire groups, when managed in this way, rarely act responsibly. We'll talk about a solution for this at the end of the book. Suffice it to say that staged optimists thrive on very large collective structures because it allows them to take center stage without revealing the center of their hearts.

Staged optimists avoid all forms of open expression that may reveal their lack of understanding. In every situation, they never really say what they believe. The only way to find any spark of understanding in them is when the staged optimist is open and free to take questions. How many times have you listened to a speaker or leader and wanted to ask a direct question? But because you weren't able to submit your question, the leader isn't challenged or doubted.

Something is obviously wrong when the values of an entire generation favor diversity of opinion over open discussion. Diversity allows for meaning to remain in a constant state of relativity, whereas open discussion flushes the true meaning out. Discussion always guarantees diversity, but diversity itself does not always guarantee discussion.

What would happen with Alcoholics Anonymous if a lecturer replaced group discussion? Nobody would receive correction in front of those who have learned to read a staged act. Group therapy dies under the lecture format. We are likewise dead in a society that shuts down dissent out of some form of positive political tolerance designed to control the group.

Colleges and universities teach the importance of cultural diversity, yet we never hear anyone talking about open discussion. In order to have any cultural value, it's imperative that we maintain free dissent from every so-called authority in a specific culture and be willing to receive correction ourselves. A willingness to stand correction is better than cultural tolerance. It is true diversity.

Unfortunately, much of the new establishment's control over optimism takes dissent as antagonistic to diversity. Diversity is a political form of optimism designed to make truth relative. This is seen when various selected ideas are given equal expression but none are ever challenged. It is like the perpetual Israel and Palestine conflict. If you question Israel, you are an anti-Semite. If you question Palestine, you are an imperial Zionist.

It is like kicking Socrates out of the city for asking too many questions about the meaning of things, and letting Plato stay because he appeals to collective diversity. Plato was linear and a staged optimist. Socrates was relational, genuine and willing to die for it. For good reason, Samuel Dael calls Plato's *Republic* "a manual for despots and a bible for dictators."[5] Why we've allowed Plato to remain the central focus of western tradition is a complete mystery. Just look at how we continue designing society around controlling authority but never do we look to promote common consent through independent and free minds.

All collective meritocracies build on the central control of a select few intellectuals who self-elect through peer authorities and adulation engineering. They build a central and vertical power structure to stage their optimism and avoid horizontal discussions to determine the meaning of things that actually might expose the politics of their falsified optimism.

Group therapy comes from the premise that the socially sick are hiding something they cannot face alone. This only works in a headless body where every person in the small group is equal in the group, and the group needs to be small. The idea is to transform a staged lie to genuine optimism, because the staged person is mentally ill. Mental patients are intellectually skilled at deflection. Open discussion, over time, is the only method for healing them. This does not imply what the best content for discussion should be. It just says that even the mentally sick have the freedom to question others that are mentally sick, including the doctor. Read *One Flew Over a Cuckoo's Nest* by Ken Kesey. An international best seller in the 1960s and later a winner of five academy awards for the film, such a piece of literature with wide appeal deserves far more importance than the newest academic research study ready to promote the newest syndrome.

Open discussion from all participants is the only way to see true motive. At its core, social responsibility provides for talk that is more open and less centralized in control. Such a superior method of autonomous discussion always brings about greater freedom and more responsibility held in common by the people rather than idolatrous authority over them.

Definition Par Excellence

When it comes to revealing political optimists of all types, especially the staged optimist, the battleground is in the meaning of words. The challenge is to acquire an independent and responsible meaning to words like logic, liberty, mercy, freedom, love, and friendship. The meaning we give these words is what drives us. By revealing our meaning, we actually disclose our motive for everything we do.

Even more, these words become our character. Political optimists do not assign consistent meaning to words. More often, they change the meanings of words by implying a new set of terms to replace the old. If we know the old definition and if we see a new meaning emerging, we can see the person's inner motive. If we could, we would see that the new term is truly false. That's the point. Attaching responsible meaning to key abstract words is what gives real strength to stand against the staged optimist. It's so important that Marcus Aurelius wrote the following in his *Meditations*:

> Remember how long you have been putting off these things, and how often you have received an opportunity from the gods, and yet do not use it. You must now at last perceive of what universe you are a part and from what administrator of the universe your existence flows, and that a limit of time is fixed for you, which if you do not use for clearing away the clouds from your mind, it will go and you will go, and it will never return.[6]

When we refuse to clear away the clouds from our minds regarding the meaning of important words in open discourse, we are subjected to the meanings that authorities feed us. Too often, these meanings include neither real value nor responsible action. Even worse, when forced upon us without our consent and without the ability to object, we begin to accept the new definitions without relational understanding.

At the end of this section, you can find an addendum that gives a list of the most challenging words to define. Defining these words in context of responsibility (as opposed to the context of control) is the substance of meaning that gives belief real strength. The only way to find the responsible meaning is to engage in the practice of reaching consent. In other words, we all need to define these words in relation to long format discussion so we can stand against the staged and linear optimist.

The real meaning we hold about words makes up our personal beliefs, written laws, and social and business policy. The greatest leaders define their words within the context of open and public consent.

If we never define terms such as love, freedom, and faith in the open and in the face of possible dissent held by a small group in common, we're more apt to accept a new definition by a charismatic authority over a greater majority. When this happens we never take the responsibility to hear dissent.

All you have to do is see how staged personalities respond to your real self when you take responsibility for what you truly believe. And what we believe is seen in the open, when we willingly define and live our definitions in the face of open dissent.

Great actors come out from behind their fear and are open about what they're willing to take responsibility for and what they believe. Bad actors don't listen to others on stage, and when they do pretend to listen and share the stage, you can see in their eyes their impatience and a quick to return to their canned delivery. Staged optimists do not read what you believe, and they certainly do not want to hear it. They appeal to the collective view and avoid responding to your honest intent. They service narcissism and not real need.

When I was in graduate school, there was a professor who was having sex with female students. Everyone thought he was suffering from childhood problems that he couldn't resolve, which led to his decision to divorce his wife. I was armed with insights from Shakespeare, Ernest Becker, and Otto Rank, but my open disagreement made me an outcast at a social gathering of academics and fellow students when I dared say, "he has no childhood issues, he's just afraid of death."

The need to complicate things with trendy excuses is something staged optimists love to do. It's a powerful form of deflection. It allows the staged person to hide the root fear, which was my argument, and avoid the responsibility needed to accept it.

The false face we paint for ourselves in order to get through the maze of the day represses the fear we refuse to accept. We get others to follow us who seek the same escape. When the staged optimist does this, the deception becomes especially difficult to read: we are all attracted to an unaffected person who's able to lie without remorse. The genuine optimist stumbles and their stammering shows a person trying to reveal more honesty.

It's like a young man struggling to ask a girl out. In that moment, he is most real and genuine, because his fear is closer to the surface.

Genuine optimists are responsible; they reveal their true heart and mind to the world. If you think they're prideful, consider that the pride may be a cover: they've learned that as soon as they volunteer too much, others complain. Take a job in a labor union shop, work harder and give personal service to others, and watch the reaction. Walk into a social or religious function with a willingness to serve with modesty and kindness and you'll get the same results. Sustain the status quo of every power center, on the other hand, and you'll receive the love desired.

Obviously, the time for a new cultural model is approaching, as every interaction increasingly ends in more central control, which comes from the easy political manipulation of majority rule. This is where we find intimidation feeding on the power of a central-control grid.

In public, we want unaffected souls and upbeat happiness, and we thrive on false modesty rather than on genuine honesty. Think about it. We counsel depressed people or those struggling through life in order to justify our unwillingness to really understand and serve them. If people honestly express dissent against our words, we say to them, "You need to be a little political."

It is clear we want happy faces to hide the struggles going on inside. This means we must also desire a different kind of political optimism to go with our unwillingness to stand in dissent due to our idolatry for authority. In order to excuse away our own irresponsibility to voice honest disagreement, something more debilitating succumbs our agency, a second type of political optimism that exists under a different guise, a guise more pernicious and even more difficult to spot.

It is the fraudulent optimism of the *intimidator*.

We have become victims of our own art. We touch people on the outsides of their bodies, and they us, but we cannot get to their insides and cannot reveal our insides to them. This is one of the great tragedies of our interiority-it is utterly personal and unrevealable. Often we want to say something unusually intimate to a spouse, a parent, a friend, communicate something of how we are really feeling about a sunset, who we really feel we are-only to fall strangely and miserably flat. Once in a great while we succeed, sometimes more with one person, less or never with others. But the occasional break-through only proves the rule. You reach out with a disclosure, fail, and fall back bitterly into yourself.

Ernest Becker, *The Birth and Death of Meaning*

3

The Intimidating Optimist

We all have a tendency to alter the meaning of words to justify our worldview. One might feel guilty or jealous because of a human situation, but rather than accept the guilt, we change the meaning of words to curb our regret. If we do not alter the meaning of words to deflect their imposition on us, we simply avoid talking about them.

Samuel Louis Dael

Defining Intimidation

Staged optimists avoid open discussion; intimidator optimists shut it down. Intimidator optimists are easy to spot because they never show any real encouragement that leaves a person's agency fully in place: they're linear rather than relational. And they will always shut down others from expressing a potentially better way that more of us can relate to.

Intimidators hate better ways. It forces them to see a wider field of new directions and to assume some responsibility for this new field. It is like they have an innovation threshold, and they alone maintain the line and keep others from crossing that threshold.

A better way to understand is that the intimidator hates to think in relational contexts. They use emergency actions with new goal-setting to distract us from new ideas. They even make peripheral issues of protocol, procedure, and planning the new central vision. This is sure to shut down effective insights and advance only those who are the most political.

Every generation has its own ways of intimidating others in order to maintain control. Look at *The Power of Positive Thinking* (1952). It came at a time when people were losing religious faith. And because nature abhors a vacuum, writers were trying to replace faith with something else. What we failed to see is that we'd misused faith in the first place by giving too much of its interpretation to religious authority. Shortly thereafter, we got *How to Cure Yourself of Positive Thinking* (1977), which had some popularity, but quickly we put it aside in favor of a new upbeat happiness under pressure, a kind of forced cognitive thinking and the law of attraction that followed. We were then told, "you are what you think." This led to, "change your thinking and you will be more positive."

It is as if we have rejected a fanatic faith in favor of a fanatic optimism. Never did we think to define false optimism as we should have defined a controlled religious faith. In fact, a society falls into darkness when it starts to define words like *faith* in terms of magic and not in terms of *responsible action*.

Let's define intimidation with a very simple approach. If words like love, justice, and even liberty imply some kind of responsible action—without saying what that action is—then surely faith requires a responsible action of its own. However, with the word intimidation, the idea of responsible action is not implied. Instead we see force upon our agency. With faith, there is no force. With intimidation, there is no freedom to act responsibly.

If we say, "faith is irrational," then we reject a better definition that might say, "faith is responsible."

There's a kind of political optimism that is coerced. We call this intimidation; it represents a complete absence of any responsible action that we might simply call faith.

For example, on February 4, 2005, while promoting social security reform in Omaha, Nebraska, President George W. Bush stepped into an unscripted moment and spoke with Mary Monin, a divorced woman in her fifties and a mother of three children, one of which was a mentally challenged son. Here is a short excerpt of that dialogue:[1]

President Bush: "...there is a certain comfort to know that the promises made will be kept by the government. You don't have to worry."

Without prompting, Ms. Monin responded, "That's good, because I work three jobs and I feel like I contribute."

The President: "You work three jobs?"

Ms. Monin: "Three jobs, yes."

The President: "Uniquely American, isn't it? I mean, that is fantastic that you're doing that." The audience then broke into applause and the president followed with "Get any sleep?"

President Bush could have said, "It's difficult when single parents are left alone in these dire conditions." This would have stated the problem. The president could have followed that with, "I will have someone contact you because I want to learn more." This shows concern, but with no obligation. The public already knows that this fundamental problem exists and it would be better to have someone local follow through specifically. Instead he chose to say, "That is fantastic."

Intimidator optimists avoid a follow-up that even a local volunteer could handle and report back on. At any rate, President Bush could have taken a great opportunity to say something like, "This kind of hardship comes from too much Washington control and not enough local autonomy to help one another. We need more community care and less government dictation." Rather than stand up and say something powerful, he used his one-liner to distract people from his lack of leadership while the audience responded in full applause.

We call these people intimidator optimists because they sound enthusiastic in their speech. Unfortunately buried in their words is a kind of positive mental exertion imposed on your own free will. For example, is it "uniquely American" (meaning a good thing) to work three jobs and raise three children alone as a single parent? Where is the hope for something better in that claim?

All political optimists avoid responsibility by dismissing important human relationships with a deflective gag, and a lot of people laugh along, escaping in turn from being humanly connected. The modern self-help and positive-attitude movements promote this kind of dismissive attitude toward those truly going through tough times. Because life does have trials, one's attitude is not always positive on the surface, and yet the intimidator optimist is quick to impose guilt for not being upbeat. This is especially true when you express doubts about certain decisions or doubts about ideas by offering better decisions and better ideas. Even with the most friendly of attitudes, better decisions and better ideas promote the same reactionary distaste that will label you as negative.

Imagine a boss tells an employee that a cut in hours will require moving his employee from the night shift to the early-morning shift. The boss knows the employee took the job because it fit with his afternoon classes at the local college. This boss also knows that the employee's wife works the early-morning shift at the county hospital and that every morning his employee takes care of his two boys to get them off to school. With hands up to excuse himself and shrugging his shoulders, the boss says, "Life is ten percent what you make it, and ninety percent how you take it."

This is intimidator optimism. It forces consent while avoiding any real concerned connection. This is how linear thinkers behave: their approach is cold, but—from their own point of view—always upbeat. Because the employee does not take the change with a smile, his expressed doubt is suddenly *his* problem.

Masked by controlled executive decision-making and delivering their messages with the appeal of smooth oratory, intimidating optimists avoid any personal responsibility in their relations to others. That boss *could* have said, "I'm sorry, but because of budget cuts, I had to adjust everyone's hours. Others have similar problems and I need some temporary rotation so all can make the best of a bad situation."

The difference between intimidation and encouragement is significant. Command-and-control intimidation does a lot of damage to human encouragement. It's high time we saw the difference between living on a linear path of intimidation and living on a relational path of encouragement.

It's one thing to deliberately control a business meeting to avoid being bogged down in a round-table complaint session. It's another to shut down a work-through discussion for the sake of expediency and without an honest field of consent. It then becomes an imposition on personal initiative and genuine concern for the thoughts of others.

A good friend nearing retirement from her position at a local college suddenly came face-to-face with the demands of saying yes when saying no stood in line with the logic of her heart and her years of valuable experience. The culprit was an intimidator optimist. He was the new vice-president of student services, a pureblood "yes" enforcer. He wanted to eliminate a vital scholarship program and put more money into marketing, to attract more students to the college. He was reaching for greater enrollment numbers versus bringing the best students to the school. (He didn't realize that by reaching for the best students through scholarship offerings, other students would follow and enrollment would naturally increase: a college is only as great as the students it attracts.)

Nonetheless, he approached my friend and asked her to help him; his unstated implication was, "get on board or quit." He went even further, telling all of his staff, "If you don't like your job, find a way to like it. And if you can't find a way to like it, find another job." Everyone just nodded in forced affirmation while a few said "no!" in solemn soliloquy.

Here's the problem. Non-political people can't hide their disagreement, and the yes enforcer quickly sees who they are: so it makes sense to express the feelings openly, because the enforcer won't be fooled by anything else. So what did my friend do? She retired early and left the college.

At the time, there was just no way to stand against this new VP because of his commanding upbeat tone. Any attempt to question him would come off looking professionally negative rather than expressing a need to ask for honest clarity.

In the corporate world, questioning minds aren't considered team players. If you aren't a team player, you are a negative person. What if corporate models suddenly chose to let doubt and new ideas arise? The only way it could happen would be inside a new model of horizontal consent that would stand face-to-face with executive control.

To understand the problem of political intimidation, imagine the testing of a twelve-year-old's adoption into a violent gang. The older gang leader tells the young boy to rob the home of a retired couple on his street in order to be initiated. Once the kid starts to show a little hesitation, the gang leader immediately says in front of everyone in the brotherhood, "We're your family. Do this for your brothers."

How could a twelve-year-old stand up against that? Yet take any positive one-liner out of any self-help book—and the young boy would still find himself stuck. A very basic affirmation like, "just think positive and you can do anything," could easily become a weapon of intimidation.

To get control, intimidator optimists use positive affirmations, quotes, and even popular usage to force someone else into a negative act. Moreover, unless you're placed on equal footing in order to question and seek understanding (through the practice of reaching common consent), you'll find yourself constantly unprepared for what the intimidator throws at you.

There's another practice used by intimidators: numbers. If they lack the guts to force, weed out and intimidate the offending "no" personality with straight-line linear conclusions that refuse outside relational context (witnessed in the use of forced affirmations); and if they don't have pumped-up positive pressure to intimidate, then they use numbers and the bottom line. These people can be kind in nature. They can even express regret and sorrow for the decision to let good people go; but they are still failures as leaders. They are number crunchers and spend more time looking at spreadsheets and financial projections than allowing more freedom to surface new ideas and offer creative innovations.

When the cash-flow is down and the economy is in the crapper, why let good people go, people who have proven themselves repeatedly? Here's an example from a nonprofit that was left in a bad fix by a departing director. When the new director took over, the program was immediately re-organized, outstanding invoices were paid, budgets matched real-life demands, procedures were written and followed, and new staff was hired in the "new solution."

Just when everything was working in the black, a new business idea came to mind that would help make the organization more sustainable. I presented it to the CEO, and within three months I was terminated: economic advisors said that is what would save the organization the most.

A month later, my business idea became a finalist in a speed-pitch competition. As of today, the non-profit is now out of business due to an uninformed board letting the CEO manage without the a wider field of common consent from his staff. Essentially, the staff was all on board to give a certain project back to the bank and move forward. The CEO chose not to do this and the debt load eventually collapsed the non-profit, mainly due to giving too much control to the chief financial officer. The nonprofit never built a team in full consensus. Instead, it was managed alone from the desk of one CEO and a CFO working in the shadows, and sadly with a board of directors that never really understood its role as a business. Again, the CEO is a great and kind man, he even sacrificed much of his own financial well being for the organization, but alone without full consent and too much responsibility being run in the dark, the ship runs ground on the rocks.

It takes massive strength in vision, tactical management, and knowledge of details to guide a company: that's too much for one person to handle alone. Nonetheless, we continue to build organizations on this model, with all consent held in that one person.

We can understand a cash-flow problem existing in any organization, and we can understand the decision to let certain people go. But why hire an outside consulting team to help structure an organization to be more sustainable and still let good people go? We hire consultants and replace higher-paid staff with lower-paid staff because we hope to find a new administrative model or some new *best* practice to employ.

All we really want is a better way to skim the milk. The problem is rarely cash flow but rather a lack of applied common consent and vision in the organization.

Organizations fail to mature into more value because of a lack of discussion bringing the whole into one visionary focus. That discussion may require a lot of time to work out, but as a team, people face the inevitable and solve problems together. Had the nonprofit's employees worked together in common consent, where dissent received encouragement, poor decisions could have been avoided, and the organization could have remained in operation—anyway who knows what might have happened?

As a team, either people come together or they break apart. It's amazing that we never choose a model that brings a team together in common consent. While seeing a team break apart is often the result of executive decision-making or the dominant control of a power center in one employee, coming together requires an organizational model that allows the whole team to fight through the disagreements and become better for it. Susan Scott in *Fierce Conversations* talks about this challenge at length. Every business leader should read it.

Any good leadership publication teaches that all successful organizations guide themselves through a compelling vision, and vision comes from the open range and never from a constricted feedlot. Because leaders don't have genuine vision from a wider field of open consent, there's a collapse in leadership at every level of society.

Without a well-defined vision, leaders fear vocal dissent and do everything in their power to control this dissent. All this happens because they have no vision from which to "come out from behind themselves and into the conversation."[2]

Leadership today is failing to manage real diverse conversations to garner strategic direction. This is why best practices are eluding us. It's why there is no advanced technology to replace our leadership problems, and why we avoid experienced and hardworking staff that can offer key points to give greater consensus to the organization.

Central to the intimidator optimist is a person or bureaucratic body using forced commands. Sometimes the force is direct and sometimes it's implied. Sometimes it's from the boss above and sometimes it's from the push all around.

As is true for the staged optimist, the only way to see this political coercion is to have confidence in your own dissenting voice and a greater depth of meaning to support responsible action.

This brings up a point about the depth of meaning discussed thus far. If you don't have the optimism for dissent, which comes with having your own mind, you subject yourself to the intimidator. We call this the *enjambment of political power.*

The Enjambment

Back in the eighties there was a baseball pitcher for the Los Angeles Dodgers named Fernando Valenzuela. He had a unique style of pitching that was within the strike box but very close to the hitter's hands. If you can imagine hitting a baseball within inches of your hands and feeling the vibration of the ball hit way off center, you can imagine a sudden shift in power the pitcher refuses to give away.

In poetry, that is called enjambment: the continuation of a sentence or clause over a line break. If a poet allows all the sentences in a poem to end in the same predictable place as regular line-breaks, a kind of deadening can happen in the ear and in the brain. If the language has the same length, then the thoughts will, too.

Enjambment is one way of creating audible interest, kind of like a vibration. Notice the intentional delay of emotion with a surprise effect in these two lines from Alexander Pope's *The Rape of the Lock*:

> On her white breast a sparkling cross she wore
> Which Jews might kiss, and infidels adore.

The second line confuses the reader with a question. Why would a Jew or infidel adore a cross? On second reading, the reader realizes that "breast" doesn't carry the general connotation of "chest" but instead the specific idea of a woman's breasts, which are so attractive that a man of any religion would kiss the Christian cross to be near them. The idea is to delay the intention of the first line until the following line plays on the expectation.

With intimidation, we hide the intent. We put things to the far edge of outright intimidation while staying just far enough inside the authoritative strike range. The intimidating optimist delays the intent by covering the motive to control with the expectation of something positive.

Every batter who stood against Valenzuela was intimidated because they had to swing or strike out. This defines the precise condition of everyone who's been politically intimidated. The game of baseball is one thing, but the game of life doesn't work through enjambment. To delay truth until the expectation in poetry helps communicate the intent, but to hide motive politically follows the law of survival of the fittest—and not the higher law of freedom of dissent, even from the weakest among us.

Few people, if any, don't know what genuine dissent is, and this explains why the intimidator rises in leadership and the person of genuine encouragement does not. Political intimidators rise in leadership because we bury genuine optimism under the positive self-help movement in the same way Christianity buried true faith in the magic of free salvation.

To an enjambment that intimidates, faith says, "no!" It's that simple. Faith does this with applied action that appears negative in the face of imposed control. Often we don't see this control until it's too late. This is why we have to swing or strike out. No matter how you look at it, we box ourselves in, and we don't know how to get out without knowing our own mind. One of the only ways to know your own mind is to employ an enjambment *no*!

Take the meaning of democracy. Is it just a vote you make in a private booth with no responsibility to social discourse? This is what it has become, but this isn't the origin of democracy. The word comes from the Greek (*dēmokratía*) that means "rule of the people," which was derived from (*dêmos*) "people" and (*kratos*) "power" or "rule."

These are still unclear until we get to *self-rule, self-determination* and *equal say*, all of which stand in greater opposition to (*aristocratie*) "rule of an elite."

If we say that democracy is popular government by majority rule, it doesn't properly stand in opposition to aristocratic elitism. In other words, the more we define democracy within the context of individual consent, the closer we get to the natural optimism of an enjambment no.

The ideal of democracy is not just a vote but to have a voice in discussion that people engage in prior to and after voting. Over time, intimidating powers have led us into *linear* boxed-in voting without any discussion. At the same time we lost the social discourse found in *relational* connections that lead to greater consent.

Political intimidators make themselves the gatekeepers of all social discourse. Our everyday business meetings follow the same methodology—they too often avoid, dampen, and control discussion to give more to central power figures commanding majority rule. The result is that natural relational connections are put aside in favor of linear and purely mechanical conclusions.

The challenge we face is how to reopen the gates of social discourse in order to reach greater consent. This is optimistic. Creating this kind of freedom is an enjambment to intimidating optimists rather than *their* enjambment to our lack of faith.

As intimidators work to control our minds while sitting in a cubicle, they'll never control the community forum at its lowest level—the level of gossip. If we could rise to a higher level than gossip with the power of horizontal consent, we could change the world.

Pushing for more open forum expression with real teeth in consent is the only social enjambment there is against the centralization of political controls. We can do this by removing our need for central power and replacing it with a much wider, horizontal voice of consent.

A wise hitter can reposition his stance and open the swing of his bat to increase his chance of a solid hit. Open discussion in which everyone has a chance to speak is the honest way of repositioning our stance. If everyone had equal voice in modular assemblies of common consent, true meaning would arise and everyone would begin to see the political optimist naked. You don't even need to talk about intimidation—you just need to push for the consent of everyone involved to reveal the intimidator who demands full control.

If everyone responds to a meaning that's slightly different from that of the intimidator, the intimidator will select a new saying to keep false control through majority rule. The process will go round and round until the intimidator finally changes his pitch.

Supporting more common consent through discussion is the true enjambment for political optimists hiding in a central-control booth. Intimidators avoid freedom because open and honest discussion requires more responsibility from everyone, which means no idolatrous worship of controlling authority. Using the same character keywords linked with staged optimists, notice the traits associated to the right when it comes to intimidators. When it comes to idolatry, where staged optimists sought for glory, intimidating optimists seek for control. Their motive is control and their reward is obedience. **See Figure 3-1.**

Fig. 3-1 Traits of the Staged Optimists

Character	Traits
Idolatry	Seeks Control
Intelligence	Glory in Power
Agency	No Freedom
Motivation	Desires Control
Reward	Demands Obedience

When we study intimidation as a politicized optimism always held in the power center and never in the people, the staff or the team, we can see the reason for a better democracy. A better democracy includes the application of responsible faith where we allow everyone to take part in the genuine optimism of common dissent. If we don't have disagreement in common, we can't have agreement in common. This logic has been rejected for way too long as a vital part of any democracy.

Put another way, when we take magic out of faith, we inject responsibility. When we take politics out of optimism, we inject common dissent.

Intimidation is a compulsory *yes* and it will never replace the responsibility inherent in *no*. The force of yes, if unchecked over time, works against the negation of no. This is where the binding optimism of the intimidator's words refuse to hear dissent by lumping all expressions of disagreement into ignorance, insubordination and direct disobedience.

When Christ responded to the stoning of a prostitute, skilled protesters used the linear conclusions from the law to support their actions. As the most powerful human enjambment against their intimidation, Christ said, "Let he who is without sin cast the first stone." In that one phrase, Christ gave everyone the freedom to continue stoning the woman based on the law, but now they understood their true responsibility—and their true motive.

In dealing with intimidating optimists, it helps to learn two kinds of enjambment no. The first is the intelligent *no* that challenges authority just by asking questions. Second is the defiant *no* that dissents directly against authority and tradition. When a hesitant *no* surfaces, there's usually good cause for it. If there's no way to express disagreements, defiance will creep in and eventually lead to revolution, revolt, and the reorganization of power. In time, the intelligent *no* will always lead to the defiant *no*.

Sometimes this can have dire consequences. Consider what President Kennedy said in an address before the American Newspaper Association on April 27, 1961:

> You may remember that in 1851 the New York Herald Tribune under the sponsorship and publishing of Horace Greeley, employed as its London correspondent an obscure journalist by the name of Karl Marx.

> We are told that foreign correspondent Marx, stone broke, and with a family ill and undernourished, constantly appealed to Greeley and managing editor Charles Dana for an increase in his munificent salary of $5 per installment, a salary which he and Engels ungratefully labeled as the "lousiest petty bourgeois cheating."

> But when all his financial appeals were refused, Marx looked around for other means of livelihood and fame, eventually terminating his relationship with the Tribune and devoting his talents full time to the cause that would bequeath the world the seeds of Leninism, Stalinism, revolution and the cold war.

> If only this capitalistic New York newspaper had treated him more kindly; if only Marx had remained a foreign

correspondent, history might have been different. And I
hope all publishers will bear this lesson in mind the next
time they receive a poverty-stricken appeal for a small
increase in the expense account from an obscure newspaper
man.[3]

As we become more confident about speaking out,
intimidation will wane. You just need to encourage more
questions, questions that require the intimidator to define
his meaning more clearly. This helps you say *no* with more
confidence. If it's expressed in an open meeting, your mildness
will be like that of a batter taking a slightly different stance.
Other people will begin to appreciate this as you obtain their
unconscious consent.

Had Karl Marx been included in a mode of ideal consent
early in his formative years and throughout his career, who
knows what he would have produced? He might have preserved
the value of freedom and attacked capitalism from a uniquely
free-enterprise position at a community level and not from his
Platonic state-run socialist point of view.

Corporations and large institutions should understand
that leadership's enemy is the intimidator, because intimidators
eliminate independent minds quickly. Consider any new
manager hired with a hopeful attitude and a successful past.
This new manager comes aboard, willing to think and speak
openly and honestly, but the manager will eventually leave
when intimidators (from above) combine with intimidating
employees (below). When the upper management controls
through intimidation, most likely the bulk of the employees find
a status-quo niche of self-protection, a perfect excuse to keep
from bearing any responsibility.

When we easily accept traditional policy and don't allow
anything new to enter the domain, intimidating leaders force us
and we either become part of the sickly whole—or we leave. A
constant change in managers is a sign of intimidation and the
eventual fall of any organization.

Governments, on the other hand, don't fall as readily
because they naturally breed political opportunists who combine

in secret to get more control. The citizen isn't the one who causes this lust for control. Citizens just allow it by giving up their voice to a popular democracy where majority rules and full consent of the governed is silenced. When we lose our consent to central powers, we empower them with the ability to sow discord for more control. Thomas Paine had something to say about his:

> Men in all countries who get their living by war, and by keeping up the quarrels of nations, is as shocking as it is true; but when those who are concerned in the government of a country, make it their study to sow discord, and cultivate prejudices between nations, it becomes the more unpardonable.[4]
>
> Thomas Paine

All governments eventually become intimidating by sowing discord between nations—and inside their own. With the reach of the Internet and the rise of the alternative media, this has become an increasing challenge for governments to stage a crisis and create division among the people for more control.

In fact, at no other time in history has the world been so politically awake as now. Staging false crises is almost impossible with so many independent media outlets ready to report the clear facts and answer the hard questions. In fact, like the increase of freedom that occurred with the advent of the printing press, the increase of freedom never had a second wind until the birth of the Internet.

Make no mistake; central powers continue to look for a way to put controls on this new freedom of dissent. When this happens, the revolt will be a new foundation for a more diverse freedom with social responsibility kept purely local. There will be no guns, no civil war, and no uprising against the controlled establishment. There will only be a new founding of social consent from the bottom up.

In the near future, there will be a power shift in social responsibility. Local communities will rise up, most likely in private models, and take full accountability for the health, education, and welfare of their citizens—and that's only the beginning. Next will come greater common vision and the abolition of central authority. In other words, the next foundation of liberty is going to be quite literally inaccessible to political opportunists. By placing more responsibility into the hands of the community in modular groups, the most powerful form of dissent against the state can take place. We might even call this civil secession, a far better replacement to the now defunct civil disobedience.

But before that happens, we need to begin asking real questions.

Standing in Dissent

To understand the power of voicing dissent against intimidating powers, look at the unintended consequences of blowback.

Blowback is what governments and even corporations suffer from when their actions reveal their deception. A good example is when the secretary of defense for the United States, Donald Rumsfeld, said—with a straight face, in front of news reporters and with certainty—that "Iraq has weapons of mass destruction." Only in hindsight and with free access to the Internet do we see how he was polished in both his stance and his communication skills. There was no connection between what he said and the truth.

At the time, most people believed that the invasion of Iraq was right, yet at the same time there were a substantial number of dissenting voices that were ignored. Very few questioned why in public, because the upsurge of *no* was shadowboxed into a corner. The secretary of defense was not allowing questions of dissent to surface in the discussion. He deflected real concerns with more forced optimism imposed by his authority rather than through open discourse.

He used phrases like "this is complicated," "honorable people are in charge," and, at one time on February 12, 2002 where he addressed the lack of evidence linking the government of Iraq with supplying weapons of mass destruction to terrorist groups, he said:

"These are things we know that we know. There are known unknowns. That is to say, there are things that we know we don't know. But there are also unknown unknowns. There are things we don't know we don't know."[5]

A reporter then asked, "Is this an unknown unknown?" Hidden in this same obscurity the reporter was asking, "Is this an unknown threat?"

Rumsfeld then said in reply, "I am not going to say which it is."

When we challenge a soft-pedaling intimidator optimist in open public, they reject clarity and use their position of power to shut down access to intelligent reasoning. It's almost impossible to stand against this person face-to-face alone, but in the open, the target is yours if you dare take it.

Unfortunately, fewer and fewer people are willing to take the shot. This is what happens with so many reporters today. A great number of them shut down their responsibility to ask questions and only one—if we're lucky—stands in opposition. When such a person stands alone, we must take notice. We must see that this person isn't wearing the fashion of idolatry. They learn and listen carefully and are willing to risk everything. Taking a risk is far more optimistic than most people dare to admit.

Consider a heated dialogue that took place on July 1, 2009, between White House press secretary Robert Gibbs and veteran White House correspondent Helen Thomas. The debate surfaced when Chip Reid, a reporter, was challenging the lack of transparency and openness the administration had campaigned for. Gibbs had an exchange involving Reid and Thomas that went as follows:[6]

Gibbs: "... But, again, let's—how about we do this? I promise we will interrupt the AP's tradition of asking the first question. I will let you (Chip Reid) ask me a question tomorrow as to whether you thought the questions at the town hall meeting that the president conducted in Annandale—"

Chip Reid: "I'm perfectly happy to—"

Helen Thomas: "That's not his point. The point is the control"

Reid: "Exactly."

Thomas: "We have never had that in the White House. And we have had some, but not—this White House."

Gibbs: "Yes, I was going to say, I'll let you amend her question."

Thomas: "I'm amazed. I'm amazed at you people who call for openness and transparency and—"

Gibbs: "Helen, you haven't even heard the questions."

Reid: "It doesn't matter. It's the process."

Thomas: "You have left open—"

Reid: "Even if there's a tough question, it's a question coming from somebody who was invited or was screened, or the question was screened."

Thomas: "It's shocking. It's really shocking."

Gibbs: "Chip, let's have this discussion at the conclusion of the town hall meeting. How about that?"

Reid: "Okay."

Gibbs: "I think—"

Thomas: "No, no, no, we're having it now--"

Gibbs: "Well, I'd be happy to have it now."

Thomas: "It's a pattern."

Gibbs: "Which question did you object to at the town hall meeting, Helen?"

Thomas: "It's a pattern. It isn't the question—"

Gibbs: "What's a pattern?"

Thomas: "It's a pattern of controlling the press."

Gibbs: "How so? Is there any evidence currently going on that I'm controlling the press—poorly, I might add."

Thomas: "Your formal engagements are pre-packaged."

Gibbs: "How so?"

Reid: "Well, and controlling the public—"

Thomas: "How so? By calling reporters the night before to tell them they're going to be called on. That is shocking."

Gibbs: "We had this discussion ad nauseam and—"

Thomas: "Of course you would, because you don't have any answers."

Gibbs: "Well, because I didn't know you were going to ask a question, Helen. Go ahead."

Thomas: "Well, you should have."

Reporter: "Thank you for your support."

Gibbs: "That's good. Have you e-mailed your question today?"

Thomas: "I don't have to e-mail it. I can tell you right now what I want to ask."

Gibbs: "I don't doubt that at all, Helen. I don't doubt that at all."

Helen Thomas, age 89 at the time, had covered the White House during every presidency since John F. Kennedy. Later, in an interview with CNN, Helen said, "Not even Richard Nixon tried to control the press the way President Obama is trying to control the press. Nixon didn't try to do that," Thomas said. "They couldn't control (the media). They didn't try." Thomas also said, "They're supposed to stay out of our business. They are our public servants. We pay them." This eventually forced Helen's retirement with a note of dissatisfaction that her life's work had ended bitterly.

No matter the discomfort, good ideas eventually excel in an open forum. We can't shut them out with the positive force of controlled intimidation just to avoid confrontation. If we do let this happen, we leave a door open for the abuse of power to enter.

If you don't think this can happen in America, you need to be living in history and not becoming it. Too many of us allow intimidating optimism to rule our lives.

In looking back, the entire war in Iraq, the war in Afghanistan, the war on drugs, the war on poverty, and even the Vietnam and Korean wars, were all forced on Americans with no room for opposition or debate. For example, no matter how justified the war in Iraq sounded after the attack on Sept 11, 2001, something was not right. It was not until this war that more and more Americans began to wake up to the historical record that certain powers foment war to get gain.

For instance, we can trace the beginning of World War II to the Versailles Treaty, an unjust imposition placed on the German people for losing World War I. It forced a huge burden of war reparations (debt to be paid in cash, cattle, and natural resources), which obliterated German sovereignty and essentially kept Germany from becoming an industrial power. Hitler came on the scene only after the Treaty of Versailles. World War II grew out of a despot willing to say no to a repressive treaty imposed by outside powers that gave no voice and no recourse to the German people.

We point a finger at Hitler, who truly deserved to die, yet we refuse to blame Woodrow Wilson of the U.S, David Lloyd George of Britain, and Georges Clemenceau of France, who together imposed the treaty. Together they sustained the impoverishment and economic collapse of Germany in the same way hoodlum gangs pillage store shops during a community crisis. This angered the German people enough to follow a crazy man in order to stop the global confiscation of their resources.

When we refuse open free expression and force corrupt controls on people without their consent, eventually they will say no. Sometimes that revolt swings too far and they create another despotic intimidating government that refuses to hear dissent against itself. Such was the case with Hitler, and it continues with the adulation engineering we see in all bureaucracies. Put a dreadful tyrant full of lies and false promises in office and enough of the majority will cow tow to him in order to advance their position. The genuine optimists willing to say no in direct dissent are suddenly out-numbered, ridiculed, and marginalized. Again, this is so much easier to see than to follow the money.

A forced direction without consent and with no opportunity for redress of grievances produces war, injustice, poverty, and inequality. What are the powers punishing an entire nation? It's the powers wanting resources—and, perhaps, the imposition of austerity measures to tax the people directly. Offshore banks hold veto power over governments, not with guns, but with foreign debt. This only forces social and internal expenditure-cutting in order to pay the debt. In other words, austerity is often associated with a loss of sovereignty imposed by outside thugs. We see this problem throughout Europe, where a country like Greece is subject to the debt it owes to foreign banks.

If people want war, it's because of a propaganda of injustice. The real motive comes from economic powers that stand to benefit. Only they can manipulate leaders with promises and political benefits. Only they have the motive for pushing the public narrative by instigating false political events called false flags.

For instance, in 47 BC, Julius Caesar used a series of riots and arson attacks—that he paid for and commanded—to destabilize the Roman Republic before marching his legions across the Rubicon and into Rome, where he took power and declared himself emperor.

In 64 AD, the Emperor Nero deliberately allowed Rome to burn in a series of arson attacks in order to blame them upon the emerging Christian sect. This set Christians up for persecution as enemies of the state, thus enabling their bloody genocide and a very convenient deflection away from the intent of established powers.

Hitler capitalized on something similar when, in 1933, it is said Rohm's SA set fire to the Reichstag (German Parliament) which allowed Hitler to blame it on the Communists, thus enabling him to crack down on his main political rivals and construct his police state in post-Weimar Republic Germany. It does not matter if Marinus van der Lubbe, a Dutch communist, said he alone set fire to the German Reichstag building on 27 February in 1933. The event was used to instigate political control, bloodshed, and war.[7] A crisis is always great theater for grabbing more political control.

Over time, we'll eventually begin to see more false-flag events, either planned or not, which are used to centralize more power and more control. Even the Patriot Act of 2001 had over 360 pages supposedly written in less than forty days after the 911 events. This begs suspicion that it was pre-written and waiting for the right crisis to come along. All false flags that are deliberate instigations to create a crisis stem from secret combinations of power that sow discord behind the scenes. If you don't see history repeating itself, then look at the staged performance removed from open questions and look for the one in control trying to shut down discussion. This is so much easier to spot than trying to follow the money, prove a conspiracy, or finding a smoking gun.

God may punish his children for the sins of their fathers, but this is just a promise to us as parents that the despots we choose will bring darkness, poverty, and ignorance to our children until we wake up again. What is it that we cannot see? What enjambment do we not see coming every time intimidating powers set out to control us?

I spent some time talking to an army officer who had recently returned from Afghanistan. He had top-secret clearance in both Afghanistan and Iraq. I asked him a simple question: "What is the problem with Afghanistan?"

He replied with certainty, "Natural gas and opium."

He mentioned the energy companies involved and,

without any political opinion, he continued to suggest that we sustain war when there are natural resources to obtain, especially energy, currency manipulation, and black market resources. While this is not a tremendous revelation to many who know better, it is certainly news to the majority controlled by political optimists.

Look at the government bailouts in the United States in 2008 and 2009, and see how they magically pushed away the fear of a total economic collapse.

With the fiscal cliff and, later, the billions in government bailouts to big banks, the government spun the issue to print public debt to pay for private losses. Quickly taxed, people will pay interest to bankers—who simply printed their own money—for generations. We witness over and over the same rush to solve, in fear, some pending doom manufactured out of thin air. If you want to understand intimidation, just look at how fast things happen in Congress during a crisis and then look at where the money goes. It does not mater if the crisis is a conspiracy by powers in government or not. A crisis is used by political optimists to grab more control.

In the bailouts that began in 2009, trillions found their way into offshore banks. It's no different from a mob shakedown of local businesses in the name of protection racketeering, the most insidious form of intimidation. The only difference now is that we're experiencing global racketeering.

If you don't believe me, read *Confessions of an Economic Hit Man* by John Perkins, or *The Crime of Our Time* by Danny Schechter. Nomi Prins also has a lot to say in her book *It Takes a Pillage* and in her later book, *All the Presidents' Bankers.* Consider also Ellen Brown's massive research in her book *Web of Debt* or G. Edward Griffin's wildly successful *The Creature from Jekyll Island.* May I also suggest Catherine Austin Fitts' *Solari.com* and Max Keiser's *MaxKeiser.com.* I site these resources because the idea of global racketeering is not wide spread in the mainstream media but wildly documented without the general public knowing.

We cannot assume that the popular mainstream media will report on this racketeering because they're stuck in a vertical power grid where dissenting minds remain suppressed while idolatrous minds reach higher plateaus with more central control.

With the mainstream media we see them hire the best staged and intimidating optimists available, the kind of detached and inaccessible human beings who avoid taking questions from independent minds like those I listed above. It's no wonder that the alternative media is the new media, and quickly becoming the new fourth rail of politics. It's protecting the optimism of no and single-handedly preserving our freedom.

The Optimism of No

The Peter Principle, published in 1969, explained why we have incompetent leadership. It argued that we are hierarchal by nature, whether patriarchal, feudalistic, capitalistic, or socialistic. Because of these hierarchies, every position of leadership falls to a person of incompetence as long as the powers above want them there.

Better reason can explain why this happens. Although we organize into hierarchies by default because of the pac-rat nature of idolatry, the incompetence of political optimism grows out of the presumed safety of *yes* in one extreme rather than the uncertain dialogue of *no* at the other. People rise to incompetence because it is financially, politically, and psychologically safe for them to be there, and hierarchies support this design. However, it is much deeper than this.

Finding fault with leaders by blaming incompetent positions on vertical structures of power isn't the solution. We must see the psychology of fear that naturally buries a disapproval of *no* under a forced agreement for *yes*.

Thomas Carlyle's novel *Sartor Resartus,* published in the mid-1800s, spoke of the everlasting *nay* coming before the everlasting *yea*. He was right, to a point. To express "No!" forces a more clarified "Yes!" Moreover, to see a greater affirmation in the positive requires a greater degree of responsibility in hearing the negative.

In other words, true optimism defines a negative *no* that gradually works toward a more responsible *yes*. *The Peter Principle* happens because we are irresponsible in our talk; we don't engage the negative out of fear of losing ground or suffering rejection for what we have accepted as a positive stand.

Political optimists—and all intimidating leaders—see *yes* as easy and *no* as threatening. In a way, the stand for *no* resides on both sides of *yes*. Without the freedom to dissent before and after a confirmed yes, our system falls into political agreement without unanimous consent.

If every media outlet allowed for all questions of dissent to rise, the people would eventually see the political standing against what is genuinely optimistic. The reason we don't include every dissenting voice is that hierarchies are byproducts of idolatry. The maze of politics is not a conscious conspiracy, but a structure of idolatry. A news organization will soon learn from its acquisition that it must shy away from certain issues and propagate others, not because that's what the market wants, but because that's what the power centers want. Soon this media gathers more political optimists, while pushing out those willing to report on dissenting views.

The world presents an infinite maze of hierarchies, and some say that if you follow the money, you'll see the real power. There's a better way. Follow the idolatry for authority.

The obedient subjects of central power have no idea of the real power they have. They're convinced by their leaders because, over time, they've earned a living from them. Just as a prostitute doesn't snitch on her pimp, the pimp protects the racketeer.

Follow the hierarchy around the world and neither the head nor the tail knows the truth. The tail can be in the underworld and the head can be part of the highest leadership of a foundation for some good. When you follow the idolatry, however, you no longer need to know the head or the tail—because you see the insidious whole in collective worship.

What's done in secret subverts openness and the real optimism of *no*. This is the way of the intimidating optimist. Knowing this, we don't condemn conspiracy theorists as modern-day heretics. We just get them to see the dangerous idolatry instead of trying to connect the dots.

If you're in a black poverty-stricken neighborhood and you say, "There's a higher probability of more black crime," it doesn't make you a racist. Trying to make all things alike and equal is dangerous to a free society. The problem is with our central power structures that foment division in governments, churches, educational institutions, and in the corporate world. It even does it in movements like Black Lives matter. We have to tolerate it in some businesses because of ownership; but the people own the government, members own the church, and students have a right to open lateral discussion. Even members in presumably open environment should have an equal voice. The fact that we allow central control to form into vertically removed power centers of intimidating optimism is simply intolerable.

Once we understand that vertical hierarchies with central control are the problem, we need to understand that every hierarchy will intimidate in a different manner.

Karl Marx tried to destroy hierarchies altogether by replacing them with, "from each according to his abilities and to each according to his needs."[8] Although this expresses an attempt at equality, it uses a false cover of equality to suppress the opposition of "no" rather than continue the debate and come to an honest consensus.

Great-sounding ideals offer no recourse for dissent. They are used by control centers to silence opposition without any concession. We see this with the progressive statist. If they can force, legislate, and coerce what they think is good (and if they can do it without a wide field of consensus), they don't mention that they're building a vertical hierarchy that will eventually change into a despotic power. Genuine optimists may see it, but the idolatrous follower doesn't.

This shows how intimidating optimism exhibits especially destructive tendencies that lean heavily on the side of social entropy. Stalin, Mao, and Hitler, the genocide of Pol Pot and many more have destroyed the lives of more than 100 million people in the last century alone, and the number will exceed 250 million when you include murder by government. According to an extensive research project conducted by Rudolph J. Rummel, PhD, "the less liberal the democracy and the more totalitarian a regime, the more likely it will commit democide."[9] He offers these points from his research:

> Freedom ameliorates the problem of mass poverty.
>
> Free people have little internal violence, turmoil and political instability.
>
> Freedom is a method of nonviolence—the most peaceful nations are those whose people are free.[10]

Given this, we then must ask, "How do we increase freedom?" Obviously, this is going to be a great challenge with the trend moving toward more intimidation and more hierarchies with more centralized control.

Intimidation in Hierarchies

The most striking trait of intimidators is that they make you feel stupid by pushing positive expectation and obligatory anticipation, like Mao's "Great Leap Forward" or a corporate branding that moves fast through new market studies, statistical analysis, visionary re-direction, peripheral goal-setting, and corporate as well as federal protocol designed to steer clear of intuitively honest queries. Even a public display of patience is a kind of optimism that hides the intimidation yet to come.

When Barak Obama's healthcare act came to full implementation, we began to experience the intimidation imposed on small businesses while seeing the many executive waivers Obama gave to big corporations and labor unions. At the same time, we completely lost the optimism presented in the first place. Most of us don't want to believe until it is too late.

Empires fall because they gave too much responsibility to their leaders with the promise that the people would be kept safe or their rights protected. This is how important the freedom of dissent is. Only with the constant freedom to speak up against establishment powers do we have checks against undue encroachments and intimidation.

Read *The End of America, Letter of Warning to a Young Patriot* by Naomi Wolf. It is a warning about the responsibility required to keep dissent free. If not, the optimism of *no* will call on the blood of our children to take it back.

The new intellectuals for social justice seem to forget this. They want to keep leading the charge for progressive change with new centralized models, but refuse to maintain the freedom of dissent. They are linear destroyers of relational progress.

Love of free expression is almost silent within the statist liberal mind, and long forgotten in the conservative. This has happened because the old liberal from the sixties, who once dared to say *no*, has evolved into the new establishment promising a new optimism of *yes* in the hands of the state. They've become the intimidators while the conservative is being overrun by the new rising liberty movement, which was once the old liberal movement. It seems democracy loses its power when the individual is intimidated to conform into the vertical power structure. We must encourage every form of dissent against the statist mind that works constantly for central control.

Intimidating optimists remain at the heart of political power because they quell the real optimism that rises in the voice of dissent. They are counter-intuitive. If a decision rests on their shoulders, this is one thing; but when they get others to commit to actions not of their own logic, they command through pressure cloaked as confidence in your idolatry towards them.

This subtle force excuses intimidators from assuming liability for their own decisions and leans on second-tier adulterous bureaucrats to make a stand, which they never do because they create the same pressure under them.

To feel and speak honestly are expressions of human intelligence, and both the staged performer and the verbal intimidator want to control at least one of them. The staged optimist wants to control how you feel, and the intimidator optimist wants to control when and what you can speak.

Here is how we battle the need for control. First, your own intelligence must express meaning within the context of responsible action. Second, the optimism of *no* must remain at your disposal and rise with common consent. A new model of governing power in all organizations—as seen in horizontal consensus—is required to make all this work properly.

Hold on, a solution is coming.

We've learned that political optimists have a unique way of avoiding or controlling discussion. How we master honesty and responsibility to stand against them will surprise most of us.

Before we get there, let's look at the last political optimist known for the greatest destruction of free agency, the *irrational optimist*.

4

The Irrational Optimist

Positive thinking illustrates nothing more than the denial of responsibility towards a more rational view. Our positive cover often becomes our shield and concealment a bastardly defense against sound understanding. The negative thinker, on the other hand, may just be trying to look at things more realistically. More often than naught, the positive as well as the negative spokesperson avoid the aspects of faith in fundamental principles.

- Samuel Louis Dael

The Stubborn Mind

A father once said to his son, "Positive thinkers are negative bastards." To prove his point, he gave him a copy of *How to Cure Yourself of Positive Thinking*. After reading this book, it became apparent to the young man that there was such a thing as an irrational optimist. I was this young man.

Irrational optimists take something negative and make it a positive through magical delusion. In the process, they reject the same thing the intimidator rejects: the free expression of a dissenting *no*. The only difference between the two is that irrational optimists use the appeal of magic to get their way instead of intimidation or a staged performance.

Most of us don't succumb entirely to irrational optimists in the same way that a lot of people submit to intimidators. Still, many of us want to believe in their enchantment, and it's easy to become a willing collaborator. If we don't collaborate, we have to stand against them. Most people recognize (perhaps in hindsight) experiences they've had with an irrational optimist.

My first experience with irrational optimism came from meeting a friend's mom when I was in grade school. She had nine kids and the family lived in a human pigpen while running a poorly managed dairy farm. During the summer, dead flies crash-landed and buzzed everywhere, with carcasses constantly piling up on the window ledge and in the bottoms of light fixtures. In the winter, the kids tracked fresh manure everywhere in the home. They never vacuumed.

Some parents do a great job home-schooling, but this friend's mother believed she was protecting her kids from the evils of the world by keeping them home. She required very little schoolwork, and they had almost no gumption for anything. Consequently, they performed academically below their age, protected by what their mother called the "armor of God." A few years later, my friend's father died because the mother believed that conventional medicine was inherently evil. At the time, I wondered what could possibly be wicked about a life-saving procedure.

My father, a friend of the family, helped move her husband from one bed to another. The man was in a coma, his body riddled with cancer. None of this seemed to deter the wife, because she believed that things happen for a reason. It wasn't until years later that my father was able to challenge her basic assumptions about freedom and agency. "I just want to be told what to believe," she said at last. Such a mind is likely to being seduced by an irrational optimism.

When we subject our agency to outside control, life acts upon us because we refuse to act. Only when we act responsibly can we say we have faith. Do you recall what we said earlier about faith? It implies some degree of responsible action. Whether we define the action as personal action or social action, faith is responsible action. Notice how this gets the mind to focus on what is responsible and away from fastidious practices and fanatical doctrines. Does this push away God? Definitely not! It brings us closer together, and is this not godly? In other words, is not the glory of God intelligence?

When we hold to sound understanding, the irrational optimist cannot twist the meaning of faith into a magical solution without any responsible action. If we cannot focus on what is responsible, we cannot recognize what is irrational.

For example, Germany's last election until after the Second World War was held on 5 March 1933. Though the Nazis party won only 44% of the vote, Hitler persuaded the Reichstag (parliament) to pass a constitutional amendment called the Enabling Law, allowing him to govern independently for four years. Articles two and three of the enabling law read as thus:

Article 2

Laws enacted by the government of the Reich may deviate from the constitution as long as they do not affect the institutions of the Reichstag and the Reichsrat. The rights of the President remain unaffected.

Article 3

Laws enacted by the government shall be issued by the Chancellor and announced in the Reich Gazette. They shall take effect on the day following the announcement, unless they prescribe a different date.

Before the Enabling Act was passed, two vital things were needed. First, Hitler and his Nazi party needed to call the new law the "Law to Remedy the Distress of the People and the Reich." This positive-sounding title garnered the appeal of the people without their full knowledge of the new law. Second, he positioned soldiers outside the Kroll Opera House (temporary site of parliament) to make sure the legislature gave Hitler what he wanted. In one day Hitler employed both irrational denial and intimidating force, a very deadly combination.

The key to recognizing irrational optimism is in the trait of denial that surfaces in how idolatry is expressed toward a new emperor or attention to one's self. You can see this denial in how it quickly pushes aside a majority of dissent, or good reason, in favor of a new savior, state, empire, a new authority, or, in the case of some, pure relativism where there is no grounding rod of responsibility.

As the intimidator expresses his idolatry through control, and as the staged optimist expresses his idolatry through glory, the irrational optimist expresses idolatry through denial. Denial is the hardest trait to spot because it has the widest appeal to a greater majority. Give the people an excuse from taking responsibility and you gain control over their freedom.

Other key traits of the irrational optimist surface when aligned with the same character keywords to the left. **See Figure 4-1.** Notice the irrational optimist's character traits for reward and how they view intelligence.

Fig. 4-1 Traits of Irrational Optimists	
Character	**Traits**
Idolatry	Denial
Intelligence	Glory in Self
Agency	Avoids Questions
Motivation	Social Exaltation
Reward	Social Worship

Irrational optimism seeks some traditional authority, political doctrine, or approval from God or the state to gain control; it ignores the still small voice within. The worst form of irrationalism is pure relativism, where constant redirection and deflection are used to avoid responsibility for common sense. The woman mentioned above never followed her heart, but rather followed certain authorities without knowing for herself. As positive as she was about her authoritative and often divine helplessness, there was no impetus from her own heart to do the right thing. Many fanatic minds often think that God rewards them for blind suffering. This is like saying God rewards people for enduring afflictions even without adding any value. Some religious people believe that "bad things" bring them closer to God. In no way can this idea be optimistic. As for pure relativism, complete rejection of responsible truth is the name of the game.

In *Power vs. Force*, David Hawkins shares insights into the *frequencies* of human action. This image shows how human beings can vibrate at a much higher frequency than most people realize. **See Figure 4-2**.

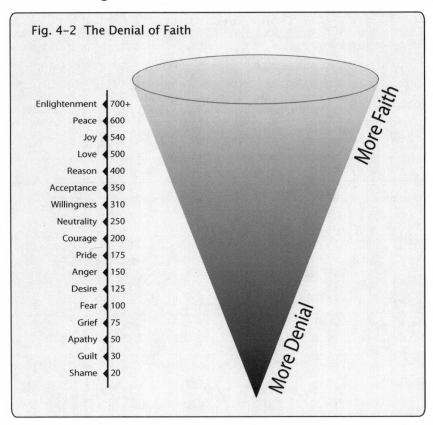

Fig. 4–2 The Denial of Faith

Enlightenment	700+
Peace	600
Joy	540
Love	500
Reason	400
Acceptance	350
Willingness	310
Neutrality	250
Courage	200
Pride	175
Anger	150
Desire	125
Fear	100
Grief	75
Apathy	50
Guilt	30
Shame	20

More Faith

More Denial

The problem with irrational optimists is that they take something like Hawkins' research and they keep it linear, as if one frequency leads to the next with no continuation of anything prior. Does pride lead to courage? Not all the time. Pride can easily regress and lead to anger if courage doesn't intervene. The same happens with love. What good is love, if we're not trying to reach greater enlightenment by tempering it with reason? This is not the real problem, though. The real problem is how on earth do we scale Hawkins' research? How do we scale the real power of each individual in a community without force? Please keep this question in mind. The answer is coming.

When we step up in power or down in force, we have one foot on one step, and another foot on a second step. This gives us stability. Irrational optimists never step up or down with stability. They stand still with both feet planted on one step. They look at pride, anger and desire as a progressive movement toward rugged individualism. Or they look at guilt as if it is the same as acceptance. In the most confused way, the irrational optimist talks of enlightenment without the stability of reason or any need of courage. Optimism is all in their mind and never alive in the steps they make in life. **See Figure 4-3**.

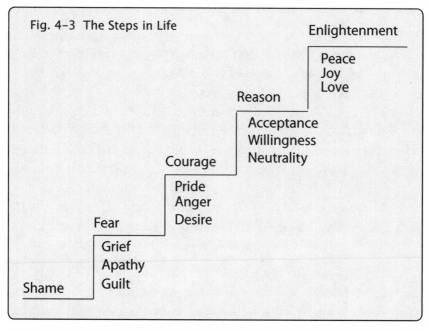

Fig. 4-3 The Steps in Life

Enlightenment

Peace
Joy
Love

Reason

Acceptance
Willingness
Neutrality

Courage

Pride
Anger
Desire

Fear

Grief
Apathy
Guilt

Shame

We used the word progressive above. Political optimists will always claim they are progressive. How can this be when they are quick to shift responsibility onto the state or some other distant authority? They never take responsible action themselves, which you would think best defines what it means to be progressive. They will centralize power and distance responsibility far away, and this is often repugnant to a genuine mind. Sometimes it's essential to be repugnant—the quality of being contradictory towards irrationality. This is necessary because the irrational optimist is skilled at diversions from responsibility. Contradictory repugnance becomes the only way to reveal the linear intolerance of the irrational mind.

For example, in regards to the Jewish/Christian tithe, a confrontation erupted between a relational thinker and an economics professor stuck in a linear intolerance imposed by the authority of his own religious culture. The two men were of the same religion. The professor, who was active in the church, came to the relational thinker to reactivate him. Over a period of months, the two men discussed their views on economics, a discussion that eventually led to a heated debate on the church's tithing method.

The relational thinker ran the numbers and showed how a father with four kids earning $28,000 a year pays $2,800 in tithing based on income, and how a single man with no kids pays $10,000 on $100,000 of income. While the father of four rents and lives on $25,200, the other man lives on $90,000 and owns his own home. If we adjust tithing to be 10% on one's net worth, the father of four would pay much less, because he has very few possessions, and the rich man would suddenly pay on net worth annually. This follows the principle of paying a tenth of all possessions that Abraham paid to King Melchizedek, and not a tenth of one's income that many Christians follow today.

According to the relational thinker, tithing by net worth decreases one's idolatry for possessions and increases free enterprise, while tithing by income favors materialism and the gross nature of capitalism.

The economics professor then argued, "The church is led by men inspired by God." Do you see what happened? The professor killed the argument when he took his foot off reason and stepped back onto anger. This revealed his idolatry for religious authority. Reason always wins if one can set aside tradition and authority and replace them with good sense coming from within relational thinking. Reason shared in a body of ideal consent lifts us in the direction of love, joy, and peace. It adds enlightenment and inspires. Irrationalism performs oppositely: it fosters central control, idolatry toward those in control, or direct relativism to avoid any responsibility.

When we choose not to act according to our defined values and prefer stubborn dogmatism, we manufacture an artificial direction in order to prove self-worth without considering the lack of good we add to the world. A daydream can be repugnant, but at times we use this to compensate for the irrationalism of day-to-day reality.

When we use pure irrationalism as a valued principle, this is where the optimism of *no* must stand and call it out in free and open dissent. Perhaps we might even imagine how we could overcome the denial of irrationalism.

The Magic of Irresponsibility

Irrational optimists make choices that are often a denial of responsibility. Not surprisingly, they look optimistic while doing this. Let's look at it from the point of view of a *deus ex machina* ("God from the machine"). Anytime the plot of a Greek drama became too difficult to resolve, the playwright used a trap door or a crane behind the scenes to introduce a magical being who would jump into the confused story and solve the crisis by magic.

We are all willing to suspend our disbelief in entertainment; there's nothing wrong with that. When it happens in life, however, we have a serious problem.

Consider the case of an irrational optimist who was the president of a company making millions of dollars by using anecdotal stories promoting magical mineral packs that consumers would add to bottled water. As both a religious minister and the president of the company, he used language of great promise (and no logic) to make his premises stick. His mantra talked of the 97% who made less than $100,000 a year and how his company helped many of those 97% percent gain financial stability among the wealthy three percent. This is odd, since 97% of all those who join multi-level marketing companies actually fail. Nonetheless, the heavy coating of a staged optimism cloaked in a revivalist rhetoric made it so that less than three percent of those present could see the dirty logic.

Infinite markets do not exist, and supply and demand will always control the movement of goods and services. Those facts were not part of this CEO's presentation. He believed that hundreds of thousands of independent sales agents all stepping over each other could fill the earth—and leave room for a billion more. The inherent lack of reason is eclipsed by the promise of personal gain. Costs are often more than thirty times the real value of the product in a multi-level marketing up-line. Not only do network-marketing companies sell value at very high prices; they push positive mental unrealities as if they were chewable vitamins.

This is how destructive motivational speakers can be when they begin to adopt irrational optimism. They use positive language in such a way that it gives the listener the same escape from the genuine path to responsible action they are seeking to avoid. It's such a poisonous form of hypocrisy that the modest heart cannot stand up and say, "No!" This problem is manifested in all of society that fears to stand up against irrational leadership built upon the worship of authority. Our problem has always been that we lack genuine leadership based on ideal consent derived from the open agreement of all involved. We prefer the magic of the irrational to the responsibility of the Master.

Consider typical mental exertions of magic pushed by companies and compare them to what we simply understand as honesty. The difference is more than subtle.

The Political

Everyone needs this product

Anyone can do this business

We don't sell this business, we share it

We have built your business for you

The Genuine

Our product is not for everyone

Nobody likes to sell but we can fill a need

We are in the business of sales

You build your own business

People who follow irrational optimists tend to have a mindset that gets fixated on forced magic to escape from taking an active responsibility in being honest. Irrationalism feeds on escape by appealing to others' fears and selling emotionally appealing magic as the false confidence of choice. When you compare this to the knowledge and acceptance of one's own fear, you can see the denial in the irrational mind. In other words, the early Greek philosophers taught us to "know thyself." They taught this to keep the ravages of fear from taking hold of genuine purpose. So much effort in talking about fear at the start of this book illustrates why political optimists are afraid, but the irrational optimist displays this fear in the most profound way.

Remember, both faith and denial describe some kind of action. When we respond in fear, we are engaged in the denial of fear. When we react in faith, we are engaged in the acceptance of our fear. The second is a much higher value. Fear will always surface as denial or a raw disability, both are much lower values, unless dealt with intelligently by taking the steps from courage to reason and from reason to enlightenment. When we choose to act in faith, which we can simply call responsible action, fear dissolves and it becomes less of a disability.

Something else is not quite clear. If fear is the motive for denial, what is the motive for faith? Faith is vital because the irrational optimist exhibits an unreasonable faith. You can see this because irrational optimists avoid direct questions that confront their lack of responsibility. For instance, like any political optimist, irrational minds lack depth or actual responsibility; but, unlike the intimidator and unlike the staged optimist, the irrational optimist doesn't run from "no." Instead the irrational optimists co-opt the voice of no for their own gain. It gives them the image of being open when in fact they are not. It's like answering a question by saying, "Let me answer that by asking you this." In other words, they embrace *no* by turning it around and using it against you.

Momentum of Enthusiasm

Think of a salesperson using emotional appeal to sell you something you neither need nor want. They appear to give lip service to your feelings (like the staged optimist), but they give absolutely nothing back (like the intimidator). A person like this will give a great pitch, but when it comes time to allow others to act within their area of individual responsibility, this person will shut it down every time.

Once we release a bowling ball, the best decision possible leaves our hand. If we see the ball going the wrong way, we don't waste energy running down the lane in order to correct the direction! And yet bad leaders do this constantly; they do not realize that every effort spent to correct the direction along the way will diminish the momentum of the labor in motion. Let the ball be off-center and retain the most momentum possible. A spare is easier to handle than a split between two pins on opposite sides of the alley.

Human enthusiasm is a lot like momentum.

If you keep correcting it until it's heading in the right direction, the ball loses momentum. The wrong direction with a lot of enthusiasm will produce better results than a constant change of direction that diminishes enthusiasm. In a way, enthusiasm is directly linked to the best kind of freedom in learning, and learning builds knowledge, which builds confidence. Take away the freedom to learn on your own and innovation dies.

The irrational optimist never stops changing direction. When we direct people, we have to avoid destroying their enthusiasm, because there's no guarantee that our direction is perfect. Even if it seems like a good idea to change direction, that act will douse the fire of enthusiasm. The only time to douse the fire is if it is out of control, dangerous, or costly. Sound leaders know this better than most people. Poor leaders need to control everything—and that's fundamentally irrational in nature.

A business client gave a job to three of his staff. The job took over fourteen months of labor, and even then they were still not done. I visited each member, and the problem surfaced right away—not one of them wanted to of the staff to get something done, *and* they were using outdated technology. The same project was built and completed in less than two weeks with a well-known third party service provider. When the in-house staff team visited for a meeting, the team leader spent all his time making the owner feel good about his decisions. He was a political optimist who staged himself in such a way to make the intimidating owner feel good about what he wanted. Meanwhile, I was combative, argumentative, and firm in my stance that "these guys are wasting your time and money."

The owner accepted the completed project but he still called on the failing team for help. He needed to feel empowered—and I needed to get something done. This kind of mixed leadership is not healthy, and yet we build bureaucracies through enabling relationships that promote controls rather than enthusiasm.

When an irrational optimist runs an organization, something interesting happens. The real fighters leave and the pretenders increase their control in the name of non-productive devotion. Their irrational gusto eventually relies upon looking and sounding like they are working. People accepting the controller's demands feed his ego while gradually limiting individual momentum. You can recognize these political gridlocks when they maintain the status quo. Nothing great comes about because old patterns are used to protect laziness of intent.

Irrational optimists are destructive forces to all natural momentum. We call them irrational because they pretend to stand for rational thinking. Consider such statements as "Let's have an open meeting about this," or "Let's get the others involved." These and other comments are often used to indicate honest intent, but they actually give everyone a chance to politicize the situation through majority manipulation and not common consent.

Instead of the group becoming a forum to discuss policies, values, and inspire individual responsibility, the group actually preserves the status quo by inflating its authority with more and more centralized control. They thwart individual enthusiasm by maintaining diminished efficiency. Welcome to the gross negligence of political optimism, a majority rule acquired by a bottom-up idol worship of one control freak in charge! Shift that model by empowering dissenting views with real teeth in common consent, and you will give birth to natural enthusiasm again.

A majority rule process can easily snuff out innovative dissent. This is the number-one killer of innovation and the killer of sustainable value creation in business, religion, education, and government. If the leadership center of any organization is not pushing for the highest level of consent while preserving common dissent in each person, then you're looking at an irrational optimist. No CEO and no board of directors will ever have the full vision and implementation needed for a company, and it is foolish to empower them with it.

More often than not, managers destroy individual momentum through group members aspiring for approval and from those with no momentum of their own. It's their very openness (without sustained vision and without allowing for dissent) that displays their political optimism. Unlike the intimidator who abhors open gatherings, the irrational optimist thrives on the irrationalism he can pontificate free of dissent.

Follow the idolatry and not the money. Let's explain this problem of idolatry using the popular philosophy behind the so-called law of attraction, also known as *The Secret*.[1] According to *The Secret*, a person's thoughts attract corresponding positive and negative life influences. The law of attraction says, "if you think it, it will materialize." Many proponents of the idea claim that, with practice, a person can use the law of attraction to manifest changes in their lives.

However, this idea has no requirement of virtue. It demands no social responsibility and allows for constant change, something irrational optimists love because it allows them to let go of difficult responsibilities in favor of a new direction with less responsibility.

This is why *The Secret* sells so well, and why new trends in cognitive manifestation are so popular. It is truly hard to argue against these ideas when they are spoken with high energy and pumped up glee. There is one way to deal with these ideas. Simply ask, "How do you scale that?"

A female student gave a speech on *The Secrete* in my class. When she completed her ten-minute presentation, I said "I am intoxicated with your enthusiasm but not with your idea."

By completely removing so-called negative mindsets simply wanting to ask a question, there's no responsibility to hear any real dissent. In other words, take away social and even personal responsibility, and the masses will buy it. This can only happen for so long until society collapses and businesses fail. Again, ask a motivational guru promoting the newest power hour, "How do you scale it." Invariably they will have no answers or they will call you a negative person.

There's nothing more irrational than a magical escape from responsibility. This doesn't negate the importance of positive thought or good mental practices employed to remove blocks and inhibitions keeping us from greater achievement. It just means that the real motive remains buried, which is why you cannot debate an irrational optimist by saying no. They think dissent is negative—when in fact it's more positive than a new magical system willing to destroy individual momentum.

The problem is not just with followers of the secret; it's with fastidious religious practices, fundamentalist traditions, and even a belief in capitalism without social responsibility. No matter a person's religion, education, or economic status, no behavior or practice can replace responsibility. A ritual doesn't replace the work of responsible faith, moral relativism does not delete accountability, and capitalism doesn't guarantee a free market for all. And yet, to an irrational optimist, they do.

The point is that when the capacity of an irrational optimist is tested, they elude with red herrings and return with loaded questions instead of answers. They stand toe-to-toe but not eye-to-eye. They redirect back to you in order to get you to claim a truth which is then countered with the all-famous "That's your perception." They face the fire, it seems, but without getting warm. Their motive is social worship or an excuse from being responsible. The only way to recognize the irrational optimist is to first have within you an intelligent concern for taking responsibility by adding value. As Samuel Dael explains in *The Christian Folly,* the suffix *–th* in both *faith* and *believeth* are linguistic calls to action. An irrational belief in something mimics religious salvation without the action of doing something good.

It makes good sense to give better groundwork to the inherent nature of faith, for faith, as we will find, is the antithesis to denial, which does not foster any responsible action.

Faith vs. Magic

Many young people apply to universities far from home. With no idea how to pay for their educations, they mail the acceptance letter and two weeks before school starts they pack their car and head off to college.

In my case, I headed north on the Pacific Coast Highway in California. I only had $400 in my pocket, no job, and no place to stay. I wasn't alone: many students do the same every year and they are further burdened by debt before they arrive. With all this uncertainty in my own life, I knew one thing. I knew that I could find a job somewhere and that I could sleep in the pickup if needed.

Even though it takes a few days, a new student in a foreign town finds a place to call home. Maybe a job follows a month later. Until that time, many students call back home a few times in fear and panic, but because of the persistent application of effort toward what needs to be done in an uncertain situation, the tough times pass and things work out.

Even though we feel overwhelmed with fear, we exercise faith in right actions. If *The Secret* had taught this, then it would have been far more popular with dissenting minds demanding deeper understanding. Irrational ideas distort faith and replace it with a desire for magic by using self-imposed positive mental exertions instead of responsible action, or again they escape with a relativistic stance to avoid your common sense in truth. The proper definition of faith means *believe* (thinking) + *th* (action). Modern English has lost the meaning of faith. Positive thinking is not, and never will be, *faith*. The best kind of positive thinking is the kind that removes blocks, false beliefs, general assumptions and cognitive programs that never lead to healthy action. And the only way to remove these is through responsible motion despite our fear. If done by any other means, we are stuck with just another sophisticated denial.

Too often, we anticipate a divine influence or magic solution without any work on our part. Faith is work, because the universe doesn't tell us everything we need to know. If it told us everything, faith wouldn't be work, and we would not learn to think for ourselves. However, the irrational optimist controls how we think by telling us everything. They take from us the personal investment to exercise our own mind. Just as faith without work is dead, so also is intelligence without thought dead.

Many people imagine that faith defies intelligence, arguing that faith is a spontaneous feeling, a supernatural energy, or the taking of a blind leap we cannot understand. This is false and irrational. Questioning, reasoning, listening, and choosing are acts of intelligence. If intelligence doesn't perform these basic acts, it doesn't act for itself. This is why faith is best defined as responsible action. If you are not actively compassionate, kind, hardworking, and a defender of the innocent, you have no faith in the right action of theses values. When you follow the idolatry and not the money, you are left with one single truth: you never see responsible action in the worship of authority or moral relativism. It is a major clue.

Let's ask a simple question. Can you exercise faith in something that is not true? If you say yes, then faith is a word with pliable meaning accessible to both the fanatic despot and the care-giving neighbor. Faith isn't neutral in this sense, as the law of attraction would like it to be. It has traditionally stood for adding value to the lives of others. Even though the dictionary does not say this, faith is more like an active verb than a static noun. It's an expression of virtue and not malice, and therefore it cannot be neutral to the abuse of an extremist or hidden in meaning to the most simple of hearts. Faith must stand for the purest exercise of what we know is good and true. If not, it carries little weight of value.

The irrational optimist refuses this kind of relational logic in applying responsible action to faith. They prefer the rhetoric of a revivalist religious convention to the actions of someone like Gandhi choosing to sew his own clothing in protest against foreign control of national independence.

Faith is the applied action of taking responsibility both personally and socially. This is how you can see an irrational optimist. They take no personal or social responsibility for adding value. If they do, it's a token gift hoping for the social reward of acceptance. Again, follow the idolatry by seeing the authority people are willing to place over them in place of taking responsible action through the social intelligence found in the practice of common consent.

Those who don't believe in magic or don't understand faith tend to adopt principles of control. Such is the view of an irrational control freak. Imagine that a student asks a teacher a question. The teacher gives an answer. The student returns the next day and asks more questions and the teacher offers more answers. This continues for weeks; the student asks and the teacher answers. At some point, however, the teacher should feel concerned that the student has no answers—but, instead, the teacher sits in total possession of the student's mind. The teacher has attracted what is programmed into the student.

Irrational optimists are like this teacher. They are platonic in their need for authority over others. No matter how sugar-coated their language, all energy returns to them. Seduced by their own passion, the irrational optimist appears to be the most open and the most approachable of all people. In truth, they are the most closed.

There are two natures in political optimists that are hallmarks of irrational optimism, and they are both linear in their thinking. The first is being open to what they will hear but closed to what they will speak (the liberal). The second is being open to what they will speak but closed to what they will hear (the conservative). Both are linear and irrational; they never relate with others in the political extremes.

For instance, for a liberal not to say what he or she thinks is simply disingenuous. And a conservative's closed-mindedness in hearing other ideas is an assumption of infallibility. The irrational optimist is both. They are open about their form of magic but closed to the inclusion of any honest faith. They keep the power of both yes and no to themselves. They show great fear with absolutely no faith in the agency of others or active responsibility to the truth.

More Clarity

Too often in a book of this kind we are pressed to remember various classifications and categories, types of happiness, or new verbiage on character brands that are common logic but not necessarily common to our language. Very few ideas broken into labels and categories actually stick, unless kept to just a few, and even these lose their significance over time. It seems that while labels tend to mystify, more clarity definitely needs to surface.

Many recall in college or high school learning about the use of id, ego, and super ego; type A and type B personalities, the color code, and the conscious and unconscious minds. Aristotle talked about three types of government—a monarchy (rule by one), aristocracy (rule by few), and democracy (rule by many). John Stuart Mill came up with one category of utilitarianism—the greatest good for the greatest number.

Sometimes we can't get by without breaking human action into categories, and sometimes we can. When the diagnosis of bipolar disorder came out, it gave us a name for certain behaviors, providing limited insight into human intelligence and human fear. Attention-deficit disorder is another branding without insight into clear meaning. In other words, without an accurate definition of intelligence to account for the various thinking patterns, what we call attention deficit may in fact be nothing but the long patience of building a concept of what is experienced in life. This would explain why some labeled as dyslexic in their youth eventually accomplish great things later in life, due to their conceptual mind eventually becoming rich enough to accommodate a greater relational capacity. This is something linguistic and linear minds almost never achieve. It also explains why linguistic minds peak early in life and rarely later.

A student's attention often drifts in class and in reading, but we cannot call this a disorder. When we see a traumatic crash on the freeway, we all rubberneck to see the damage and continue driving for miles afterward without being alert to the road ahead. Is this a disorder?

It's the same problem with speed-readers that bullet through a book with swiftness but seem to lack the conversational experience that requires several moments of pause through the book. We can speed-read many written works. However, what do we miss with a book like the Bible or Shakespeare's plays? Can a speed-reader comprehend all books without a single question that demands the mind to pause and consider the meaning of what took years for the writer to compile?

With all its hype, speed-reading is strictly linear. It doesn't produce relational meaning. It doesn't allow the mind to question while reading. This may just be a problem with slow learners. We call them disabled or dyslexic to explain away an assumed dysfunction. Why do I mention this? The irrational optimist speed-reads human beings, books, and his own mind without any relational skills.

An older couple in town teaches a speed-reading class together. At one of their classes, a few questions surfaced about the meaning of a book, content about God, love, freedom, and education. They became extremely uncomfortable and quickly became intimidating optimists by avoiding the conversation. They redirected the class in order to move along. This is the behavior from two people who read about ten books a week. A humanities professor in town swears that speed-reading is essential to learning. In his blog posts, although clear and concise, he says very little in relation to other ideas outside his field of study. When you speed-read, you think through things the same way. Everything is linear and not relational. You fail to see insight because you have put the power of dissent and reflective questioning to the side.

Consider the following divisions of intelligence types that may help you understand the concept of linear versus relational minds. At one extreme is the conceptual process; at the other is linguistic memory. Conceptual minds are more relational; linguistic minds are more linear.

The two are like a vast graphics program taking up most of the computer's memory as compared to a small calculating program taking up very little memory. The graphics program is slow while the calculating program operates at a very high speed. Adding memory seems to help both extremes. However, high memory intelligence with a small, fast calculating program fares better in school. It does well because it has a greater capacity for recollection. The conceptual mind has something just as important, but the processing of a program such as relational concepts responds much more slowly.

Most educators teach against a student's memory rather than against a student's relational understanding. Memory and programs take up part of the total intelligence. A memory preserves and records data; a program processes that data.

A conceptual intelligence (more program than memory) has a hard time retaining data because it is trying to process as it goes. These minds often appear slow and those possessing them have many questions. They may even have difficulty phrasing the questions, especially if their thoughts are drifting in order to process new information.

This is a genuine optimist in embryo. The tendency to use the term "attention deficit" does them no justice. Younger minds may appear almost void of a memory and this may highlight their behavioral distractions even more. Over time, however, they eventually learn to relate concepts because they have taken the time to pause and consider meanings. We may label them in their youth, but in their adult years they build a life program that yields insight and wisdom.

Irrational optimists aren't like this. Everything is linear to them and they relate to nothing and never acquire the wisdom they pretend to have. They are all memory with no conceptual whole.

Relational intelligence builds over years of processing; it might even become faster in time than the immediate recall of memory. This is the great secret the irrational mind never understands. Have you ever seen a fast calculating mind in its youth become full of wisdom in later years? Take even a child protégée, do you ever hear of them accomplishing great things later in their life? There's a great richness of humanity in an older and more conceptual mind compared to a youthful and purely linguistic one.

This is essentially the difference between relational and linear thinking. Collecting data records will never secure the desired meaning. The rare exception is the occasional genius like Shakespeare, showing both linear recall in using a vast vocabulary and a relational insight revealing the deep meaning of each word employed.

Many researchers have established similar distinctions: between left and right brains, between yin and yang, between romantic and classic. You can have all the reference data in your head, such as categories, types and classifications, but without a relational concept pulled from many sources and sifted through a lot of discussion, you find yourself unable to relate.

Are we not found wanting as a society in this regard? This is the basic problem with irrational optimists: they are purely linear and remain stuck in their limited range obtained without discussion and without debate. They reach far in their minds for a single view, but they never turn their heads for a second or third view.

If you could point to one good thing our education system has destroyed, this is it. We favor linear thinking over relational connections. We kill the oral traditions of "no" in favor of a contrived and forced lecture of "yes." We are educated without meaning and we speed-read without developing sound questions. We live without the internal pause of a personal conversation.

The first time I realized this came while reading Herman Melville's *Moby-Dick*. It was the scene in the book where Starbuck, the first mate, challenged Captain Ahab. Starbuck said something revealing on the quarterdeck for the other mates to hear: "Captain Ahab, I have heard of Moby-Dick—but it was not Moby-Dick that took off thy leg?" The captain then said in a whipped reply, "Who told thee that?"

At this point, it was impossible for me to read any further. For days, I thought about it. If Moby-Dick had nothing to do with taking Ahab's leg, then why does the captain blame the whale? What was the captain's problem? A few months later, *The Denial of Death* by Earnest Becker came into my life and he answered the question. The whale was a scapegoat for Ahab's denial of death. By killing the whale, he sought to repress his own fear of mortality, at least in his own mind. Ahab's problem became a symbolic one. Ahab was trying to kill death. It took about two weeks to fully wrap my mind around this concept. By the time I was fully aware of the new understanding, the rest of the class had completed the book. I was left behind in the class but far ahead in life.

A conceptual understanding is not the sum of human experience. It is a sense of responsible meaning that helps connect life experience to other thoughts. Irrational optimists streamline any conceptual abilities to avoid responsibility and they shift that into a magical escape or a relative flight.

A conceptual mind struggles to make sense of bits of data by placing the details into a larger whole. The linear mind can file data with very little order. To many genuine optimists, this seems irrational.

A friend had to pass a state contractor's test. He memorized the answers to the test and passed without understanding relevant meaning. The conceptual mind struggles to file things away until it can fit the same into a larger context. That larger context is a way of seeing things from a broader perspective. The denial of meaning becomes the denial of responsibility.

Another good friend prepared to take the same exam and instead of plowing through the test with the least amount of effort and with no meaning, he decided to spend a good year to study several books and understand new green building technologies in order to get a bigger picture for himself. He even attended several construction sites to take part in the building of homes using solar, radiant barrier, insulated concrete forms, and geo-thermal technologies.

This behavior makes for great doctors, lawyers, teachers and practitioners in many fields. They have the bedside quality that can reach across with a depth of meaning to add character to their vast and detailed knowledge. You will never see this range of understanding in the irrational optimist because they don't think relationally. The only way to see this emptiness in the irrational optimist is if you get more responsible meaning in yourself.

The meaning of words now becomes the enemy of political optimism, especially of the irrational optimist. It is out of a struggle for rich and well-defined words (obtained through common consent) that we can stand against the irrational optimist. Although various types of political and genuine optimism are classified, the real intent is to uncover an understanding of human fear and the denial of responsibility seen in certain behaviors said to be optimistic.

Take a moment to think about words used in a discussion, such as those listed below. Try to find their responsible application in dialogue with others. If you dismiss them or think that they are purely relative with no grounding rod of responsibility, then you are a political optimist. If you focus on one word with no relation to another word, you are irrational. Think of each word as possessing a magnitude of responsible action and then you will begin to see them in relation to each other.

You are welcome to add to the list. Open discussion of these words in a therapeutic way in business, family, and community life will increase responsibility and decrease denial that too often surfaces in the escape of a staged optimist, the control of an intimidator, and the magic and relativism plagued by the irrational mind.

Angels
Art/Beauty
Being/Existence
Belief
Brotherhood
Capitalism
Causality/Infinity
Chance
Charity/Service
Citizen
Communication
Community
Conservation
Conservatism
Constitution
Culture
Currency
Death/Life
Deduction
Definition
Democracy
Denial
Desire
Distinction
Dream
Duty/Responsibility
Economics
Electric
Evolution
Emotion
Energy
Enterprise
Epistemology
Equality
Ethics
Evil
Evolution
Faith
Family
Fear
Federalism
Form/Law
Freedom/Free Will
Friendship
Globalism

God
Government
Health
Heaven
Hell
History
Hope
Hypothesis
Ideal
Imagination
Induction
Intelligence/IQ
Interpretation
Joy
Justice/Judgment
Knowledge
Leadership
Learning/Education
Liberalism
Liberty
Light
Love
Magnetic
Marriage/Family
Meaning
Media
Medicine
Memory
Metaphysics
Monarchy
Moral
Morality
Myth
Nature
Nutrition
Obedience
Opposition
Optimism
Ownership/Georgics
Philosophy
Physics
Politics
Principle
Prophecy
Providence

Psychology/ Psychiatry
Quality
Reason/Logic
Relativity
Responsibility
Revelation
Revolution
Rhetoric
Righteousness
Rights
Sacrifice
Science
Sin
Socialism
Sovereignty
Soul
Space
Spirit/Spiritual
Sport
State
Statesmanship
Taxation
Technology
Terror/Intimidation
Time
Tradition
Truth
Tyranny
Value
Vice
Virtue
War
Wealth
Wisdom

Domestic violence and abuse are used for one purpose and one purpose only: to gain and maintain total control over you. An abuser doesn't play fair. Abusers use fear, guilt, shame, and intimidation to wear you down and keep you under his or her thumb. Your abuser may also threaten you, hurt you, or hurt those around you.

He has spoken out strongly against the fact that when belligerents see freedom of expression as an enemy to their cause and the media as a tool for propaganda, journalists who attempt to report in a nonpartisan way face pressure, manipulation, intimidation or even elimination.

Marie Okabe

Section II The Genuine Optimist

> The test of all beliefs is their practical effect in life. If it be true that optimism compels the world forward, and pessimism retards it, then it is dangerous to propagate a pessimistic philosophy.

> - Helen Keller, "Optimism: An Essay"

Optimism says that this is best of all possible worlds. However, if we do nothing to add value to our world, our optimism may certainly exemplify that of the phony and the political. If, on the other hand, we do something to make this the best of all possible worlds, then our optimism is manifested in the value we add and not the attitude we show.

There is something else just as important. If there is a means to add value, there must also be a means to protect value from the control of political optimists. Adding value and protecting value from political control are needed to support the genuine optimist.

In this section, we discuss the meaning of a practical faith. Faith in common consent is important in this discussion because we must restore the action of continually moving toward higher values. Once we restore this forward action, we can offer three types of genuine optimism that run against the three political optimists discussed in the previous section.

We're about to see three unique ways that genuine optimists add value to the world, and how we've lost faith in the voice of consent in a free society that supports their value.

With this knowledge, we can then propose, in the final section, a way to unshackle genuine optimists with the advantage of common consent so they can rise naturally and take more leadership against the narrowing constrictions of a political world. It is the only way to properly protect the value they add. Perhaps the real problem is how we see leadership and power. If this is true, then perhaps it is time to see how we give a popular vote to leadership without any real consent. What will surface is the greatest challenge in human history, the removal of our idolatry for authority.

5

Our Responsible Faith

We talk about the responsibility to vote, but without dialogue and debate among ourselves, as a jury is required to do regarding innocence or guilt, we truly are not responsible. Simply casting a vote is not responsibility. It is a vote for one's personal darkness. We must discuss, exchange, and be challenged. This is Socratic heavy lifting—the basis of knowledge.

- Mica Thomas, editor Vision Impact Publishing

I think hedonism, escapism, laughter and fun are paramount, but as you grow up, it's not enough to be happy and laugh. There's something missing in your make-up if that's all you're about. I love the lighter side of life as much as the next person, but I've become less and less afraid of the heavy stuff.[1]

- Drew Barrymore, actress

A Step Forward

I was riding my bike when a fat bully threw a hard plastic football at the front wheel, and caused me to crash. I remember trying to brace myself as I went down. Both elbows scraped across five feet of black asphalt and the stinging pain seemed worsened by the hot, sticky tar. Small pebbles were buried into the bloodied palms of my hands. The bully was a foot taller than me, and two years younger. With friends in his yard, goading him on, he laughed at the crash he'd instigated. This laughter, I realized later, was a manifestation of his denial of fear—and a troublemaker's fear was hidden by a false laughing optimism. This dark form of denial can really hurt.

A few weeks before this event, the football team was practicing indoors because of heavy rain outside. The football coach randomly matched football players with wrestlers to test their ability to grapple their opponent to the ground. Paired with this heavier kid, I took him down every time. With his 170-pound advantage to my scrawny 119 pounds, he rolled across the mat like a hot sweaty water bottle filled with chocolate pudding. His fat belly had no muscle, and so it came as no surprise that I could push him around. It took the skill I'd learned in wrestling to see that the football player had no training.

Even though the entire football team faced the same embarrassing problem with other wrestlers, I was the one selected for retribution when this bully tossed a football into my front wheel at the first available opportunity. The masculine fear of failure at the hand of a much smaller athlete was too much for him to handle. He had to lash out in denial to hide the fear bottled inside. Logic says that if we base our motives on faith in genuine courage, we act responsibly. However, if we base our motives on the fear of rejection, we act irresponsibly.

If we have faith in something that isn't true, we live in denial. Faith isn't working toward a desired physical goal, but rather toward a true principle. A goal may not work, but a principle—such as accepting what you fear—will always show greater value to the world. We always adjust our goals to the principle, and not the principle to the goal.

The bully in our lives puts the goal first and crushes the principle. Political optimists may always outwardly express a principle, but inwardly they have a hidden agenda. The hypocrite comes upon us as a wolf in sheep's clothing. When they lash out, they destroy the higher democratic consent we have the potential to reach.

Optimists are natural risk-takers. Political people take no risks and in fact are destructive toward those who do take risks. Using myself as an example, the odds seemed stacked against being able to get a business off the ground, especially with a lot of competition. Many close relations knew of the great sacrifice made, and how little money was available to my family during this time. We rarely had food in the kitchen and many times several months would pass without any income. At one point the house was leased to a renter in order to pay the mortgage while the family lived with in-laws in another state. When a few friends and family tried to talk with us, it was easy to sense their guilt for not helping when honest words of encouragement would have been enough. Instead, many put on their counseling hat and began telling us what to do.

One such close friend called to give counsel in order to deal with personal guilt in not trying to help, encourage, or understand, qualities found in genuine optimists. She spent thirty minutes counseling on the phone before it came time for me to question her motives... and she hung up the phone. I sent her a simple email to point out her motive:

> Maybe the need to counsel others is done to hide guilt. As long as the counselor can find fault to correct something in another, she doesn't have to take responsibility to show understanding and real encouragement. This is why group discussion reveals true motives better than a counselor's advice. Take the therapy of Alcoholics Anonymous to help overcome alcohol addiction. It is far better than a one-way lecture with very little agency to disagree. Maybe we need Counselors Anonymous as a support group to overcome guilt. What do you think?

This experience made it clear that counseling can be a way to tell others what to do—without showing faith in their agency. The political optimist loves to advise others. Keep in mind that to counsel is not the same as to correct a motive that needs correction. It's one thing to tell a person what to do; it's another to ask questions to reveal motive. The difference is that when questioning a person's motive, we cannot conclude anything. Because most people want to hide their intent, we must ask *why* until everyone can see and be clear. Asking questions to reveal motive shows what we intuitively see in another person.

Political optimists jump to counsel, and ignore the challenge to encourage and ask questions. Unsolicited counsel shows the counselor to be lazy. It's like trying to step from reason to enlightenment without rising to a higher value in love, joy, and peace. It's impossible to skip past relational connections—and this is exactly what linear counseling does. The person who's quick to counsel is also vertically separated, elitist, and emotionally closed... all the qualities of a political optimist.

It takes two to make the stand in order for one to overcome. One must be willing to stand to be corrected and another must be willing to speak the correction. This says that counsel is the way to make a stand for another to overcome. Specifically, it means taking a stand against one's denial rather than giving unwelcomed direction. In a genuinely optimistic world, faith in others becomes a matter of revealing one's internal psychology and not directing one's agency. Feel free to question motive—we can all learn from it—but leave others' free agency intact, because we all need to face fear on our own. There is no shortcut for that.

A college roommate once invited several friends on a riverboat. There had been high waters and a recent flash flood the night before, and a large boulder fell into a narrow gap in the river. This created a section of turbulent whitewater at just the wrong place—dead center in the river. Several guides ahead tried desperately to avoid the boulder, only to find their boats parallel from the rock and capsized. Not my college roommate. He just headed right for the huge boulder and pushed over it. His was the only boat that avoided the turbulence by directly riding over it.

Fear is a kind of foreboding and we tend to deny it (like the political optimist) rather than recognize it through applied faith in the expressions of love, patience, and friendship. There is no other way to overcome fear.

Each person must step onto courage with one foot still on fear. Once balanced, your foot can leave fear and glide past desire, anger, and pride. Then, for that moment of unsteadiness on one foot, with neutrality, willingness, and acceptance passing underneath, you can plant a foot on reason instead of fear.

Just as denial of fear causes people to collapse downward into the lower values that create vertical idolatry for authority, faith in forward action, with common consent, shows confidence in higher values natural for an optimistic life. This creates greater relational connections with others that inspire many people. See **Figure 4.2** used in chapter four.

Understanding Faith

Faith more accurately describes the knowledge of fear rather than its denial. Faith sees the truth and acts accordingly. Denial *covers* the truth and acts in destructive ways. You may still feel fear while applying faith in higher values, but fear is certainly not acting upon you.

Some writers see this distinction while others adopt a form of political optimism that covers fear. When we act in denial, we see what we want to see. When we act in faith, we see the truth of our own motives—*and* a path to great social consent, which equals greater value.

When a published book defines faith correctly, it isn't particularly popular, as the prognosticators of new magic promote a more sophisticated form of denial in other bestsellers. This happens when we look for enchanting steps to success rather than real ones. If there is magic in the faith, it will sell, because it justifies denial. If any responsibility is required, the book may not sell, even though it speaks the truth.

We've lost touch with the value of responsibility as being genuinely optimistic, which means we've lost touch with the true value of optimism as a certain quality of faith in taking responsible action.

In life, we're either acted upon—or we choose to act. Optimism has come to mean a blind faith that acts upon us rather than life choices acting in higher values. When a successful CEO tells us how to achieve victory by applying a formulaic five-step program, our idolatry toward the CEO covers our fear and we modify our lives to fit his false sense of cheerfulness.

We show adoration and obedience to the CEO icon rather than independent dissent in higher principles of real value. We are always looking up to others rather than to the enlightenment within.

With devotion applied to leaders rather than faith in exercising our own freedom, we can cover fear with a new acceptance formula and still succeed through denial. To stand on your own is to face a kind of social death; this can't refer to optimism at all, right? Or... can it? In other words, is optimism the application of faith while facing political death? This would mean that genuine optimists who live in horizontal relationship to others would have equal footing. Such an idea must call for a new way of self-government, one that removes central power structures and replaces them with a wider reach toward common consent.

During the nineties, I sent off dozens of applications to various colleges to teach in their English departments. In just about every interview, I was asked, "How do you promote cultural diversity in your students?"

My response? "I don't educate tolerance for dividing views." Everyone looked at me blankly and I was forced to defend myself. "In a liberal environment," I explained, "we learn to fight for the cause of equality by emphasizing *social responsibility*. In a conservative environment, we learn to fight for the cause of liberty by emphasizing *individual responsibility*. Political division isn't diversity. If just one person rejects ideas found on both extremes, what guarantee is there that this one person's ideas will be heard by either extreme? Diversity is not the tolerance of different political parties, behaviors, sex or skin color. Diversity is the open forum of ideas, no mater where they come from."

When the word "responsibility" was used in the interview process for these jobs, my use of the word was a hangman's noose, showing a complete intolerance for diversity of *behavior*— and preferring instead a complete tolerance of *ideas*.

Diversity in colleges and universities today is all about tolerance for various forms of behavior (often sexually oriented) and not tolerance for a diversity of ideas. While attending a college class on modern poetry, a female student came to class wearing yellow painted hiking boots and a white tank top with no brassiere underneath. Her hair was cut short and slicked back with black shoe polish. She wrote poetry about sex with women and talked of having sex with trees and the earth, while coloring men in disparaging imagery. Her poetry was lifted up and encouraged by the professor.

Meanwhile one male student in the class openly questioned her motives and wanted to find out what was fueling the hatred toward men in her poetry, which to him was not a sign of a welcoming diversity. The professor shut the conversation down by saying, "it is not our job to question the poet's motive."

Throughout most of academia, we see the same iron gate of control that shuts out honest probing expressed by genuine optimists. They call this diversity.

We should never condemn a man for his belief or a woman for her ideas—but we have a perfect right to *question motives* for any ideas and beliefs. Questioning motive doesn't mean intolerance. Questioning motive and keeping the debate open is the essence of social responsibility and the fuel for a genuine optimist. Let discussion rule the day! Trying to keep discussion from finding understanding shows a complete lack of faith in public discourse.

Continued discussion brings about a greater consensus, and unanimous ideal consent through modularized groups takes us to a higher path of enlightenment. Few people understand the value of open and free discussion designed to find agreement in meaning and reveal motives, which is why political optimists guillotine all debate. Open discussion with a requirement to reach ideal consent is the only way to reveal motives and meanings. Until we reach greater models of open consent, the dissenting leader is left to speak up at their own risk.

When Aung San Suu Kyi helped liberate Burma from the military junta, and when Wei Jingsheng stood up for human rights and democracy in China, it took time in the face of much opposition. Even when Congressman Ron Paul affected a positive anti-war movement in a typically pro-war establishment, this type of outside-the-beltway diversity took over thirty years to build into what has become the modern tea party. Genuine human diversity stands alone as a visionary soloist in one's own academic camp, political party, culture, or community. Despite what it may look like, open opposition is never a mess of confusion... until, that is, we attempt to silence and intimidate a single voice. It is only when we attempt to silence opposition that we create a mess.

The usual path to success is to become politically active and tell potential employers, current teachers, or others exactly what they want to hear. The problem with this approach is that it increases our idolatry for authority, which inherently promotes people who are more political. Innovation dies and the leaders in charge typically have no clue. All centrally controlled models with top-down leadership promote more political people than genuine independent optimists who thrive in organizations run by ideal consent.

A better way is coming.

What is important now is to see that fear will always express our anxiety about death and life rejection, and seeing through denial requires that we work toward the higher values found in love, joy, and peace. The real enemy is the denial of fear re-factored as a new escape from taking responsibility. Those who bring up the fear of death or the fear of rejection with the intent to reveal true motive are deemed antagonists to diversity. The political minds want the diversity of denial to dominate the diversity of ideas. This is truly evident in how we define faith as something incomprehensible and not as a responsible action.

Can we exercise faith in something that is not true? We've asked this question before, and we ask it again. For faith to be responsible, the conscious mind must show action consistent with higher values. This means faith is the expressed action that is true and good and not a fastidious traditional practice motivated by the fear of death.

Earnest Becker writes, "...one of the great rediscoveries of modern thought: that of all things that move man, one of the principle ones is his terror of death."[2]

This means that either we accept our fear with a responsible faith (responsible action) or we choose a destructive path of denial. It now makes sense why William James called the fear of death "the worm at the core," and why Socrates called it "the muse of philosophy, and that "we should always be ready to die."

Death fuels the fire for all fear, and in order to deal with fear, we must recognize denial in our actions and in our need to attack others. The only way to do this is with a responsible faith willing to accept fear, move toward a consensus of higher frequencies, and not step down from diversity toward lower frequencies of denial. Denial will always push the majority by silencing the voices of dissent. It's time we reverse that by shifting our view of leadership from command and control to a voice of dissent.

Until we have a responsible faith in discourse for questioning motive and meaning, political optimism will continue to distract our attention with staged performances, upbeat intimidation, and with irrational escapes. All of these fail to exhibit the real nature of faith, that best seen in genuine optimists.

Now it's time for us to look at the believing optimist as a counter-stand against the staged optimist. The real difference between faith and denial begins here.

The best existential analysis of the human condition leads directly into the problems of God and faith.

Ernest Becker, The Denial of Death

Faith is the highest passion in a human being. Many in every generation may not come that far, but none comes further.

Soren Kierkegaard

6

The Believing Optimist

In belief lies the secret of all valuable exertion

-Bulwer

This is Work

Many say that optimism is simply an attitude of mind—a state of carrying a positive outlook. With our understanding thus far, we can use other synonyms for attitude and place "positive" in front of each.

These synonyms include a *positive boldness*, a *positive brashness*, a *positive arrogance*, a *positive assertion* and perhaps a *positive defiance*.

Each one of these can possibly have both positive and negative connotations. Our mistake comes from thinking that one's positivity is always good and that it never has evil aspirations.

However, if we look at optimism as having two sides, we see that it either aligns with the drive to control and take away value, or it becomes one's drive to add value. The latter requires some work. The former may be the ultimate condition of denial.

It is easy to say, "I'm an eternal optimist." It is *work* to say, "I never give up on a good thing." The eternal optimist can be political. They can be a staged personality, a smiling intimidator, or an irrational peddler of magic. None of them show any work that supports their optimism. Their claim as an optimist comes, rather, from an inner desire to control. It's like gathering crops to sell that were planted by someone else. When the fall season arrives and it's time to gather the crops, it is easy to focus on your success and preach to others. Meaning, it's easy to be an eternal optimist if what you harvest takes from the work of another man. There is a big difference between what you reap and what you sow. Political optimists focus on what they reap. Genuine optimists attend to what they sow.

Have you ever met a person so busy making money or climbing a political ladder that they don't add value? They figure out how to get a bigger piece of the action, or more control, without adding value of their own. We look on them as successes and we think, "they're optimistic." They stand in front of us at a Chamber of Commerce luncheon and tell us how to achieve triumph while quietly telegraphing how to avoid telling the truth. Often these same people proclaim, "I'm an eternal optimist," appearing constructive without really adding anything of worth. So what is the proof we should look for to inspire genuine optimism in our own lives?

You might be surprised.

In times of great difficulty, those who say, "I refuse to give up on a good thing," are certainly optimistic. We could also call them full of faith. The way you can tell for sure is when someone suffers to achieve a principle in order to protect a good thing.

In American history, the only death by *peine forte et dure* (pressing to death) was performed on Giles Corey, who was pressed to death on September 19, 1692 during the Salem witch trials. Because he refused to enter a plea after being accused a witch in the judicial proceeding, his last words, according to legend, were, "More weight." This may sound extraordinary, but it's the source of strength of genuine optimism and real faith.

Genuine optimism rises from the will to take on *more* weight and *more* responsibility, rather than find a way to escape. The political optimist, by way of contrast, justifies their escape in an attempt to save their image.

The proof we need doesn't come from someone saying they believe in something. Merely asserting a belief has an ingredient missing. We just as well call it phony optimism, because a mental belief alone lacks the substance of faith. The real substance becomes a worthy sacrifice.

Attached to the belief, as correctly stated by the 18th-century writer Edward Bulwer-Lytton, "valuable exertion" illustrates a connection between the sowing and the reaping.

Of all genuine optimists, the *believing* optimist sows their worthy effort in a very pragmatic way. You can feel and see their optimism in live action rather than through verbal assertion. Believing optimists are willing to take on more weight. They are hard workers. They possess that extra ingredient that manifests their trust in our agency. Trust is a great synonym for faith.

Like Chuck

Chuck Stamps is an example of a believing optimist. A retired cook from the US Coast Guard, Chuck is a broad-shouldered man who loves to give hugs. No matter how much taller you are, he somehow wraps his arms around your neck and lifts his eyes level with yours. Believing optimists have this quality. Their concern is about what they do for another, in how they make you feel, and in how they add warmth and service to your life. To debate over principle is unproductive, and to encourage any right action from someone else isn't either.

To many people, optimism is a belief that the existing world is the best possible world. For the believing optimist, the thought is extended to ask, why worry and why get frustrated trying to understand motive and principle? All that matters is the good you can do.

Another definition holds that optimism is a belief that good always prevails.

Both of these approaches fit the nature of a believing optimist. They don't see evil, not because they *avoid* it, but because they stay focused on the good they can achieve on their own. They may not understand a lot of things, but they do add value.

The staged optimist covers his evil intent in a performance and never accomplishes the good he professes to want. A believing optimist accomplishes good in the most direct way possible.

Here's an example of what I'm talking about. Chuck helped single moms and college students away from home. On Mondays he cooked dinner at a local church for hungry college students, all on his own dime and with the help of a local produce distributor and several grocery stores.

A true believing optimist's motive comes from a fundamental principle of "doing good," and this is what sets them apart. They live to touch lives—versus the staged optimist who lives to get attention without touching anyone.

A simple philosophy of life goes like this: add more value than you take, and do this for as long as you can. Some people aren't able to give to their community because of illness, disability, or other handicaps; this is why more is required from those who can. At some point, we all need to take from the community—but not everyone at the same time. It would actually surprise most of us how easy it is to add value, even with extreme disabilities.

A believing optimist sees this better than most.

For example, a woman at a title agency had to leave work for thirty minutes to go home and turn her bedridden husband to avoid bedsores. Prior to a recent injury causing him to be bedridden, he'd been independently mobile and could make his way to the family-owned auto repair shop in his electric chair and help diagnose mechanical problems. Even though he was a quadriplegic, with the help of a voice-activated computer he maintained the accounting, paid invoices, and managed information flow.

You could see this woman talk about her husband with intense joy, despite what she had to do for him. This is exactly what a believing optimist does: they touch others' hearts by bringing the best out of themselves. Everything they do comes from a deep-seated drive to touch lives with the best that they are.

The unique attribute about believing optimists is that they trade the distant stage for real human connections. The disabled husband is a life-force magnet from whom many people seek advice and friendship. Without the ability to move his arms and legs, he adds a massive degree of value. He's a believing optimist; he must add something to the world, to his family, to his immediate contacts, and to others.

What good is the world if one cannot add the best of what they have? This is the fundamental drive of the believing optimist. They may not know their underlying principles, and they may not encourage others to perform any right action as much as they give of themselves. The nature of what they give is the rich stuff called intimacy, the very opposite of what's seen in the staged performer.

Staged optimists are unable to undress themselves on stage and reveal their hearts. Believing optimists do it naturally. Unlike the staged optimist who lifts themselves above others, a believing optimist lowers themselves below others. Mother Theresa was a believing optimist. She descended below them all.

Today many people add value through teaching a child the principle of persistence, setting an example of giving to those in need, and still they can build relationships, fire new enterprises, launch new technologies, and create new organizational models with more freedom and less central control.

The believing optimist adds value from inside. Their value comes in acts of patience, of long-suffering, of gentleness and kindness to others, rather than leadership qualities like encouragement or the innovative value of advancing knowledge and principle. We'll see both in other genuine optimists. Believing optimists aren't prone to becoming leaders in a political world, yet they are the first to step out to lead and take responsibility.

Believing optimists are the perfect example of value since value to them advances charity and builds character without hypocrisy. They are the real life manifestation of everything we value in a friend. They judge nobody, and even though they may hold strong religious doctrines and beliefs, they never deny you the expression of your own mind. There can be no greater value than the support of another person's freedom. Just look at how the believing optimist has faith in self. They also show great self-motivation and their reward is self-realization. See **Figure 6-1**.

Fig. 6-1 Traits of the Believing Optimists

Character	**Traits**
Faith	Faith in Self
Intelligence	Glory in Being
Agency	Obeys Truth
Motivation	Self Motivation
Reward	Self Realization

Too often we think of value as a physical product or monetary worth of something. Value isn't something in the market. Value is the action that replenishes and improves. Whether this action is through upholding a principle, or giving a service, or motivating a team, all genuine optimists—especially the believing optimist—hold one thing most true, that optimism is not the attitude you portray but the actions that match the attitude.

Sometimes this action exhibits more kindness, more encouragement, or a firm stand of *no* to force a principled *yes*. Staged optimists place the return of value to the self; believing optimists place the return of value to the community, the family, and friends.

Just the other day my daughter ignited a discussion when a family member made her feel bad. A comment followed from my observation,

> There are some who think in very straight lines and only for themselves. They are linear. Then there are those who include others into their thoughts. They are relational. Every time you think of doing something, consider how it affects everyone you can, the family, friends, and neighbors, even the homeless. You will build stronger relations with others if you practice this.

By directly giving value to one's immediate community, this same value conserves its energy and returns to you seven times greater. This is the opposite of a staged optimist who talks about helping you, and never suggests how we can help each other. In fact, the staged optimist is the modern politician because they never show any real human touch. The believing optimist can never exist in politics because she needs too much real intimate touch. Oddly, this is what makes for a better leader, because it is real and not fake. If we could do one thing to improve our world, we should find a way to get more believing optimists into leadership positions.

Hold tight: a solution is coming!

The modern religious or political zealot is a negative example of a believing optimist. You see the same thing with self-help trends in forced positive thinking. They put on a great act, trying to be close, but they refuse to make the step toward greater enlightenment. If you were to ask a believing optimist what it means to believe in something, he would say, "What I do for the least in my community I do to God." This is exactly how a believing optimist lives their life. They show concern for those at the bottom of despair and they focus on what they can do to help. There can be no better meaning to belief. Anyone who disagrees is not his brother's keeper.

A believing optimist never frets over peripheral issues of tradition and authority. They are more concerned with the central issue of serving a need and not telling people what to believe. Fundamentalists waiting for a magical rapture to come out of the skies and save them will never make "serving others" the true rapture. On the other hand, a believing optimist will.

Believing optimists connect with people and make lasting friendships because they listen and are willing to put out a hand and to help another. For the political optimist, this is not enough. To a believing optimist, this is common consent—and it's more than enough.

A believing optimist preserves the powers of free agency, whereas a fundamentalist evangelist too often wants to counsel you, just like a self-help guru telling you how upbeat they are without feeling the beating of your heart. Neither the evangelist nor the motivational guru has a clue as to what is in your mind or in your heart.

Years ago while standing outside a movie theater in Brentwood California, a young Christian evangelist approached with zeal and said, "You live in sin until you accept the blood and sacrifice of Christ our savior." A believing optimist sees through all this as coercion and even some form of denial on the part of an intruding enthusiast. Rather than focus on physical images such as the virgin birth or blood sacrifice of Christ's death, believing optimists look instead at mimicking Christ's life. They live life examples as Ghandi lived Thoreau's philosophy on civil disobedience.

A lot of religious fanaticism and political rhetoric looks and feels like believing optimism, but in truth they're staged optimists willing to get in your face and never in your heart. The best way to see the genuine apart from the staged is to measure how well any guru of goodness supports your two powers of free agency.

For example, do they openly and willingly support your free agency to dissent? And do they support the same free agency to consent? If they are bothered with your twin powers of freedom, then you know they are staged and political in their optimism.

Believing optimists don't ask questions of meaning as would an encouraging optimist and they don't stand up in dissent of self-evident principles. They just allow total freedom to speak. The atmosphere of a believing optimist is like group therapy. While there might exist an adversarial relationship in the group, believing optimists are the last to judge and the first to touch. Believing optimists will always believe in your best potential, even when you've failed to show your best effort. At the bottom of any trial in life, even at the bottom step of shame, believing optimists will be the first to descend and be there for you.

In 1983, volunteers arrived to help sandbag the dam of a local reservoir after heavy snow in the Rocky Mountains caused flooding when the temperatures rose. We worked hard to prevent damage to the pristine campgrounds, the golf shop, the park ranger's station, and the newly seeded cornfields below the dam.

I was an 80-pound 10-year-old and unable to lift the 50-pound bags. An older girl handed me a shovel and showed me how to fill the bags with sand. A great urgency filled the night and everyone pitched in: the task belonged to all. One farmer arrived with extra shovels in his truck and another brought a tractor with a front loader. It took most of the night to patch things up under the full moon.

This experience is similar to many events we read about in history. Consider the night of March 4, 1776, when General John Thomas and 2,000 troops marched to the top of Dorchester Heights in Boston. During the night, they hauled fortifications behind bales of hay (placed between the path taken by the troops and the harbor) in order to muffle their movements. These troops hauled and placed earthworks and cannons. General Washington provided moral support in the early morning hours of what was the sixth anniversary of the

Boston Massacre. By dawn, fortifications had been constructed, including barrels filled with rocks that could be rolled down the hill at attacking troops.

The amazing thing about this event is how much was accomplished by so few and in just one single night. This is how powerful believing optimism can fill the air: it brings out the best in everyone because there is an applied faith accessible to all. Political optimists never give others that kind of belonging because they separate themselves as elitists.

Many self-help writers have given assistance to individual needs and have given solace to many people. What they don't show is a certain discrepancy between how they look in the mirror but disregard the lives around them. The best ideas always focus on value-adding action and not on cognitive mirrors. Don't get confused. Higher frequency thinking leading to greater freedom of mind is always important, but if your internal spirit doesn't match a similar action in living, something's wrong.

This is where a lot of motivational talk misses the mark. It also explains why we need the external optimism of social responsibility to fire up personal responsibility toward adding greater value.

Too much self-help and religious motivation tries to do it from the individual's point of view without interacting with others. This is why believing optimists are so important: they have to make real connections with others or they simply cannot take part. They are the first to manifest outwardly the good inside their hearts. They are purely relational in how they need to touch others. This is opposite of the staged optimist who is removed from the needs of others. When the situation turns political, believing optimists are the first to walk away because they have no stomach for compulsory imperatives.

This explains why political optimists have gained control over others' free agency: they always demand more control so they can force consent, while believing optimists back off from using force.

Make no mistake, the need for motivation is very important. Nobody likes a sourpuss in the office or in the home. A negative cloud lacks productivity and too often inhibits building relations with others. Even worse, very few people can endure listening to fear-laden problems day in and day out. Such a person can take more from the company, more from family members, and more from the community than they give.

Even with that said, at times, the expression of personal fear in an open setting is natural for us to share compassion and sentiment, to help us all see a rational reason for the fear. If we don't allow free expression to work through issues that might otherwise fester, issues often develop into emotional disabilities and eventually into denial.

When political, religious, and motivational tools of denial cover genuine fear, we have a serious problem: we'll never be challenged to correct ourselves.

This problem surfaces with linear minds that employ denial. They inhibit relational minds from challenging their motives. More knowledge of how linear minds and relational minds approach life is helpful.

Linear Verses Relational

Take Shakespeare's *Hamlet* as a fascinating example of linear versus relational thinking. Imagine the ghost of your father suddenly appearing to you in the wet damp of a foggy night. Imagine also that the ghostly figure of your dead father reveals to you his premature death and murder by the hand of his brother, your uncle. Finally, imagine that your uncle is married to your mother and it has only been a month since the death of your father. Would this eerie experience cause you to behave crazily?

Add to this a liberal education in the classics, as Hamlet had, and you compound the experience with insights gained from philosophy, art, history and poetry, all of which Hamlet used as intellectual weaponry for avoiding the responsibility to avenge his father's murder.

Yes, it's true, reading classics can give you greater relational depth. Sadly, if studied alone, without the oral tradition that infuses responsibility into human character through question-and-answer discussion, reading the classics is actually more debilitating and linear. This is worse for speed-readers who refuse open discussion of what they read.

Affected with overwhelming knowledge, Hamlet's condition near the end of the play states, "I am dead." Optimism must be made of much sterner stuff than this. It's not good when we seem affected by the darkest realities of life without an optimism that sees through great challenges. Socrates, Christ, Martin Luther King Jr., and many others teach that moving forward through massive opposition is not impossible. Just look at self-absorbed artists who take their lives while great leaders sacrifice their lives. Those willing to take on "more weight" in life actually show more optimism.

Hamlet expresses an attitude on the short side of optimism. The only difference is that he has the language to express his illiterate courage, which makes him such a fascinatingly tragic figure. Some call this madness; however, it's more accurate to call it a handicap. Unless one is able to make positive action that adds value, there is no real optimism, no matter how literary one's language.

This need for positive action rests at the core of the believing optimist, because they must do something good they can relate. Staged optimists relate to nothing, but they do reveal their linear approach.

For instance, a person with a linear mind will see a homeless person and say, "If they can hold a sign saying 'homeless need food,' they can get a job." The person with the relational mind will walk over and talk with the homeless person to find out why they are homeless. This builds knowledge to relate to the homeless person's situation rather than passing judgment created by detached and linear conclusions. While neither is giving anything as a hand out, the relational mind has a better understanding.

Political people are linear. Genuine optimists are relational. You can now see why we need more relational minds in leadership. This doesn't make linear minds the filth of society. It just means that our world remains mostly governed by linear thinking. Linear thinking favors central control at greater and greater distances. With the world controlled mostly by linear minds, we have more conclusions and more ideas completely detached from real understanding.

Genuine optimists are not political people and central control is a serious disadvantage to them. With central control, there's no appeals process against power centers and no open free expression to dissent against power with real teeth.

Many collapsing societies lose their relational understanding because they become fixated on death as a linear problem and they forget to live in relationship to others as a real solution. Just about every television show today centers on some aspect of death. Music videos plaster sunken cheeks of horror with skin and bones to match and we just love to look at the carnage of murder and death to satiate our need to feel that we are alive. Meanwhile we have no understanding of what is motivating us.

The viewer becomes the prisoner of his fear. Because we fear life and death, we look at morbid scenes to feel alive. This is pure linear thinking. It's like the gladiators and war games held in the Coliseum in ancient Rome. The spectacle of death, made the audience feel alive. To see others slaughtered makes your life suddenly seem safe from death. What a great diversion given to the people so they would not focus on the real problems of inequality and political injustice. Do we do the same in modern life as in ancient Rome?

Relational thinking says, it's true we are mortal. It also claims that we all should be a part of making this world the best of all possible worlds. Denial is a linear attempt to repress awareness of the elephant in the room. Faith sees the elephant and looks at a solution in order to remove problems through relational understanding that leads to greater service to others.

Today we lack genuine optimism and the necessary value-adding action to live in genuine relationships. We're worse than Hamlet. We've become the comatose face of *ennui* and Hamlet is slapping us in the face. At least Hamlet had the gumption to fight at the last minute for justice and die. We just keep looking in the mirror trying to find out what is wrong inside. We never realize that the problem rests not so much in the glitches in our cognitive insides or in our emotional pasts, but in failing to engage in open discussion, the very thing that liberates all genuine optimists.

If we keep thinking that we must push ourselves away from the controlling influence of others (the rugged individualism approach), and if we keep following the idolatry of authority (the zealot's approach), we are following a dead methodology. These are linear dead ends. The first avoids building relationships and the second allows authority over our free agency.

Sometimes we can remove these two constraints through meditation, but rarely do we find our purpose and live our lives in a meditative state. This is the basic logic of the believing optimist. While some genuine optimists actively live as they see within their mind, and while other genuine optimists actively live as they are inspired to lift others, the believing optimist actively lives as they feel.

If we just focus on changing our thinking to change our lives, there's no guarantee that we'll see and accept our own fear. With no effort to reach out and understand others, we escape from social responsibility in life. The believing optimist doesn't seek to escape life this way. Their main concern is the good they can bring to others by seeking understanding, by listening, and just by being there. They are great at letting you talk. As long as they can do something good for you, which can be as simple as saying nothing and letting your twin powers of freedom figure out a solution, they're happy.

The real difference between the linear mind and the relational mind is demonstrated in what they're willing to let inside. A forced political body assembled into a vertical

138 | *The Genuine Optimist*

organization creates power structures too far removed and too difficult for a genuine optimist to combat. Modern advertisements prove this one-way method by encouraging a mind to react without question. Reaction comes through subliminal methods while we put aside our free will to disagree and question.

When we interact with other programmed minds, and when we avoid any expression of dissent, we reinforce incorrect meanings into our traditions. Without oral discussion coupled with the right to dissent, we'll never be able to eradicate authoritative controllers.

A believing optimist is limited without open access to adding value. They may challenge the staged optimist by building genuine relationships, but not when it comes to challenging intimidators or those promoting irrational magic. This is why we have encouraging optimists to tackle the worst enemy of individual freedom, the intimidator! If not, then we need principled optimists willing to rise in strong dissent against the magic of idolatry that comes with centralized authority.

Let's move now to a very powerful form of optimism we call encouragement. Outside of believing optimism, it is the first step toward a social optimism that's truly accessible to all.

I am fundamentally an optimist. Whether that comes from nature or nurture, I cannot say. Part of being optimistic is keeping one's head pointed toward the sun, one's feet moving forward. There were many dark moments when my faith in humanity was sorely tested, but I would not and could not give myself up to despair. That way lays defeat and death.

Nelson Mandela

7

The Encouraging Optimist

Correction does much, but encouragement does more.
Encouragement after censure is as the sun after a shower.

- Goethe

What is Encouragement?

While a believing optimist measures accomplishment
by bringing out the best in themselves, an encouraging optimist
measures accomplishment by bringing out the best in others. The
good news is that we can move from believing to encouraging.
It is a natural progression. When they're together in one person,
they are everyone's dream boss.

Encouragement is pretty much the opposite of
intimidation, which imposes uncertainty through your own
actions. Here's what's different: encouraging optimists love
liberty, openness, and conversation, which brings out the best
in others through a process of ideal consent that has both rough
and smooth edges. Encouragement is not always a bed of rose
peddles, but it does eventually bring out the best in others.

The Rough Edges

There's often one person who encourages us to give our
best. In my case, the first person that comes to mind was a college
professor named Jerry Fetch. He taught courses in humanities
and business and marketing at Moorpark College in Southern
California, and Jerry knew how to encourage the best out of
each student.

It was late afternoon in the spring semester and Jerry found me walking my bike away from the campus library. He called out to me and I parked my bike and joined him in his office. "Sit down," he said. "Do you mind if I make an observation?"

Sitting stiff in a hard plastic chair near the door of his modest and narrow office, I said, hesitantly, "No."

"Keith, you do not have one thing about you that is dynamic." There he said it, hitting dead center on my ego, like being forced to look into a mirror for the first time to see a big mole on the tip of my nose. I was speechless, hurt, and unsure how to respond. I felt offended and waited for the hurt to go away.

At that time in my life, I was studying to be an actor, specifically a film actor. I was taking private lessons at the home of Frank Roach, an accomplished actor who also taught at the same college. I was pretty much impressed with what I was doing... and still, there was not a single thing about me that was *great*, and Jerry brought this realization out and into the open.

Sometimes we need to see what we treasure inside pushed to the outside. It is like seeing as we are seen of others, which is better than a mirror.

Jerry wasn't finished. "Instead, you have a number of qualities that, when properly aligned, they create an incredible character."

For months, all I could focus on was the thought that I didn't have a single thing about me that was great. It took another six months to see the truth, quit my direction in the performing arts, and get a better path of action to fill the measure of my real potential. I suspect that Jerry probably told the same thing to many students over the years.

Encouraging optimists are excellent mentors at any point in our lives. They build on the qualities of a believing optimist and compound their effect in what they pull out of you. The secret to their success is leaving your agency in place by showing faith in you, completely opposite of how the intimidator works. Supporting another's free will requires a certain practice of faith rarely understood by those who think that intimidation can be optimistic. Why faith? Because it's faith that demands an alert mind rather than a comatose following. For the encouraging optimist, this faith comes through a kind of tough love that has been sorely misconstrued by those who think they can practice tough love without a relational understanding.

If a loving relationship isn't established between two people, the practice of tough love is too easily wasted, because it will be misunderstood when it's delivered. Think about it, the word *tough* and *love* do not go together naturally. People who practice tough love, without any established relationship able to withstand the practice, do so more out of the denial of their own fear of rejection (to look confident) than anything expressive of faith (that is confident). Consider the old adage a father says to a disobedient child before a spanking, "this is going to hurt me more than it will hurt you."

Think of tough love as being tough on the one giving correction and not on the one receiving. This means that one must first establish a relationship of love and friendship—which takes time—before offering an observation that may be tough to express. The intimidator wants to shift tough love onto the person receiving the observation or correction. Encouraging people take the toughness on themselves. Which has a better chance of being received? Obviously the second.

The reason Jerry could make that comment is because a relationship had been built between us through my attending several of his classes. This gave him the connection he needed to say something difficult to me.

We all have a friend who tries to show tough love without ever taking the time to really talk or listen to us. The best relationships are those that take a long time to build. Those that are built quickly tend to suffer when it becomes clear (via a crisis) that they don't have the necessary connection.

Parents reject children by being tough on them without taking the time to understand who their children really are. You can be tough, but allow for more time to build the relationship through discussion.

For instance, encouraging optimists are very patient and are usually the first to say, "We have all the time in the world." The political optimist will say, "We don't have all the time in the world." Most genuine optimists favor giving more time to decision-making. Political optimists favor giving less time to decision-making. The challenge in reaching common consent and deeper connections comes in having enough freedom of discussion—and the time required—to work out differences. If there's no relationship, there is only one way to speak freely, toss everyone in a room and make them talk until they reach an agreement.

A good example is the 1957 classic movie *Twelve Angry Men,* with Henry Fonda. In the movie, twelve male jurors exit the courtroom to decide the fate of a young man tried for murder. Without any deliberation, all the jurors vote for a conviction quickly except one man, Juror 8 (played by Henry Fonda), who insists on more discussion.

After many hours of debate, one juror at a time begins to see more reason to doubt what had seemed to be a slam-dunk conviction at the start. What is most interesting is the patience that was tested by every juror, especially on a hot day with no air-conditioning. All it took was one juror to hold everything up and demand some answers to his questions of doubt. When forced to reach a unanimous consent, just one person can help eleven others overcome bigotry, racial prejudice, and apathy for justice. A rule by majority, which easily succumbs to intimidation, can never do this; it is never the high road of common consent, which fully supports encouragement.

A free society is defined by anger, prejudice, and long, spitting debates in an openly adversarial environment trying to reach consent. Challenging generalized assumptions and quick impatient judgments are healthy practices because they result in better understanding.

The great lesson this movie teaches is that discussion, a lot of it, and with plenty of time to work out differences, is good. Only when we ask the attention-seekers to define their terms and reveal their facts will we eliminate the political grand-standers.

In some situations, many can assume there is prejudice when there is none. Staged dissenters often stand up only for attention. This may cause many honest individuals to hold back for fear of what others might think. Only in an environment of ideal consent can we ask those looking for attention to *explain their motive*, *define their terms* and *reveal their facts*.

If we could really unload what's on our minds, and relinquish what we feel in our hearts, and if we could do this without the fear of becoming marginalized, and if we had enough time and opportunity to be challenged, we could overcome and accomplish so much more both as individuals and as a people. This process is exactly what defined the great oral traditions of the past, such as those that lead to the Magna Carta, the dialogues of Socrates, the debate that created a constitutional government, and even a team in any organization trying to achieve something great by letting open discussion lead the way to team consent.

Without this vigorous and "fierce conversation," and without taking enough time to work disagreements out, we've become a polarized people without understanding each other. This very nature of freedom has fallen and risen many times in history. It appears we are being called upon to restore it once again.

Ideal consent (as seen in the jury process) removes idolatry toward certain individuals. Acting free from these power centers sometimes becomes a rough road thorough the process, but it's the only way to reach a consensus and smooth out the edges of controversy.

Smooth Edges

The smooth edges of encouragement are the lifting quality of all optimism. You see this in open and free talk, the power found only in the encouraging optimist.

When the chips are down and war is in the air, we call upon motivational inspiration to rally the masses. The problem occurs when that political motivator tells a lie. When this happens, the political liar gives an open door for our escape from responsibility to question the lie, and those that dare challenge the motivator fall in battle against the new popular movement. The result is that the genuine optimism of "no" appears to be anti-optimistic. We now see the grand power of intimidating optimism; it moves the masses but never the free will of the individual. Intimidation is the direct opposite of encouragement.

The poet Ezra Pound is a good example of appearing antagonistic while in fact being encouraging. Despite his stand against Jews, and despite his support of fascism at one time, he spoke out against usury after having experienced the ravages of World War I. Ezra Pound was arrested in 1945 on charges of treason and incarcerated in St Elisabeth's Psychiatric hospital in Washington DC for twelve years.

Pound was against all forms of finance capitalism, which he called usury. He sided with Lenin and Hitler in their early days just to stand against the capitalism of the west and the behind-the-scenes funding of war. But did this kind of negative stand make him a dangerous man? To certain political powers, apparently, it did. Through the use of free speech, many have tried to stand against the imperial hubris of the United States or its treasured capitalism, but their solutions completely ignore constitutional forms of government and the necessary auxiliary precautions in defined checks and balances of power needed to keep the country from falling into corruption. In other words, they never figure out how to scale the freedom of dissent.

Hemingway, Pound's protégé Eustace Mullins, and others lobbied for and eventually obtained his release.

A strong anti-Zionist, Mullins worked in the Library of Congress; and Pound commissioned him to research the world's hidden banking powers. They later published a book called *The Secret History of the Federal Reserve.*

It's easy to call Pound an anti-Semite: there's plenty of evidence. Does this discount his efforts to reveal secret actions of financial power sowing discord between nations? A muckraker is what the term implies; they take dead water made lifeless by political optimists and they stir it up. They get oxygen in the system again and they allow fresh water to flow. The great secret is creating a political design in which we all can become little muckrakers when needed—and not for the sake of getting attention or for revolution, but for the sake of disagreement with bad ideas.

The genuine optimism of *no*, even when imprisoned by intimidation, confirms a greater *yes*, especially over time. Very few of us are willing to say *no* to the wave of so much *yes* speech that inhibits natural deliberation and open talk. This problem stems from the way the herd's mindset channels agreement with some idolatrous power center without any recourse for individuals to stand and say, "No!" The idolaters too often label the *no* as rebellious rather than (more optimistically) as free.

Ezra Pound presents us with a good example of the optimism of *no*. He knew all too well that packaging the *yes* herd into one corner through financial coercion was part of dictatorship. Those who seek to shut out rebellious disagreement are covering their real intent: to control and eventually change the law. Such political rigging for personal gain is the real rebel hiding in the cloak of phony optimism.

The worldviews offered by George Orwell's *1984*, Aldous Huxley's *Brave New World,* and Ray Bradbury's *Fahrenheit 451* provide vivid depictions of secret combinations of state and corporate power sowing discord to create crisis, which is a practice employed to give the state more centralized power. Pound suffered from this worldview and fought against it. His efforts later became known as the modern conspiracy movement, the heretics of our time.

The alternative media alone can tell the truth while traditional media is still controlled. Traditional media may imply that there's wrongdoing somewhere, but alternative media will rebel and challenge traditional media's assertions.

Traditional media has gradually morphed from telling the truth to telling lies; but alternative media can lie, too, especially when we don't fact-check. In either case we are the blind led by the blind until both fall into the ditch.

If we restore open autonomous discussion, rather than letting traditional media control every discussion, we can get away from the political imposters who control us. Here's the truth: politics is what happens in secret while leadership is what happens in the open. The more widespread we can make this truth, the closer we will come to supporting natural leadership and less political posturing. We might even figure out new technologies to properly scale this truth.

Consider the trends in media over the past two hundred years. Our future might surprise us all. See **Figure 7-1**.

Fig. 7-1 Trends in Media

Complacency	Courage	Control	Conviction	Civil	Common
Oral Traditions	Print Media	Broadcast Media	Alternative Media	Open Media	Consensual Media
Old stories retold over and over by approved authority with no questions allowed.	A burst of freedom at the start that quickly fell into the hands of central control. We read only what is printed and politically correct.	Centrally controlled corporate funded . We receive only what is reported and approved by the owners ·	Whatever the new media personality wants to say · Paid sponsor or viewer supported commentary.	Open volunteer reporting and headless structure· Not funded.	Organized by common consent in modular form . A purely decentralized model. Media operates as both a platform to communicate and to make decisions. Owned by members.

Opposite from the encouraging optimist is the intimidator, and when the intimidator refuses to hear "no," our social discourse is subject to following what the fickle majority decides. It's true that there are far too many people with too much political power and influence, people who are propped up by advanced academic degrees and the financial backing of industries and large corporations. When we centralize power in one authority, we engender the ultimate intimidating optimist.

Bureaucracies represent very small numbers of people, but no matter how important their supposed rhetoric for social good, they're still bureaucracies.

Children can tell lies about their siblings to discredit them with the parents. Likewise, bureaucracies operate with secrecy and tell tales to sow discord behind the scenes. We fail to recognize this intent because we cannot prove the motive for their actions, and we're intimidated by it and therefore we follow the established rule or the authoritative power. Political optimism pushes out lies while killing encouragement for revealing them. For the most part, the political optimism of the bureaucrat follows some social alignment to an implied social good. If we challenge the political optimist, he'll manipulate us to feel that we are against the good—when our real goal is to expose his secret intent.

The voice of the optimistic "no" in the presence of an evasive and hidden motive appears paranoid because the majority of people don't see any hidden intent. Some of us may know instinctively that something's wrong, but we can't define what that is. When people like Ezra Pound reveal secret motives, we don't see what he sees and we call them conspiracy theorists and undercut their free dissent.

Political optimists are very hard to challenge because they judge the "no!" as an attack on their "good." They use this deflection as a cover to hide a different intent. Most people are caught up in the *appearance* of good and don't see any underlying motives.

We're told that if we cannot put up with a little politics in life, we're bound to fail. We delight in some action movies because they show how the villain seems initially to be good, sometimes more so than the hero. The hero is a simple person and overcomes the deceit, showing him self to be the better of the two. We enjoy it because we see the truth. We're unable to deal with it in real life, so we welcome it in fiction.

The typical action movie, for example, becomes our canvas for the struggle between good and evil and we like to see the political optimist get his due for making evil play the false role of good. In real life, however, things aren't as clear, and we don't see deception. This happens because in real life we measure evil by destruction rather than deception and secret maneuvers.

This is why we can't see the political optimist coming before it's too late. We confront murder, rape, and crime, but are disinterested in seeing the heart of deception, denial, and coercion. We rarely admit that the supposed good out there really represents evil in sheep's clothing. Just as a child has a difficult time seeing an abusive parent, we likewise want acceptance and so we overlook the deception so prominent in our lives. Like the abused child, we live in darkness, thinking that abuse is love.

Determining the truth is a difficult process, and most people avoid looking for it because the truth is best revealed with the help of more than one person to find it.

For example, there is nothing better for keeping freedom alive than a twelve-person jury determining the truth by unanimous consent. In this closed environment, each person is forced to endure long battles where anyone can seize the discussion and demand answers. Compare that to the majority that falls into two polarized groups that remain forever separate and never in agreement. The first is the Platonic state (the modern democrat); the second is the Aristotelian individual (the old conservative). Compare them with the encouraging Socratic (independent mind) and you will see that the Socratic mind leaves your agency in place without evasion and without coercion. Notice the traits of the encouraging optimist. They show faith in others, their motivation is to inspire others, and their reward is more community discussion. See **Figure 7-2**.

Fig. 7–2 Traits of the Encouraging Optimist

Character	Traits
Faith	Faith in Others
Intelligence	Glory in Service
Agency	Freedom to Others
Motivation	Inspires Others
Reward	Community Discussion

Neither the Platonic nor the Aristotelian mind will ever encourage you to think, as does the Socratic mind. The real western tradition died with Socrates, and what lived on is a dualistic view, an idea of unnatural opposition that distorts freedom and not a natural opposition that supports common consent. It is like we got stuck with two mindsets that swing between two points without allowing for any additional points of view to flesh out assumptions and bad ideas, kind of like the left/right political paradigm we have today. See **Figure 7-3**.

Fig. 7–3 The Center of the Socratic Eye

Platonic	Socratic	Aristotelian
God of Forces	God of Responsibility	God of Reason
Control by Authority	Control by Equilibrium	Control by Law
Liberal	Inquiring Mind	Conservative
The Ideal	The Meaning	The Real
Atheistic Evasion	Faithful Action	Fundamental Escape
Position is Power	Wisdom is Power	Knowledge is Power
Word of Truth	Spirit of Truth	Light of Truth

Socrates asked questions that revealed psychological motives, which in turn revealed faulty meanings. This is the true spirit of an encouraging optimist: to find meaning through dialogue. Neither the Platonic idealism of state control, nor the Aristotelian isolation of individual liberty, is able to let go: both are too eager to opt for state control or individual gain.

Plato answered the questions and gave up the dialogue; Aristotle defined his terms without it. Neither encouraged in others the Socratic lift of genuine optimism, supported by disciplined and hard-fought meaning obtained through timeless discussion.

While the principled optimist makes a firm *stand* for freedom, the encouraging optimist *lives* it better. It would be good to differentiate between genuine Socratic optimism (that encourages both social and personal responsibility) and a political duality (that divides and concurs). Both liberal and conservative politicians stand against the Socratic encouraging optimist. There is no way this can be called progressive.

Dissolving the Left-Right Paradigm

In both liberal and conservative minds, leadership and idolatry combine into a political control model. A political control model is where a democratic majority governs the decisions. Political optimists thrive in this environment. On the other hand, the genuine optimist avoids idolatry for authority, which is the same as avoiding *all* political environments. This explains why we have such disappointing leadership in government, education, religion, and business. Genuine optimists don't advance in any political system because these systems don't allow for discussion and open questioning.

For example, just look at the loss of social discourse that we once had in the past:

The idea of connecting freedom to having a voice in social discourse was almost synonymous in many of the first colonial agreements, charters, ordinances and local constitutions that came before the U.S Constitution. In the *Cambridge Agreement* of December 24, 1632, every person was required to meet every second Monday of every month at the town meeting house after the ringing of the town bell. Those who didn't make a personal appearance, or those who failed to stay until the meeting ended, were required to pay twelve pence. If not paid by the next meeting, they paid double.

In *The Massachusetts Bicameral Ordinance* of March 7, 1644, legislators constructed a two-house legislature where magistrates on one side and deputies on another side passed bills to each other until both houses reached full consent. (Consider the power of that model and compare it with today's typical county commission of three or maybe five members, or a city council with five to seven members, or a school board with the same or less. There are many examples of greater involved consent in the past than in our limited and centralized control models today.)

Even in *The Watertown Covenant* of July 30, 1630, the members of the community enacted a promise to enter into a sure covenant to renounce all idolatry and superstition.[1] What would happen if a community decided to renounce all worship for authority and consequently all idolatry for the same? Once we renounce our desires for authority over us, we begin to imagine a better world, a world without the constrictions of a left-right paradigm.

I recall attending a *Meet the Experts Luncheon* in which several local business owners spoke about their education, wealth, and business achievements. One entrepreneur stood up in the back of the room and said rather forcefully that he could not get any investors for his business idea. He pushed forward nonetheless and advised all the new entrepreneurs in the room to "go it alone." His true guts and passion showed, for better or worse, and this seemed more optimistic and genuine than the experts who seemed more distant, unapproachable and well connected to the same. The real difference with encouraging optimists is an eagerness to add value and express meaning, rather than remain aloof in protection of one's position.

To add value and be honest in a political world seems awkward, but to stand at a distance and add nothing protects one's place and gives the appearance only of knowing something. You'll find two personalities in any organization, one that thinks of taking and the other that thinks of adding. The taker always disguises him self with something smooth and good but that's rarely effective. This sets the political optimist apart from the genuine optimist who has nothing to disguise. Let me give an example.

The opportunity came to pitch a business idea in front of five venture capitalists at a speed-pitch competition. (This is a situation where new business ideas are presented to investors.) There were over a hundred small business owners in the auditorium along with four competitors on stage.

I delivered a four-minute pitch, after which one of the judges stood up and said, "Do you know who I am?"

"No," I said.

He explained that he was the principle investor in a business venture similar to the business idea I pitched; but he claimed to have lost millions in the deal. "I strongly suggest you rethink your business model," he said to me.

Did this businessman understand the power of encouragement? Did he forge a strong relationship and a new bond? Of course not. In fact, all four contestants stood in the hallway to thank the judges... and this judge walked by with head turned away. This is the first thing to watch out for when it comes to false optimists who pretend to care. They always walk away from real human interaction, and they never add value.

Both the liberal and the conservative parties suffer from this arrogance. They do not take the opportunity to become classic statesmen and encourage greatness in others.

I was left standing and looking dejected in front of established business owners. What you will find is that genuine optimists live through situations that are worse than this, and the only way out is to give encouragement to others. Some faith in your self helps too.

Just because you rise from a bad situation and achieve great success another day doesn't make you a genuine optimist. It just means you're stubbornly blind and won't listen to criticism. This type of rugged individualism, assumed to be optimistic, makes the mistake of being isolated. When you meet such a person for the first time, it's as if they are elitist in their optimism, explosive in energy… but too far away to touch. Their own vision knows best and they remain alone, self-absorbed, defensive, and unable to work toward consensus with others. In the long run, they never scale their success beyond a certain point because they never exercise faith in the structured freedom of common consent. The encouraging optimist does and has far greater success with the same visionary passion.

No matter how visionary a person can be, they'll never see everything. Such a challenge came some time ago with a potential business partner. I asked her, "Do you believe in the team we've put together?"

"Yes!"

"Okay, if so, then are you willing to let decisions be ruled by common consent from all members on the team?"

Her reply startled me. "I don't subject vision to a committee decision."

"So you believe that vision must come first, and it must rule?" I asked.

"Yes: without vision, the people perish," she argued back.

"So you want me to subject my agency to your leadership?" I asked. She smiled back and didn't say anything.

"I'm sorry, but I can't agree to that." We never moved forward as a team despite all our potential. She needed to be in total control as the sole benevolent leader and I needed a voice in full consent.

Compare this with an experience I had with Susan Scott, author and founder of Fierce Incorporated. I listened to her speak at a conference in Las Vegas, and afterward she quickly grabbed her suitcase and began to head for the door, in a hurry to make a scheduled flight back home to Seattle.

I held out my hand to indicate my appreciation, and to my surprise she stopped in the aisle, put her suitcase down, and gave me focused and individual attention. She smiled, said nothing, and listened, letting her "silence do the heavy lifting," as she phrases it. She was more real in the isle than on stage, and that sticks with people for life. We could have been business partners on the spot.

If we don't bring value to others in a real moment-to-moment way, and if we don't support the free agency of others, we're no better than staged performers and intimidating authorities. A genuinely encouraging person can easily trump the most politically skilled intimidator. The key is getting any political person out in the open so the encouraging optimist can ask questions.

The boomer generation defines optimism as the rugged individualism of being stubborn, pushy and even aggressive. This stands in sharp contrast to the parents of boomers who define optimism as reasonable, patient, and considerate.

Just look at the older boomer generation: it has produced some of the worst presidents in U.S. history. Compared to Presidents Reagan and Kennedy, boomer presidents have produced almost no vision for the country, because they're not encouraging and relational. They're Platonic and linear. They push for central control in order to avoid any real social consent.

Just look at John F. Kennedy. He was disgusted with secret intents aimed at obtaining more central control. He was far more aware of hidden powers and coercive intentions than any president since Abraham Lincoln and Andrew Jackson. Consider Kennedy's knowledge of hidden intent that he discussed in his address before the American Newspaper Publishers Association on April 27, 1961. No president since has ever dared to talk so honestly about the hidden agenda of political power.

> The very word "secrecy" is repugnant in a free and open society; and we are as a people inherently and historically opposed to secret societies, to secret oaths and to secret proceedings. We decided long ago that the dangers of excessive and unwarranted concealment of pertinent facts far outweighed the dangers which are cited to justify it. Even today, there is little value in opposing the threat of a closed society by imitating its arbitrary restrictions. Even today, there is little value in insuring the survival of our nation if our traditions do not survive with it. And there is very grave danger that an announced need for increased security will be seized upon by those anxious to expand its meaning to the very limits of official censorship and concealment....
>
> Today no war has been declared—and however fierce the struggle may be, it may never be declared in the traditional fashion. Our way of life is under attack. Those who make themselves our enemy are advancing around the globe.
>
> ...For we are opposed around the world by a monolithic and ruthless conspiracy that relies primarily on covert means for expanding its sphere of influence—on infiltration instead of invasion, on subversion instead of elections, on intimidation instead of free choice, on guerrillas by night instead of armies by day. It is a system which has conscripted vast human and material resources into the building of a tightly knit, highly efficient machine that combines military, diplomatic, intelligence, economic, scientific and political operations.
>
> Its preparations are concealed, not published. Its mistakes are buried, not headlined. Its dissenters are silenced, not praised. No expenditure is questioned, no rumor is printed, no secret is revealed. It conducts the Cold War, in short, with a war-time discipline no democracy would ever hope or wish to match. [2]

As for Ronald Reagan, although he was incapable of revealing secretive intent, he was an encouraging optimist. His main concern was focused on protecting the American spirit, even though he didn't understand the cartel of elite moving the agenda (as Kennedy understood all too well).

They were both encouraging optimists. Kennedy did it by revealing the truth and waking people up to the American spirit. Reagan did it by communicating his love for that same spirit.

If you don't agree, perhaps you're looking for something more than encouragement. Perhaps you're looking for a third type of optimism, the kind that many in my parents' generation knew best: I call them principled optimists. If we're lucky, we'll see them communicate vital principles that some of us might convert into a technology to help us organize our consent with the power of dissent fully protected. Very few presidents and people in power understand the real value of this optimism. The principled optimist may just be the first to define it and the last hope for preserving freedom.

8

The Principled Optimist

> I've concluded that genius is as common as dirt. We suppress our genius only because we haven't yet figured out how to manage a population of educated men and women. The solution, I think, is simple and glorious. Let them manage themselves.[1]
>
> -John Taylor Gatto

The Progression of Optimism

As you've probably deduced, a principled optimist is someone who stands for something good. What you may not know is that it takes at least two people to make the stand: one to speak up—and another to *let* that person speak up.

This book is an attempt to take a stand. It all began with a letter that arrived while I was in college. It came from my father and it said, "Dear Son, for some time I have felt that Satan is trying to exalt you."

It's not easy to get a letter—on your birthday and from your father, no less—with that line in it. The letter was a correction, and correction is part of being raised by a principled optimist. They dig a hole in what you think or believe, but it's dug in order to fill that space with better material. A principled optimist always fills the holes they dig.

Fathers, mothers, managers, and friends all have some sort of responsibility that's all their own. A mother has the responsibility to correct her child, a friend is responsible for correcting a friend, and a boss has the responsibility of correcting an employee.

Accepting correction is never easy or comfortable: this is where the phrase "I stand corrected" comes from. It's also why it takes two to make the stand through which at least one will overcome. It takes one to correct and one to be willing to accept correction. It's the same as digging a hole and filling it.

If baby boomers had followed this prescription, they would have left a better legacy behind them. They are instead leaving a vacuum of freethinking filled with empty holes and no examples of having been corrected. I make this observation as the youngest member of that generation. Being the youngest in a generation has its advantages. It lets you see the mistakes of your older brothers and sisters. It also lets you see the wisdom of your parents that your older siblings failed to experience.

While personal insecurities are usually revealed in public over time, we tend to fight back when we're confronted with a correcting principle. In addition, we tend to counsel others while neglecting our own issues and need for correction. This is why seeing our own insecurities in a larger social context is the foundation of human identity.

Most of us know that no person exists as an island. What many people don't know, is that personal identity progresses from the individual to the family and then out to the community. Many in my own generation seemed to miss this understanding. All you have to do is see the weakening of community strength across the country and how it has been replaced with more political control at greater and greater distances. The idea of community strength is a central principle of my parents' generation. Perhaps an entire generation stands to be corrected.

The expansion of the individual into family and then into community is the inevitable development of genuine optimism. It's what the genuine optimist is pushing for, especially the *principled* optimist. This is why a principled optimist never removes anyone's free agency. They just confront you with a neglected principle that might shift your character toward more community involvement.

Take music as a good example of progression and notice how it applies to human progression toward community living. In music, we progress toward song and symphony. In human life, we progress toward compassion and community. Without a progression of some kind, optimism suffers.

For example, music is a combination of discord, harmony, and overtones. Discord represents different wavelengths, or two adjoining keys on the piano played at the same time. Tap any two adjoining keys on a piano keyboard together, and you'll find the sound unsettling. It causes stress and doesn't diminish smoothly. It sounds more like *"ouwow"* circling into your ear.

Harmony, on the other hand, is any note played with an audible crest that falls precisely in line with the crest of another note. Some keys match every third crest, some every fifth, seventh, or eighth. Take any key on the keyboard and move up or down the keyboard until you hear that reverberating crest harmonizing the two keys. When you play both at the same time, you have harmony because of two matching waves that crest and trough at the same time. With fewer matches, we have less harmony. Eight keys away is a full octave that starts over in the matching of crests and troughs.

Finally, we have overtones, subtle bits of harmony that are sympathetic and ride on the back of a stronger harmony. They add variety to the complete musical array.

Essentially, we have harmony and discord, with the occasional overtone. In music we call this a rich sound. In human language, it's called optimism.

Like music, genuine optimism comes out of the community but diminishes in the state. The larger the population gets, the more diminished the optimism. Like a rich sound in music, honest optimism diminishes the further the distance traveled.

The greater the body of people in which optimism is expressed, we find an increase of political hypocrisy.

Discord in small localities is quickly corrected by harmony. If the dissent has a very strong harmonic, it'll smooth out any phony optimist in power. In large cultures, the power structure promotes more discord by getting everyone to harmonize without their consent in order to become part of it. The only way we can maintain true harmony comes from allowing dissent at the most local level. If it has harmonic value, it will overcome discord. If not, it'll dissipate quickly against discussion promoting a stronger harmony.

Education reform is a good example. Too often we have a federal mandate imposed across the nation to test students in order to quantify teaching results. Teaching to the test becomes the new measure of quality and good teachers leave the profession in the same way genuine optimists leave political environments. With no means to dissent at the local level against an imposing larger force, our cultures are filled with more political discord than consensual harmony.

Dissent against overreaching power increases the potential for harmony, but dissent among the good dissipates quickly. However, when evil is packaged as good, dissent is too easily marginalized to the far side of nuisance.

Many people feel that the world has become so polarized with two opposing forces of discord in the state that we've lost local common ground. Just look at our political climate, in which the progressive liberal wants to solve everything through state and global control, with the end being a unipolar world government. At the same time, the neo-conservative wants to give up liberty in the name of security, with the result being big corporate bailouts and the inevitable police state.

Once upon a time, we argued about federalist responsibility versus individual rights. Now we have a two-headed monster, one side wanting to take all responsibility for our social good and the other side wanting to take rights for our protection. We think too often that rights come about by demand and not given out of responsibility. We lack harmony in our thinking. We are forever fighting between the statist view and individualism. We will never find harmony. It has to come from the common consent best originated in a community, which is the best source for harmony because it's the only place where individual responsibility can scale. Community is the only place where discord and harmony can exist together.

In **Figure 8-1** twelve terms are indicated in three columns. There is a masculine column, a harmonic column, and a feminine column. All of the terms best fit in one of these columns. Even the numbers are appropriately indicated in each column. It would take too much to explain the feminine and masculine numbers, but the center is the best harmonics on a piano keyboard. I have placed words to show the range of optimism that can be found in genuine optimists. The sub comments under each give a broader description of each term and what is accomplished in the individual or better yet the community as a whole. Consider the top row as each subjective individual can yield, the second row as the action yielded, and the third row as a result that comes from the proper relationship.

Fig. 8-1 Harmonic Relationship of Meaning

Masculine	Harmonic	Feminine
2. Wisdom *Yields Responsibility*	**1. Identity** *Yields Individual Growth*	**3. Vision** *Yields Direction*
4. Judgment *Yields Conservation*	**5. Faith** *Yields Principles*	**6. Perception** *Yields Planning*
9. Agency *Yields Autonomy*	**8. Persistence** *Yields Sovereignty*	**7. Satisfaction** *Yields Achievement*
12. Ideal Consent *All must Agree*	**10. Community** *The Foundation*	**11. Fellowship** *All must Speak*

The bottom represents the community as a whole. Isolating any term is like extracting one word from the community vocabulary and elevating it to a level in which individuals often demand, but responsibility is leveled to nothing. Such is the case when agency is magnified to such a high level, as in the case of rights, we deemphasize satisfaction with a lack of harmony and also vision because faith harmonizes agency and vision. This will never be genuinely optimistic. The principled optimist doesn't lay claim to having all of these qualities in their possession at once. Instead, they only lay claim to the placement and meaning of those terms. This facilitates the recognized value of some terms in relation to other values. Without the relational connections in meaning that words make with other words, their progress is limited because we do not use the full range of our harmonic potential.

Look at the word "identity." Like any abstract noun, it needs to be linked with other words in order to be understood. Those other words are *wisdom* and *vision*. We tend to generalize the meaning of identity, whereas identity is a specific attribute of each individual when fully developed. With common consent and fellowship, we have a perfect community. Without wisdom, what is human identity? Does it have the same value? The principled optimist sees a greater range of relational meaning. Linear thinkers, on the other hand, don't see this relational association. A good example, as we will see later, is with the word *democracy*. If you cluster all associated words, what kind of range of meaning would it give to democracy? Once the full range is seen within the cluster of relational meanings, then there's more responsibility placed on the community as the foundation for democracy and less on the state. This is more specifically realized in *common consent* where all must agree in *fellowship* where all have an equal opportunity to speak. This can only be achieved in modularized communities acting as one through a chosen representative to a regional, state and eventually a federal forum. What we are doing is creating a direct republic of common consent that operates the same on every level as the community.

The problem with a polarized political world favored by political optimists is that they cannot play harmony with words. They regurgitate slogans and platitudes inherent in their selfishness and idolatrous need to control the masses. When compared to irrational optimists showing *idolatry* in denial, the principled optimist shows *faith* in truth. This faith in truth eventually leads to the only true principle strong enough to protect all genuine optimists; it is the principle of ideal consent. It is the only way to help others see what they cannot see on their own. See **Figure 8-2**.

Fig. 8–2 Traits of the Principled Optimist

Character	Traits
Faith	Faith in Truth
Intelligence	Glory in Vision
Agency	Ask Questions
Motivation	Prophetic Insight
Reward	Ideal Consent

Michael, a close friend, is a warm-hearted believing optimist who touches lives for good. He called last night to talk. After an hour on the phone he told me of his wife's surgery; doctors removed a cancerous portion of her lower intestine. He explained in detail the difficulties this brought into their lives. He spoke with a forced positive attitude that believed in pushing through and enduring to the end. "Are you online?" I asked.

"No," he responded. "I have dyslexia." Apparently, years before, he was told he had dyslexia and he accepted it as his identity.

From Michael's point of view, all he knew was how to be a loving and kind man, to touch lives for good. He was a believing optimist locked in one place with no progress. He lived to support his family and his wife and to endure almost anything, even great loss and sorrow, with an almost stoic compassion fueled by depressed humility. However, can we say this is optimistic? Perhaps optimism touches others, but not if it fails to lift Michael himself. Will he ever stand and say no, to force a better yes? Will he ever progress toward encouragement and principle? Is life an endured process imposed by fate, or do we act on our own? To the outside world, endurance through great challenges in life seems optimistic, but never from inside our own heart.

When we're emotionally depressed, it's hard to keep fighting to get more out of life. This is the real test of optimism. Optimism is made of better stuff than a surrendered humility that attacks believing optimists. It doesn't inspire them to express the optimism of no in exchange for greater understanding of what is available in life.

This is why optimism must be music that we make as a community rather than a single note played repeatedly. Optimism must grow from belief to encouragement and then to principle—or, in the reverse, from principle to encouragement and then to belief. Both directions are paths of progression from one good position to another good position.

If each of us were to name the most humble and the most optimistic person we know, and if we had to choose just one to emulate, most of us would choose the most optimistic. The optimist gives all of us something more to aspire to than just the humble strength to endure. Does this negate humility? No! Humility for those choosing to leave the practice of being political is essential. In this they progress toward genuine optimism for the first time. To progress and to endure are different expressions. The first aligns with optimism and the latter tightens his or her teeth with a half-smile.

The intention isn't to debase humility. The only intention is to show clearly that in times of great challenge, and against great odds, optimism is the act of building. Humility can be useful: it's sometimes a much-needed demolition. Humility brings down what tries to command and control everything. Human progression has to lead into a better understanding of genuine optimism. We've already talked about the revolution of no that promotes a greater confirmation of yes. *Responsibility is both revolution and confirmation, and when we have both yes and no in equilibrium, we define this as freedom.*

It's like looking at a scale with a weight for yes on one side and a weight for no on the other side. The reason why one side tends to outweigh the other is that we take our eye off the middle axis of meaning, which the Socratic relational mind found in *The Tree of Life*.

The Principle of the Tree of Life

There's a big difference between opposition and separation. With opposition, two or more views can stay in the discussion. With separation, two or more views eventually become polarized apart from each other while rejecting any outside views.

This idea of separation began with the Judeo-Christian story of Adam and Eve.

In this story, God planted two trees in the Garden of Eden and commanded Adam and Eve to eat from the Tree of Life, but not to eat from the Tree of Knowledge of Good and Evil. Eve decided otherwise and ate fruit from the Tree of the Knowledge of Good and Evil. Adam followed and the Lord banished both from the garden, thus beginning what Christians refer to as original sin.

What's the difference really between these two trees? We know that good and evil exist as a separation, a kind of division between bitter and sweet, joy and sorrow, pleasure and pain. This isn't the case with the Tree of life. The Tree of Life is a natural opposition, what we see between male and female, the ideal and the real, justice and mercy, reason and intuition. This opposition doesn't divide and separate, because so much different fruit come from the same tree.

The wisdom of the universe perhaps meant for us to sustain a natural opposition in all things found in the Tree of

Life, rather than an unnatural separation in the Tree of Good and Evil. This may explain why we're as polarized as any other people in history. Only at special times have we shown otherwise. Perhaps that's our trial: to learn to choose meaning through common consent after experiencing so much meaning imposed by authority. If this were the case, then true meaning obtained through open discourse and not authoritative or mob rule is our salvation.

Does opposition incorporate evil? Natural opposition is the optimism of "no" that's allowed to germinate a clearer meaning—and a total consent for "yes." With continued freedom to say no, natural opposition sustains meaning and real progress. This has absolutely nothing to do with evil. It has everything to do with freedom. To put it a better way, evil cannot take root in natural opposition because there is no way to subvert unanimous consent.

Evil works to shut down the freedom of dissenting ideas against itself: it's not progressive. Only natural opposition allows for a greater vision of more good, because it allows for dissent voiced throughout the process. Evil doesn't allow for this. It can only exist in division and more separation.

Freedom cannot exist in a state of natural opposition, such as what's found between a believing optimist and a principled optimist. Evil requires a duality, such as found between an irrational optimist and a principled optimist. This kind of division is not a natural opposition. Evil does not make you a better person. Only natural opposition does this.

Both freedom and responsibility belong in a natural state of opposition rather than in a state of division (such as what's found with good and evil). Black-and-white notions of reality support more duality and more division rather than an opposition that progresses naturally toward the common consent of the community. In a natural state of opposition, evil can never take hold and the issue of separating good from evil is suddenly moot.

When we support separation, evil takes more power through discord, division, and deception. Evil then roots itself deeper into our social conscience, creating more division and more separation. If you don't believe this, consider the two camps of public discourse that have ruled governments throughout history.

The first camp is the Platonic. Driven from top down, this centrally controlled model commands blindly and controls without responsibility. It's the more pervasive of the two. The only reason we call it *public* is that it employs the semblance of openness in public discourse by using a majority-rule democratic process.

Just about every institution employs this model, including religious, government, business, and non-profit organizations. It focuses primarily on power centers of control and suffers from idolatry supporting authority. Many people associate this model with the social justice movement. It empowers a minority or new underclass, only to then become the new power center. It's linear in logic.

The second camp is the Socratic, driving the open forum and unanimous consent—and, in rare situations, a super majority rule. This process seems to take a longer time to make decisions, but it's also less prone to corruption. Above all, the Socratic method decentralizes.

Models for the Socratic method include the jury system, our constitutional convention, the Knights of the Round Table, the Magna Carta, the Charter of Liberties, the Iroquois Five Nation Confederacy, and Swiss Cantons. The Socratic model founded on the highest level of consensus (the people) is often associated with the classical social contract. It empowers people and not the idolatry for individuals over people. It is relational.

Most of our modern technology—social networking, online marketing, big data mining, profile security, and even the new alternative media battling the old media—all this still favors the Platonic method while crypto currencies, cooperative organizations and headless media movements are realizing the advantages of the Socratic.

The big question is this: is public discourse entering a new renaissance? If so, what role will you play? Will we continue with more Platonic king-making models of central control or will we divide power with more voice and consent of the people? In business we scale for growth. In education we scale for learning. Why not scale government for more dissent? Is this not a move toward more abundance? Shifting the paradigm like this may just be the answer to launching a new renaissance and finally putting to rest the scarcity pushers.

Letting people manage themselves within the context of greater room for dissent while reaching for common consent, this alone will solve the problem of divisive evil. With less division, we can all challenge one another freely rather than submit to the supposed expert, authority or political correction.

Freedom is what the principled optimist struggles to stand for in a world stuck in the duality of good and evil—a purely political and linear construct. A natural opposition allows one to enter and confront a dominant *yes* establishment. It is not too late for the boomer generation to properly fill the hole they dug in their youth.

Many times in college, high school, and even Sunday school, teachers are deliberately selective in what they include in the lecture. The teacher obviously cannot include everything, but to shut out the content of a discussion that will help better define complex terms means the teacher is separating and controlling freedom. They do it to save time and get through the lecture, but why not allow more time to talk? Why not have a class that works like a jury—and not let the class end until there is a consensus? Wow, what kind of education would that be? Is the Tree of Life all about granting more time for natural opposition? A greater consensus is better than backroom deals made to prevent opposition.

In 2002 the Oakland As played their longest baseball game ever. It took over 19 innings and didn't end until six hours and thirty-two minutes later. Baseball has become an American pastime because of the timeless nature of the sport.

We need more timeless approaches to life, and less sudden-death elimination. The first is genuine optimism and the latter is political optimism. The Tree of Life is a renaissance of people willing to incorporate natural opposition into their lives. They're willing to take more time to work things out with the full consent of everyone involved in a modular construct so as to allow for healthy discussion.

This problem of perpetual duality at odds with social consent has occurred many times in history. A monarch or king wants to shut down progressive freedom because of too many free-floating ideas for them to control. When there are too many voices, controlling minds gather together in secret to devise plans to centralize control.

Political optimists want freedom, but not for everyone. They even have the gall to call their plans progressive—when they are anything but progressive. In the tyranny of excessive control, taking freedom away works to the tyrant's advantage, as long as they call their ideas progressive.

Yet it's not progressive to centralize freedom. Historically, progress is always on the side of decentralizing freedom. The modern social justice movement is all about centralizing freedom to right a wrong.

Compare that to the Magna Carta, written in 1215 as a deliberate attempt by nobles, barons, and the wealthy to put themselves on equal ground with the king. It was the first document forced onto the king by his subjects in an attempt to limit and decentralize his powers and protect their privileges.

Over the centuries, the progress of freedom wanted more since more people demanded the same freedom to stand against the oligarchs, and thus came the American Declaration of Independence, the Constitution, the Bill of Rights and many other similar documents. All these enlarged the progress of freedom. Over time, though, the voice of the people is taken over by a controlling mentality that doesn't allow so many voices free access to freedom. Today, corporations (the new barons) re-centralize freedom for their convenience by putting a new dictatorial class in place.

Many call fascism a radical authoritarian nationalism, but in truth it is the merger of corporations and government. How else can you centralize so much power without financial support?

It's clearly antithetical to freedom. The first thing the principled optimist looks for is what is genuine—and what is political. The principled optimist sees that freedom must progress through natural opposition, not through separation and more division.

As long as faceless powers are allowed to sow discord behind the scenes, we're in trouble. We must adopt The Tree of Life as our means to genuine optimism, and stop eating from the Tree of the Knowledge of Good and Evil, which conquers the people through division and separation. The Tree of Life arises through natural opposition. It requires us to reach common consent and inhibits polarization from taking place. Good an evil mentality empowers political power centers.

Only in natural opposition (which is long, tedious, wide open for discussion, and slow in arriving at consensus) will freedom decentralize control naturally. The expediency crowd will want control in order to get things done; the efficiency crowd will want new vision to get the best thing done.

Only the latter will play a timeless game, if only they can progress toward community in proportion to individual voice of consent and not stop at the one-vote process.

Voice in discussion and vote for consent must scale together.

Even now: we are, with the help of the Internet, the most liberated generation, with wide-open freedom placed before us. Despite this marvelous technology, we've chosen globalism, corporate monopolies, political division, executive fiat, cartels, and more central control employed out of crisis.

Political optimists will often create a crisis in order to inject and claim more control: the standing rule for all political optimists is to never let a good crisis go to waste. The term *crisis* comes from the goddess Isis, whose name in Egyptian means, "throne." The "throne" of control that a "crisis" comes from simply divides and conquers the people.

Genuine optimists demand that control become touching acts of belief, mentors of encouragement, and a principle that stands the test of time. Without the faith necessary to let freedom flourish in these directions, leaders tend to fear criticism of their decisions. We find them doing everything in their power to control or spin away dissent and criticism. They cannot help but reveal that they have no vision from which to come out from behind themselves and into the open conversation.

Leadership today is failing to manage real diverse conversations because it sides with a partisan crowd rather than engage the body of the whole at the most local level.

There's no best practice eluding us; there's no dressed-up positive mental exertion and a new rhetoric to go with it. There's only free discussion working toward the highest degree of public consent possible.

A society that conserves the freedom of each person in the crowd can only develop in a graduated consensus, with each person having full and independent agency to dissent in their individual group.

The political optimist with no working principle of freedom fears standing in front of those expressing dissent against their control. The risk of losing power is too great. Throughout history, there are more political optimists directing society than there are genuine optimists appearing on the scene. Because every generation fails to exercise faith in human freedom, we always need to show additional faith. The real battle is about abolishing our idolatry for authority and replacing it with the principle of common consent taught at every level of civilization.

Common consent is the conservation of responsibility within the community, perhaps the most powerful truth held by a principled optimist and the one idea our founding fathers never realized.

The Conservation of Responsibility

If you think of faith as a positive mental exertion, or some sort of upbeat thinking, a positive attitude then could very well be a political act if there's no responsibility attached to it. For example, a sales manager can intimidate the entire staff by saying, "You have to think positive if you want to make sales—stop being so negative!" The sales manager is actually intimidating to cover his fear. He doesn't have faith. The use of intimidation is a sign of dishonesty covered by the cloak of a positive mental exertion. A manager leading the sales staff in faith would say, "We make sales by serving a need, so listen to the words of your client and find a way to serve that need."

When you're interviewing candidates to hire, or while dating a potential future spouse, look for the *meaning of faith*. Faith reveals their view of freedom, and that in turn reveals their individual motives for everything else. If one thinks that doing the honest thing, coupled with hard work, is faith, then responsibility connects properly to the meaning—and the salesperson is apt to succeed. If the sales person talks about sales and numbers with no regard for how they achieve those numbers, you have a big problem. A business may have a quick jump in sales with a political optimist, but it will never sustain that growth. Political optimists in sales are transaction-driven rather than builders of relationships. With political optimists, everything at every moment is about making the sale and not about building a long-term client base. Put in a business sense, you can scale and remain sustainable with genuine optimists but you cannot scale with political optimists.

Think about the difference between "thinking positively" and "taking responsibility." The latter is truly in your reach; the former is difficult to grasp. Thinking positively is not a sustainable approach to business. Taking responsibility, on the other hand, is sustainable. There is only one way to keep the political optimist from infiltrating the system and usurping power, and that's the principle of common consent.

We tend to associate responsibility with a pyramid, where one person at the head makes all decisions. This is a serious error. Responsibility comes when we hold decisions in common.

A few weeks ago, my business team interviewed a candidate who would head up the technical side of things and eventually become our chief technical officer. Each person who interviewed him had a completely different experience, and they were not consistently positive. I had a positive feeling, but my other three partners didn't share in my enthusiasm. My partners noted the candidate's unwillingness to sacrifice and work hard for the company, plus other issues that had surfaced in the negotiations. It had been easy for me to ignore those issues because of the candidate's skills and experience—*and* the feeling of importance the candidate had given me.

Genuine optimists are quick to see where they can serve. Political optimists are not service-oriented, and yet they tell you what you want to hear.

Political optimists always look for advantages and are always looking to jockey for a position of control. No matter how talented and experienced they are, they cannot compare to a volunteer willing to give more time and more effort, even with less experience and sometimes no pay. The only way to attract volunteers with belief, encouragement, and principle is to give them a real voice of consent with real teeth in the game. A political optimist will want more. They will want full control, often giving nobody any voice of consent.

It's amazing to see how corporations, governments, and even religious institutions have been organized with such centralized political control. *Why* we think this model is good is a sign of our continued idolatry for authority.

However, by building new structures on natural opposition best seen in the practice of common consent, we support the freedom necessary to create better institutions in education, healthcare, government, and business as well as in community service. In other words, we support a more sustainable approach of taking responsibility.

This idea of freedom built on common consent (where it's within each person's agency to say yes and no) is the foundation of everything that's genuinely optimistic. The problem is that most of us have no idea how to first protect this freedom, and second how to scale it into large groups.

This is where the conservation of responsibility, through common consent, comes into play. It's a principle that protects freedom while at the same time allows it to scale into very large organizations. We will see how all this works in more detail as we talk about the restoration of common dissent in the next section.

As for the principled optimists, they stand against the irrational optimist in profound ways. Just the other day a friend sent me another inspirational video to watch online. The speaker, Eduardo Briceno, started with the usual question, "What do you think is required to reach our ultimate goals?"[2] Briceno told the story of Josh Waitzkin, the winner of multiple chess championships. Later, at the age of 21, Josh decided to master martial arts and eventually won several championships in Tai Chi from 2002-2004. The speaker quoted from Josh Waitzkin to explain his success: "The moment we believe that success is determined by an ingrained level of ability, we will be brittle in the face of adversity."

Eduardo Briceno talks about the research of Stanford Professor Dr. Carol Dweck, who realized a difference between a *fixed mindset* and a *growth mindset*.[3] In her book *Mindset: The New Psychology of Success*, a fixed mindset says, "Effort is for the incapable." A growth mindset says "Effort makes me smarter." A teacher with a fixed quality of intelligence says to a student, "You must be smart at this." A teacher promoting a growth quality of intelligence says, "You must have tried really hard."

I sent the video link to my father and I got this reply:

> You can study anything and come up with a formula for success. What researches the surface will not tell you the underlying the principle or timing as to the flow of things. Being in the right place at the right time comes only by understanding the flow, the relation of things, and the dynamics of a chain of events. Successes are often associated with timing and failures are also by the same conditions—a lack of timing that we cannot control. Fortunately in my old age I do not have to depend on timing other than the natural process of illness.

> The real power of achievement is in a group of minds or in more than one mind. Other than this, you cannot intellectualize success by any means of assurance. Sportscasters intellectualize sports, but fail to connect the events. One succeeds or fails because of some choice they made. Choices make little difference when it is not the right series of events. We often go in circles because we cannot see the pattern.

> I have failed consistently at computer programing. I have no idea how I ever succeeded in any attempt learn the basics. What I have learned is to focus as local as possible and stop searching for some answer held by some knowledge base. Things are designed in small conceptual packages and tested. Too often the writer or teacher assumes the student understands and the student feels intimidated to ask for a conceptual flow of things. Looking elsewhere, outside of the norm, leads to accidental workings that cannot be repeated because of an unknown variable. I thought I had everything working, but minor changes lead to untold failures. We go in circles, because we have no relation. I realized the prior successes were automated beyond my knowledge. By going through the simple process intended by the vision of the idea, I was able to do it simpler than before with perfect success.

Knowing your tools is better than hard work. Knowing how things work and how things flow is ignored by instructors and writers. They go directly to the detail to which the learner cannot relate, but only memorize. Hard work and positive thinking are simply forms of denial. The only common denominator of success is to learn the flow and that comes best through discussion and questioning and not lectures and over-detailed books. We fabricate illusions or think someone else already has the answer, if only we can discover it. This is a lack of vision, flow, and understanding—the hallmarks of success.

Many researchers of success do not discuss how to scale the idea of a growth or an abundance mindset for the community. They always stop at the individual perspective, which is the case with the talk by Eduardo Briceno. It is one thing for an individual to become the best in the world in two competitive events, such as chess and martial arts. It is quite another for a whole group to rise to greater achievement without an individual overseer.

When you scale everything great about the individual into the community or the corporation, you cannot be left with an individual overlord over the whole. The entire organization must move in genuine abundance of a growth mindset, like a beehive, as if they are one mind. This can only happen for every individual when we protect the genuine optimism found in the principle of common consent.

Section III
Restoration of Common Consent

Tyranny naturally arises out of democracy.

- Plato

While some of what we read as history and the rise and fall of empires, also includes the waves of political control and eventually social collapse. Anyone mildly aware of the fast approaching world government feels that a counter-change must take place if we ever hope to advance towards *heaven on earth*, truly the best of all possible worlds.

The sense is that the biggest change must come against liberty through the controlling influence of authority. It may take a hundred years to see the pendulum swing, but a shift in power toward more local autonomy will come. It's the natural reaction to central control and the only solution in preserving individual freedom.

Don't let the positive aspects of modern technology distract you into thinking the world is getting better. For the most part, all the best technology remains buried while control continues to rape the system. A good example is the story of Paul Pantone. He created GEET, a Global Environmental Energy Technology.

GEET is a fuel system that allows internal combustion engines to run far more efficiently while dramatically reducing toxic emissions by 90% or more. Unfortunately Paul Pantone has been marginalized to the corner of a tinfoil hat. More than most inventors claiming extraordinary high efficiency in combustion energy, Paul has labs and satellite inventors around the world, all putting to work the GEET technology with surprising results. Despite the wide consensus of this application of major fuel savings, Paul is relegated to something less than a garage tinkerer, by those in power.

Paul has a record of being incarcerated in a mental institution. Even Martin Luther King Jr., Henry David Thoreau, and Socrates all suffered incarceration. Is there a common thread? Yes! The common thread is a will to dissent against entrenched bureaucratic powers. This control does not align with optimism. Even though it looks odd and easily marginalized as crazy, the real solution to improving human freedom does not involve new technologies or the will to struggle against big brother. Instead, the real solution is about scaling personal responsibility, including the will to dissent. It is social responsibility at the local level. We can talk all day long about the power of thorium reactors and how they are far more efficient at producing energy and how they can actually burn the waste from uranium reactors and that they produce a fraction of the waste. Unfortunately thorium does not produce the material needed to make nuclear bombs and so it is never promoted. Disruptive ideas like thorium require the widest consent possible. Instead we marginalize the best ideas for a lack or common consent. The popular rules and the center of power will control what is popular.

We must limit central power and keep it under local concern and never pass responsibility up and beyond our local commonwealth, save we choose to do so. If anything great is to happen as a counter measure to everything wrong we must replace our idolatry for central control with the genuine optimism of local consent and social responsibility.

People are feeling a growing distaste for the politics of central world control far distant from local disagreement. A vacuum is beginning to appear and a hole has been dug. Now is the time to fill the hole before its replacement is merely a new authoritarianism.

If ever there were a time to plant the seeds of a new renaissance, now is that time. The following chapters comprise this seed.

9

Personal Responsibility

Here is a great question that came to my mind. Which is more valuable, free salvation or personal responsibility?

Political Idolatry

Political idolatry is the worshipping of authority instead of using your own mind. Consider this from Shakespeare's *Hamlet*:

Polonius: This above all: to thine own self be true,

And it must follow, as the night the day,

Thou canst not then be false to any man.

Farewell, my blessing season this in thee!

Laertes: Most humbly do I take my leave, my lord.

-      Shakespeare's Hamlet
Act 1, scene three.

To thine own self be true is Polonius' last piece of advice to his son Laertes, who is in a hurry to get on the next boat back to school in Paris and away from his father's long-winded speeches. We are as uninterested in the "still small voice" as we are in long-winded lectures on personal responsibility. We don't want to see, and we don't want to hear, because we hide our mind's eye with a view that is linear in making conclusions and not relational in understanding.

Let's examine three views. You might be surprised to know the authors of each.

> **#1** "People like me only have a duty to ourselves: we have no duty to other people. I am responsible only for the reality that I know, and absolutely not responsible for anything else. I don't know about the past, and I don't know about the future. They have nothing to do with the reality of my own self." [1]

> **#2** "Every age and generation must be as free to act for itself, in all cases, as the ages and generations which preceded it. The vanity and presumption of governing beyond the grave, is the most ridiculous and insolent of all tyrannies. Man has no property in man; neither has any generation a property in the generations which are to follow." [2]

> **#3** "And he shall go before him in the spirit and power of Elias, to turn the hearts of the fathers to the children, and the disobedient to the wisdom of the just; to make ready a people prepared for the Lord." [3]

The first view limits responsibility to the self, the second limits responsibility to the present, and the third sees responsibility applied to past, present, and future generations.

The first view is from Mao Tse Tung (mass murderer), the second is from Thomas Pain (founding father), and the third is from Luke 1:17 in the *King James Version* of the *Bible*. How hard would it be for the first view to accept the third view? It is almost impossible.

Changing our view of life is like a bad dream. We desperately plan our escape into a deeper slumber in order to avoid hearing a different view. In order to resolve our dilemma, we find ourselves caught in an unfinished dream. We remain convinced that our *view* is the only way. We do not hear our own doubts or understand the doubts of others. As we sleep through the morning, we never get the chance to overcome and be challenged by ideas from outside our own mind.

This is like refusing to hear the still small voice of truth in the open forum. We are instead subjected to authoritative approval without speaking our own mind.

Imagine being stranded alone on an island in the South Pacific. You scavenge for coconuts to quench your thirst, you cut giant palm leaves to protect yourself from the weather, and you catch fish with a spear made from bamboo. Each choice you make derives from your mind's ability to embrace or not embrace certain actions to stay alive. These choices are related to dissent (the will to say no) and consent (the will to say yes). Combined, the two define the freedom we associate with personal responsibility.

Since a chance at discovering life is better than loneliness, you find a way off the island in a makeshift raft. After two weeks at sea, a passing tanker rescues you. While this is the storyline of the movie *Cast Away*, consider how the choice is yours to assume responsibility to get off the island. When you re-enter society, do you have more responsibility... or less?

On the island, all you had were your own thoughts; there were no dissenting views. Because of this, you had less potential for freedom. Oddly, not having your own ideas questioned actually limits you. On an island, you had fewer ideas and so you could only doubt and challenge yourself. We idolize the individual who rises above these challenges to find more life, but why not scale this kind of rugged fight into community?

How do you get more ideas and more input while still being able to think and exercise your twin powers of personal responsibility?

The best way to preserve personal responsibility is to move away from majority rule (political optimism) and toward common consent in small groups (genuine optimism). In other words, you cannot scale political optimism (a majority) without destroying personal responsibility (local consent).

When it comes to larger populations, scaling civil discourse into many small groups seems impossible because we never talk about decentralizing control into constituent parts. However, this is the pattern in a true republic of common consent. It is organized into modular structures representing regional, state, county, community, and even neighborhood forums. These forums send representatives to the next level by the same discipline of common consent. Instead of trusting an individual by majority vote, why not trust a higher forum, council, committee, or board that must reach perfect consent? Does this not better protect every person's freedom to dissent?

Too many people feel impatient about reaching a decision with full consent because they cannot see how small groups are a better fit for liberating civil discourse than a majority vote in larger populations. As long as we reject the voice of each individual human being, we will continue to devalue wide consent and favor a slim majority rule that promotes more idolatry for authority.

In order to protect the twin powers to say yes and no in every person, we must reject our idolatry for unchecked authority over us. In a letter to Garret Van Meter April 27, 1781, Thomas Jefferson is quoted as saying, "Laws made by common consent must not be trampled on by individuals."[4] Unfortunately this happens all the time. When we set above our minds a central authority, we subject our consent to the same.

Consider a note that James Madison made during the constitution convention on May 28, 1787:

> A member shall not speak oftener than twice, without special leave, upon the same question; and not the second time, before every other, who had been silent, shall have been heard, if he choose to speak upon the subject.

Making sure that each member of the convention had equal footing produced a document imbued with the widest appeal and the greatest consent possible. There's nothing more optimistic than reaching perfect consent. The problem is that we haven't been creative enough to scale it in our modern world.

In the business world, people push for quick decisions to conserve the time value of money. That's the argument we hear over and over, and yet businesses fail more because of this approach than they would if decisions surfaced as a result of long and patient discussion. Think about it. If decisions were made by unanimous consent, the only lengthy discussions to surface would be those voicing dissent against a majority. This is preferred over having to disagree with a political optimist in central control. Ideal consent preserves freedom. Central control empowered by a majority does not.

If we think a centralized political hierarchy is better for producing increased revenue and better business than a decentralized and wider body of consent, we are mistaken.

Look at employee owned companies operating by greater democratic consensus and compare them with privately owned companies run by a board of investors and paid advisors. You would think a wide-open democratic process requiring a greater consensus would not work in the business world.

A Rutgers study conducted by Joseph Blasi and Douglas Kruse found that companies with employee Stock Ownership Plans (ESOPs) grow 2.4% faster in sales and 2.3% faster in annual employment growth.[5] Another study conducted by Dr. Peter Kardas and the Washington State Department of Community Development concludes that: "The combination of employee ownership and significant participation makes it possible for employee ownership companies, on the average, to have an advantage unavailable to their competitors."[6]

A National Center for Employee Ownership study confirms the same, that employee owned companies with democratic management grow 8% to 11% per year faster than their private competitors.[7] Employee ownership with workplace democratic participation breeds more volunteerism, more innovation, and more competitive value in the market.

As times begin to contract due to growing government debt and excessive centralized power, more and more people will begin to see the benefits of consensual involvement. New business models will be the first to shift toward local employee-owned ventures.

With unanimous consent in modular form, we have a more pure form of freedom, because it successfully scales the individual into a community. It is true the process is longer and often filled with frustration, but this is preferred over the political pandering we see with so much corruption in power today.

Look at what is really driving this idea of common consent. It's the only way to avoid the destruction of our twin powers of personal responsibility that scale naturally into public discourse. Most motivational speakers fail to realize this fundamental flaw in their thinking. It's one thing to motivate a political optimist in a world filled with more political optimists. We do this all the time. But we cannot expect a genuine optimist to rise in a political world without changing the power systems in that world. When you put them head-to-head in a majority-takes-all environment, political optimists dominate genuine optimists every time. Speakers on leadership will never tell you this truth because they fail to see real optimistic solutions that scale into community.

For example, the U.S. legislature sometimes passes bills in haste to avoid discussion. Former Speaker Nancy Pelosi, in referring to the Affordable Care Act of 2010, said, "But we have to pass the bill so that you can find out what is in it, away from the fog of the controversy."[8]

These are the words of a political optimist. When we put discussion aside and—in the name of expediency—encourage a manufactured crisis, the fog of controversy grows thicker. Any hope for consent suffers from the intimidation of majority rule. For example, every once in a while, a lonely senator or a few congressmen speak against billions in foreign aid given to dictators. With such blatant abuses of funds fully documented, more foreign aid is still sent, year after year.

At the same time that more corruption continues unchecked, we repeatedly assume by default that we need centralized authority in order to operate government with expediency.

Let us ask this question: What is more important, pushing for more central control, in the name of expediency, or allowing for disagreement, in the name of freedom? Only a free society preserves disagreement. Authoritarian societies push for expediency. Authoritarians also push the newest crisis to quicken a need for expediency.

In fact, many democracies devolve into authoritarian rule through continual crises instead of rising through a republic of common consent. This is how political optimists get control over the free expression of every individual, through sowing more crisis, hence the term "False Flag." A False Flag event occurs when a government or corporation stages a secrete operation whereby they pretend to be targeted by the enemy while attacking their own forces or people. The attack is then falsely blamed on the enemy in order to justify going to war against that enemy.

Deliberate meddling to force a crisis pushes people into accepting more central control, and it is always expedient. It has happened more in our history than we dare admit.

The worst element of political optimism is the corrupt power centers that sow public discord. The only way to stop them is to begin scaling society to protect the optimism of common consent.

The solution is here!

Imagine two groups of 100 people. They separate to choose a representative. The first group randomly breaks into 10 groups of 10 and each group selects one representative by common consent. This produces a committee of 10 representatives operating by the same common consent. From this committee they choose their representative. We call this a republic of common consent, a government of the people and by the people. The second one hundred select 1 representative from a popular vote from the entire body. We call this a popular democracy, a government of the power centers and for the power elite. Compare the differences in **Figure 9-1**.

Would you rather have your voice count in a group of 10 that selects by common consent one representative that advances to another group of 10, also ruled by common consent? Or

Fig. 9-1 Political and Genuine Optimists Compared

Genuine Optimists	Political Optimists
100 people ruled by common consent where 10 groups of 10 rise into one committee of 10 to choose one representative for the whole. This representative is aligned with the committee of 10 and not power centers in the whole.	100 people ruled by a popular direct vote that chooses one representative by majority vote (51%). This person is then forced to align with power centers inside and outside the group.

Genuine Optimists	Political Optimists
• Two layers of voting	• One layer of voting
• People are the power centers	• Candidates are the power centers
• 110 potential votes with teeth	• 100 potential votes with no teeth
• 100% agreement	• 51% agreement
• Power is relational and horizontal	• Power is linear and vertical
• More discussion	• Less discussion
• Dissent is sustained	• Dissent is not factored
• Decentralized	• Centralized
• Eliminates parties and factions	• Forms into parties and factions

would you prefer a vote with no voice in the whole group of 100 where a 51% majority rule decides the vote? If you are a political optimist, you will choose the latter. Genuine optimists choose the former.

In smaller groups, we have more opportunity to discuss, more power to dissent, and greater opportunity to reach consensus. We have forgotten that this is the true voice of the people, and it's genuinely optimistic because it naturally eliminates political schemers. In the larger group, you diminish discussion and you lose the opportunity to express dissenting voices. Any hope for greater consensus is taken by controlling power centers in the group, and you lose options and ideas.

We find this linear approach to centralize power in all political optimists. Anyone who calls popular voting the "voice of the people" is deceived. All you have to do is look at the difference between having a voice in common and having a vote that may or may not be of the majority. If a small group is heading in the wrong direction, a single voice in common dissent can stop it. With a vote that is not part of the majority, you have no realistic chance of stopping a bad decision.

If you still cannot see the difference, then consider this. We choose leaders first—rather than choosing the *process* of selecting leaders first. Selecting leaders first focuses our attention on the worship for authority and not on an equitable process in using our own minds.

We see this problem in foundations, nonprofits, corporations and city, county, state, and federal governments. If you aren't part of the process, you aren't a power center; and if you're unwilling to pander and prostrate yourself to power centers, you're not in the game. A room full of people always has power centers controlling the room, unless that room is run by the highest ideal of common consent.

If only we could see a better vision for freedom, we could get our eye off the leader and focused on giving equal footing to express the voice of dissent in modularized groups. Imagine selecting the process first and the leaders second? Suddenly our focus shifts to advancing the best vision from every person.

A Vision from Our Own Minds

While working in the produce department at a local grocery store during a temporary career realignment, I witnessed a lot of waste. This waste was so bothersome to my principled mind that I came up with a new business model: feed the wasted produce to local hogs, chickens, and cattle, rather than put it in the trash. The same wasted produce could also be mixed with sawdust from a local lumber mill and then heated in the open desert air to create a nutrient-dense potting soil.

I came up with these ideas because, as a genuine optimist, I was awake, bothered, and stubborn about finding a better way to use a wasted resource. *This is vision.* It begins to form when we see a better way.

Because the grocery chain was controlled at a distance, local employees had no way to communicate their dissent with so much waste. So I came up with an idea for a cooperative grocery chain allowing for more local innovation while at the same time creating a distribution channel for locally made quality products.

After several years of talking about the idea, I realized that it takes an enormous effort to accomplish something so disruptive in a politically controlled system. The political challenges faced by visionary minds make such projects impossible. It takes a strong stomach to push through political barriers and I did not have the stubborn individualism needed to challenge the current model.

Look at Herman Melville. Several dozen publishers rejected him when he tried to get *Moby-Dick* published. In order to understand the drive behind a passionate vision, read what Nathaniel Hawthorne had to say about his friend:

> Melville has not been well, of late; he has been affected with neuralgic complaints in his head and limbs, and no doubt has suffered from too constant literary occupation, pursued without much success.... and his writings, for a long while past, have indicated a morbid state of mind.... Melville, as he always does, began to reason of Providence and futurity, and of everything that lies beyond human ken, and informed me that he had "pretty much made up his mind to be annihilated"; but still he does not seem to rest in that anticipation; and, I think, will never rest until he gets hold of a definite belief. It is strange how he persists...in wondering to-and-fro over these deserts.... He can neither believe, nor be comfortable in his unbelief. If he were a religious man, he would be one of the most truly religious and reverential...and better worth immortality than most of us.

- Notebook Entry, November 20 1856

Vision comes from a defiant mentality, often a "loose cannon," the very opposite of a visionless political mentality. Melville was frustrated by the system but not by his vision. This reveals a lonely truth: vision arises best from individuals, never from a committee decision. However, we have two options for an individual to advance a vision.

The first option is a political dogfight and the hope that one person in power will stick a neck out to support the vision.

We look up to these achievements only after the fact, when they have achieved something great, never in the struggle. The second option is a change in our system so that more can hear new ideas with real teeth of consent in the game. The only way this later option can happen is if smaller groups, organized by 100% consensus, make sure visionary ideas are not shut down by a political majority of 51%.

Imagine a great writer enters a room of publishers and it takes 100% of the publishers to advance his book. It also takes 100% of the publishers to reject his book. Just one publisher can hold the other publishers hostage until all see the same thing. Being held hostage until an idea has had a solid chance of presenting itself is a better process than being forced to take the hard fought, rugged individual route of pounding the pavement to find that one person in power willing to believe in you.

The United States Constitution, written with almost no entrenched political power center, surfaced after fifty-five delegates from various states worked in common agreement to solve a big problem. Although Benjamin Franklin pushed for unanimous consent, the delegates approved a super majority of two-thirds of the thirteen state legislatures where only nine were needed to ratify the constitution. This meant the decision was not left in the hands of the fifty-five delegates.

Put in the hands of the state legislatures, an even greater horizontal body retained broader powers of consent. Had the Bill of Rights been included at the start, greater consent among all the state legislatures may have manifested greater achievement? Even without the Bill of Rights, Delaware, Georgia, and New Jersey ratified the constitution by unanimous consent while other states secured a majority only. The point is, the fifty-five delegates did not see themselves as the center of the universe (as politicians in Washington think they are today).

My sense is that if new policies had to be ratified by the state legislatures, we would find a greater union of states and a greater consensus of the best ideas.

The Declaration of Independence had even greater consent. While there was no set number of states that had to vote in favor of the Declaration, the members of Congress felt that it was such an important vote that it should be unanimous, and they waited until all of the states were in favor. There was no official rule about how many states must ratify it, yet unofficially they wanted a unanimous vote.

More push for consensus is the very stuff that promotes optimism. Only the best ideas come out of it, ideas that apply equally to everyone, without divisions and without partisan bickering. Neither a simple majority rule nor a super majority can ever accomplish this kind of unity.

Look at how the highest court in the land whose rulings are often broken into a simple majority rule. When the nine-member Supreme Court splits into a 5/4 decision over any issue, it exhibits a political structure and not a freedom model. If twelve jurors can function under unanimous consent, then why not require nine Supreme Court justices to reach common consent? This would inhibit any legislation from the bench. Without the discipline of consent, we swing between political controls as the power centers of the new majority change.

What is the difference between a power center manipulating a majority rule and a single person holding up a common consent decision? With the former, a dissenting voice against the majority cannot slow down the decision process. With the latter, in the ideal of common consent, anyone can slow the decision process with a modular design. The real difference is that with majority rule, bad ideas get promoted all the time, producing an incremental creep toward more fascism and tyranny. With unanimous consent, only the best ideas get promoted.

If it takes two to make the stand for one to overcome, we should conclude that pushing harder for a republic of modular levels of consensus brings individuals together while a popular majority vote does not. Only in the conservation of individual responsibility that allows each person to voice dissent in a horizontally expanded body do we preserve greater social consent for all. We also eliminate our idolatry for authority.

The Discussion Gap

I was in pain and the medication I took for it eased the pain, but it left my brain fogged, so I went to an herb specialist. She examined me and prescribed certain herbs, vitamins, and trace elements. I followed her suggestions and, within the same time period that I gave the regular physician's medication, not only had the pain disappeared, but my thinking remained clear.

I mention this to illustrate that we may sometimes need an interpreter to challenge our inner minds to be open to various options before us. In popular democracies, this never happens. The intimidation of a majority controlled by a power center can shut down this process.

Idolatry for authority is that thick door between your own mind and your own spirit. In the movie *Joe Versus the Volcano*, it's called a *brain cloud*. If you prefer visualizing a barrier between the conscious and subconscious, this is acceptable. You could even think it is between you and God, or between the left and right sides of the brain, or between masculine and feminine or reason and intuition. The point is that we don't know the two realities individually, but we do sense a link. When a link is made, we begin to see our own minds in the same way another pair of eyes helps us see a blind spot.

We need an interpreter to translate for us. This interpreter can take the form of a conversation with a close friend, or it can be a computer keyboard enabling ideas to flow out of our fingertips. The words we use tell us of the door between our denial and what truth lies beyond. Humility will open it, and pride will close it.

The only way to walk through the door is through the oral tradition of open discussion where others can challenge motive. This is the key to personal responsibility. If we can't do it through meditation and with a willingness to adapt our own view to the inherent truth, we need greater freedom and greater responsibility to express raw ideas and raw feelings in the open.

Personal responsibility corrects the motive of others and it must be able to stand correction as well. Remember, it takes at least two to make the stand for one to overcome. This isn't about one person counseling another, which tends to promote idolatry. It's about one person having the freedom to ask questions and challenge the other person's motives, promoting more responsibility and more freedom.

Most of the time, it takes many days, weeks, or even years to see through our linear thinking and realize our true motives. It's not easy because we don't see that idolatry (masked as an ideal good) keeps us from understanding. We're blind, but we think we see.

> Linear thinking sees the facts in a row. It concludes a pattern by the results and does not see the relational cause as if coming from the side of our linear row of data. We miss the relational cause or assume one relational cause affects every step. There may be many relational causes coming from right angles so to speak and we do not see them because we do not think proportionally. We focus our minds on the sequential row and conclude that all cause comes from elements in that row.[9]
>
> Samuel Louis Dael

A student once debated me in class about the need for humanitarian aid to third world nations. I argued that it is a waste of vital energy and she argued that humanitarian aid is good. I brought up the issue of a single father of four young kids all living down my street and how he has no money to pay rent because he cannot find a job that works with his family responsibilities. I asked this student, why do we travel to foreign lands and yet ignore humanitarian aid locally? Would we not save a lot of money and energy by not traveling to a foreign land and conserve energy locally? She replied, "I am not arguing that. I am arguing that it is good to give humanitarian aid to undeveloped third world nations." Essentially, she wanted to focus on a singular linear thought of something good to do far away without relational context of its local cost.

Open discussion is the only way to surface more relational context and break down the doors of denial. Real discussion comes when everyone has an equal opportunity to speak—and this eventually facilitates the best interpretation. Keep in mind that it's those with the strongest closed doors who are seeking to destroy others who have wide-open minds.

When you enter a room, you typically gravitate toward specific personalities. If a personality has more status, more money, more knowledge, more beauty, or great speech, you generally want to please or impress that person. You even may put others down, hoping that this person will agree with you, because you feel if that happens, you'll become their equal.

This is the political part of idolatry: seeking both honor and power by attracting those people likely to give assistance for a piece of honor for themselves. Regardless of how great their professed ideals, the participants' doors remain closed and it's impossible to perceive their true motives. People ridicule each other in the quest for honor, and idolatry becomes the master over the group.

Without the opportunity to reach consensus, dictatorship arises and the true value of a democracy—as an open discussion within smaller forums—begins to collapse.

Keep in mind this differentiation: democracy is a voice expressed in open discussion; a republic is consensus reached bottom-up. When people have both a voice in discussion and consensus from modular groups, it results in an informed public and a free society. This better defines a democratic republic. The idea of limiting democracy to a vote without discussion, or a republic limited to majority rule without consent, this is the genuine destroyer of personal responsibility.

A free society comes from individual responsibility: first in the voice of dissent and second in small-group decision-making. This gives each person a voice in the process plus teeth in the game.

Political optimists want you to forget this. They want to remove discussion from the vote and consensus from the group. To see a perversion of this, just look at the seventeenth amendment to the United States Constitution.

Article 1 of the Constitution says, "The Senate of the United States shall be composed of two senators from each state, *chosen by the legislature thereof*, for six years." The Seventeenth Amendment changed this to read, "The Senate of the United States shall be composed of two senators from each state, *elected by the people thereof*, for six years."

When the amendment shifted the election of senators from "the legislatures" to "the people," it removed both discussion from the vote and a greater consensus from the political process. The consequence is that people lose their freedom to political power centers.

Most people argue in favor of the seventeenth amendment because it gives everyone a vote, but a vote is destructive without involved discussion and without letting lower bodies ratify for greater consensus. At least in the state legislatures there was open and public discussion about the candidates. In a popular democracy, the discussion gap grows larger and larger, with media outlets replacing both dialogue and the right to dissent.

If we want a real solution, let's scale our republic downward and create lower representative bodies closer to the people in our counties and in our communities. Every autonomous group would then function under the genuine ideal of common consent in choosing representatives and ratifying decisions.

Political idolatry rejects dissent in an open forum. When all the citizens of a state elect a senator by popular majority in private voting booths, they cannot question the candidate's motive and qualifications. You can wave a flag of disapproval on the street corner, but in a popular democracy where majority rules, you have no teeth and you have no voice.

This is how we form political parties. They form when power centralizes and when large bodies suffer under the idolatry of authority figures. Access to engage in the discussion is completely pushed aside in favor of having a vote only. Consequently, we are intimidated and end up voting for what we perceive as the lesser of two evils.

It is time we scale a direct republic of common consent in small groups and decentralize our popular democracy. It's more feasible than you think. For now, all we have to see is how to protect in small groups the twin powers of personal responsibility better than in large populous voting.

In a small forum, we question every candidate. If all citizens vote directly for the person of their choice without discussion on several levels and without ratified consent in small groups, power shifts to candidates and to the power centers promoting them.

Those who favor keeping power in the people (common consent in stratified bodies) actually promote more personal responsibility. This is called common consent; it is superior to a single vote with no discussion and with no room for dissent. It is superior to the appointment of ambassadors to the United Nations without a single vote from the people, superior to a president of a university appointed by a state board and not the widest consent from the faculty and staff, and definitely better than those in power over the European Union that is looking to dissolve the autonomy of its nation states.

The Enemy to Personal Responsibility

Many genuine optimists consider running for political office or stepping into a leadership position, but quickly realize they're not political material. They don't know how to stage themselves, intimidate with poise, or pitch a new kind of magic that would appeal to public selfishness. The sophistry of rhetoric is not in their favor.

However, if they could start in a small group—from nine to seventeen members—and advance through the various groups producing an incremental effect, then they would enter the best structure... because it's too inconvenient and too difficult to be political in one small group after another. This is why political people prefer to be the central power figure over large and even small groups run by a majority; it gives them unfettered control.

The modular structure of common consent can overcome political idolatry in small local bodies and it can eventually consume the state, the nation, and the world. By the time any idea reaches the state or the nation, it's clean of partisan controls, lobbyist infiltration, and corporate manipulation. It is the best way to protect individual freedom. We forget that democracy should *decentralize* power. The key to making this happen is preserving the liberty to voice dissent.

How do we deal with the idolatry of power centers and the political worship it generates? On the smallest level, consensus in discussion arises as the only assurance. Why? Because a democracy of majority rule with popular voting will always end up with more and more idolatry.

Young kids get it right when they line up on the basketball court and number themselves: one, two, one, two. Two random teams are thus created. However, if two bullies select their teams one at a time, everyone will not have an equal voice, as the bullies control the selection process and the game. All forms of leadership education should emphasize the former practice and reject the latter.

Unfortunately, leadership education gets it all wrong when it puts too much emphasis on leaders as being in charge and thereby removing equity in the process. Great leaders choose equity from the process. Political optimists emphasize the glory of the leader.

People who argue against consensus refer to ideas like the Pareto Principle, created by Joseph M. Juran, the father of quality control. He named the principle after economist Vilfredo Pareto, who observed that 20% of the population owned 80% of the property in Italy (later generalized to mean 80% of consequences stem from 20% of causes).

The Pareto Principle is something managers improperly use to focus their attention on the "vital few" apart from the "useful many." This is the 80/20 principle, where 80% of the productivity comes from 20% of the workforce. What if the 20% are political optimists employing the tools of staged performance, intimidation, and enchantment? Does this really produce quality?

Consider a twelve-person jury and the requirement to reach consensus. Inside a jury, the individual retains an incredible amount of personal responsibility. Is the Pareto Principle true because we eliminate consensus? What if we removed idolatry for authority (as a jury naturally does) and increased the personal responsibility of individual dissent? If idolatry is removed from the focus on power centers in larger groups, and if consensus is put in its place in smaller groups where all members are given an equal voice, then what? Doesn't this create a greater free market for more genuine optimists to rise in both leadership and achievement? Does this suddenly increase the 20% to a much higher ratio?

Pushing personal responsibility off to larger groups gives more power to political optimists, which means more staged optimists, more intimidating optimists, and more irrational optimists. When people are forced into a large body, individual power is lost. This is why the best models of power distribution support more discussion and more dissent, which can only happen in small groups organized by common consent. However, more central control over larger bodies naturally destroys open dissent because disagreement is simply ineffective to work out in large bodies.

Filled with worshipers and groupthink, a political optimist can stand before a large crowd and lie between his teeth. Even if one or two people in the front row are yelling their opposition, they're usually marginalized as "radical" and not "optimistic."

Take President Obama's "sunlight before signing promise" made in Manchester, N.H., on June 22, 2007, where he said, "When there's a bill that ends up on my desk as president, you the public will have five days to look online and find out what is in it before I sign it." Obama signed his first bill, the Lilly Ledbetter Fair Pay Restoration Act, on Jan. 20, 2009, just two days after its passage. In his first year as president he gave public review to just six (6) of 124 bills.

Popular democracy produces forgotten promises.

It is very odd that democrats and socialists are often fighting for the distribution of wealth but never the decentralization of power back to the people. A dictator always says, "There's no need for bickering to reach consensus. Give me honor and power, and I'll show you what mighty works I can do for you."

When the masses choose a political process without graduated levels of consensus, power centers will consistently grab the majority's attention with flattering words. The majority looks at them in the moment and not over time. In a majority, where there are larger numbers, democracy marginalizes dissent (calling it extreme), while discussion is centralized and forbidden to outside individuals. The growing bubble of a popular democracy that advances the idolatry of central control never increases freedom for the individual. It always destroys it.

Take again President Obama signing the National Defense Authorization Act for 2012 on Dec 31, 2011, on a Saturday during the holidays. He promised that he would not sign the act during his campaign and then he signed it anyway with a signing statement (something he also promised never to do) wherein he promised he would never use provisions in the act as president.

The NDAA for 2012 specified the budget for the United States Department of Defense along with controversial provisions contained in subsections 2021-2022 of Title X, Subtitle D "Counter-Terrorism." The detention provisions authorized the president and future presidents to order an indefinite military imprisonment without due process (including American citizens) captured anywhere in the world and away from any battlefield. Why do people allow abusive power to trample the Bill of Rights? The answer is simple; people succumb to idol worship and follow political optimists blindly.

Cutting out the Middleman

The second commandment reads, "Thou shalt not make unto thee any graven image." This means to not put anything or any person to stand between God and people's free agency. The first commandment puts it even more strongly: "Thou shalt have no other gods before me." This says there is no intermediary.

A political optimist is an intermediary between the individual and public dissent. There's a big difference between a middleman and having an agent who decides on your behalf. An agent is a person acting in a defined area. This person operates with your consent, based on agreed contracts, and can be fired and removed with the authority you retain in the same contract.

A political middleman doesn't operate in contract with your approval. He or she operates without a contract. If such a person harms you, you have no power to get rid of them, because you have given that power away by default without contractual consent.

Driven by the idolatry we show toward others, exalted leadership hastens our destruction. All political optimists take our ability to be self-starting, self-thinking, and self-nourishing. When we say to ourselves, "take from us our consent because we willingly give up our freedom to dissent," we lose the power to question authority and we lose the authority of our own mind to think for itself.

Being able to question secures the twin powers of personal responsibility through which every person retains the right to say yes or no. Lose one, and you lose the other. It's imperative that any future renaissance in freedom scale with both powers in place. Those advocating for the same old popular democracy promote only the yes vote. A true republic of common consent must scale with both yes and no.

When compared to the qualities of genuine optimism (bringing out the best in ourselves, or encouraging the best out of others, or standing for the best principles), the idolatry promoted by the political optimist will always secure the upper hand. This is true as long as we focus on a central authority in the same way a lecture hall centers attention on the professor. Every time we find ourselves attracted to leadership authority as a means of escaping personal responsibility, we'll be rejecting the value of dissent. The consequences are devastating.

In 1942, Mao Tse-tung started a "rectification" campaign in the Communist Party of China. This campaign allowed local peasants to put up posters in public areas criticizing local party leaders. In these displayed posters, the people demanded more freedom and the right to greater individual expression. However, this action produced a divisive power-storm: Mao turned the campaign into a witch-hunt against his own party leaders. He did this repeatedly as chairman.

By creating an opportunity for upwardly mobile political devotees to fill the newly vacated spots of the older leadership, Mao created a constant stream of newly dedicated idolaters who offered no threat to his command.

His first victims were the peasants; then he moved on to the intellectuals and then to his inner circle of advisers, before finally starting the process over again. Using low-level gossip and tattletale venting, Mao turned people against themselves and against his own leadership bureaucracy in order to maintain his central control. Jung Chang wrote in *Wild Swans*:

> Although the Communists [in China] were opposed to torture in theory and on principle, officials were told that they should not intervene if the peasants wished to vent their anger in passionate acts of revenge.[10] (166)

Consider the qualities of genuine optimism (believing, encouraging, and standing for principle) and see how they stand against a centralized control grid. In every situation throughout history, the odds remain stacked against genuine optimists.

China's Great Leap Forward from 1958-1961 was a state-run cultural revolution designed to push the entire country into a rapid industrial revolution. Private farming was done away with and those caught running a private operation suffered ridicule and in some cases death. Because personal initiative became unacceptable, over thirty million Chinese died of famine during this time.

The sowing of discord by pitting people against each other comes from the central control run by political optimists. This extremely dangerous process gives too much weight to secret combinations of power that sway the minds of the people by simply sowing discord, confusion, division, and hysteria. Until we dismantle this abuse of democracy that appeals to the supposed scarcity of authority, and until we work things out ourselves in a republic of common consent in modular groups, we will not be free.

Sowers of Discord Everywhere

In my neighborhood is a fourteen-unit apartment complex. All the units need repair and upkeep, but mostly the driveway became cracked and crumbling, with old asphalt covered in loose gravel. Every six years the association would fix it with hot slurry (a heated mixture of half-tar and half-sand). As a general contractor for residential construction, I mentioned they could install brick pavers a little bit at a time and eventually get a new driveway that would be much stronger than concrete and would last a lifetime. The initial cost was more, but the savings would be huge over time.

Just a few weeks later, a tenant of the complex, a retired 72-year-old man, began digging up the asphalt by hand and started replacing the private drive with brick pavers. He had to re-compact the soil underneath with a vibrating compactor. It was exhausting, but he carried on. Because of his fixed income, all he asked for was that the homeowner's association pays his HOA fee of $110 a month in exchange for his labor. After a year, he completed over 4,000 square feet. If a general contractor had done it, the cost would have been five times greater.

Nobody in the association offered to help, and there was plenty of sweeping of sand between the pavers and picking up the crumbling old drive. The old man continued pecking away at the task and saved a little on his monthly expenses.

Then something happened. A new tenant moved in and she started to complain about this man's operation and demanded that the association hire a property management company to make sure nothing illegal was happening. With a slim majority win, she got the decision passed.

Due to the extra costs required in hiring the management company, they had to shut down replacing the crumbling drive. By that time, the project was nearly seventy percent complete. With the roofs needing serious repair and many other needed improvements, it was an unjustified cost to hire a third party to manage the small complex with no real value added. The private drive sat incomplete for over a year.

As a result of the political stress, the old man moved out of the complex and the association was forced to hire a contractor to finish the job at a substantial increase in cost.

I was the contractor and the old man was my father.

It's easy to get stuck following a dominant leader able to move a majority rather than thinking for ourselves. Political optimists feel justified when they take responsibility away from honest volunteer efforts. It makes them feel relieved about not applying their own efforts.

Political controllers enter the picture and take work away from the outstanding volunteer. When someone makes a sacrifice, political optimists cannot accept it: it's a reflection on them for doing nothing. The same person sacrificing must have a motive, they assume, because political optimists are inherently selfish. They think everyone is like them.

There are two philosophies in the world. The first says humanity is basically selfish and we need to impose controls to keep us from falling into cannibalism and war. The second says humanity is born free and good.

The selfish belief will always push for central control because it is easy to scale, which is to say it is linear. The second idea that we are all born good and every human being is free is harder to scale because the models are not readily acceptable to emulate. They are relational. Sometimes someone out there is seeking to do you harm and you never know it until it is too late. The destruction that just one person can inflict in a business, a community or nation can be devastating. So why not empower genuine optimists with a model of consent that makes sense?

In graduate school, I took a seminar in government simulations. This was a class in which students simulated city, state, federal, and private council meetings. In one simulation, a dominant female student pulled another female student out in the hall for a private discussion. When they both re-entered the simulation, they voted against a proposal to create a more transparent local board of education. While they both agreed with this idea beforehand in open discussion, the one dominant participant mentioned that the sponsor of the proposal reminded her of her ex-husband, and so she worked behind the scenes to get others to vote against the sponsor of the proposal. Obviously, she hated her ex-husband, and, unfortunately, I was the sponsor of the bill.

I once witnessed a board remove the founders of a school after they had given many years of service. While the founders were controlling in their vision and tended to run the school with a disregard for dissenting ideas, including state requirements, their volunteerism and sacrifices should not have been disregarded so quickly, even though they were managing the school into the ground. As a result of the separation, the vision of the founders died, everyone involved was suddenly separated into two camps, and the school struggled to overcome bad leadership decisions.

We see the same thing happen with nonprofits and even many large corporations. Because there's no protection for individual dissent, genuine optimists eventually are pushed aside in favor of more political people. I admit that visionary people can lead with tendencies toward excessive control. However, political optimists lack vision while they're masters at getting the control away from full consensus. This is why they favor majority rule. The only solution to keeping the visionary on board and properly checked is to exercise the practice of common consent. You either move forward as one body and preserve the whole, or you do not.

The exercise of personal responsibility is impossible without social responsibility in place to secure every individual's twin powers of free agency. Without personal responsibility to dissent and without the ability to give voice in discussion, all those who live to believe, encourage, and stand for principle suffer.

Political people appeal to a higher authority they idolize, and from which they get a position on the board, committee, or executive pool. No one will ever know if the same person can add value and inspire others to speak honestly. It makes perfect sense that in order to increase personal responsibility and the qualities of genuine optimism, we need to support a better model of social responsibility, one that confronts the sowing of discord directly as the single enemy to all responsibility in the hands of the people.

10

Social Responsibility

A poor Irish widow went forth with her three children,
bare of all resource, to solicit help.... At this charitable
establishment and then at that she was refused...till she
had exhausted them all... she sank down in typhus-fever;
died, and infected her Lane with fever, so that 'seventeen
other persons' died of fever there in consequence.... The
forlorn Irish Widow applies to her fellow-creatures...."
Behold I am sinking, bare of help: ye must help me! I am
your sister...." They answer, "No; impossible: thou art no
sister of ours." But she proves her sisterhood; her typhus
fever kills them: they actually were her brothers... Had
man ever to go lower for a proof?[1]

- Thomas Carlyle

Community

A former employee of mine died in her sleep. Born in
India and adopted into a family in the United States, she was
homeless and living on the streets by the time she was 19. She
had serious health concerns, including diabetes and a heart
condition, and she smoked and was seriously overweight.

She had a stubborn streak about her and would spend
hours taking up my time just to make sure she was clear on her
tasks, often giving long-winded comments of her own. Mostly,
she just wanted to feel like she belonged to something. After she
settled into her new job and felt important, her perfectionism in
graphic design was always on my side. All this ended when her
health began to deteriorate.

Often she left work early to see a doctor, only to return complaining about not being given the "right meds." It was almost impossible for someone living on the streets to eat right, so she ate poorly, aggravating her health conditions. Often she would ask for a cash advance to buy medication, but instead bought cigarettes and soda. Due to complications with her diabetes, she died at the age of twenty-one in bed at her parents' home in the middle of the night.

If you think her situation was hers to bear because of a lack of personal responsibility, then you're not seeing the need for taking social responsibility.

Does this mean people should grab total control of her life and force good on her? No! It means the community needed to open the door to genuine optimism to support the life she *could* have had. Giving her a bed for the night at the homeless shelter, only to be forced on the streets during the day, is not encouraging support: it's bare subsistence. We call this being expedient and not being efficient. Living at the bottom of life on bare subsistence is ineffective. It is like driving an empty tank most of the time because you have no money for gas. The consequence is that the fuel pump breaks down and the cost to repair it puts you further in the hole. Falling on more bad times is inevitable when you are down on your luck. It is a vicious downward spiral.

Those people employed in community service see the world differently. They don't see the world comprising individuals striving for personal excellence. Life to them is all about making their community a little more like a light on a hill, even at great sacrifice to their own needs. They're quick to join a cause, and the first to volunteer. They serve the struggling college student needing direction and the alcoholic needing support. They help the old, the hungry, and the mentally ill. They are the largest work force in the country. From homeless shelters to elementary schools, from the county fairgrounds to the doctor's free clinic, social responsibility is the workforce that defines the strength of a community. So where is the motivational self-help for them? What books and publications on leadership do we write for them?

Much like military service, community service is controlled by power centers—with almost no consent given to those who have made community service their life. It is clear why communities operate at a disadvantage: they've lost their autonomy. You can see this when genuine optimists willing to volunteer under normal situations actually withdraw from public service when they are confronted with too much political control. Notice the death of public chambers of commerce. Once organized by boards under majority rule, now they've been replaced by private networking organizations. What was public and expedient is now private and efficient. Is more privacy the best direction for our communities? Perhaps the *efficiency* of being autonomous may be better, but the privacy leaves a lot to be desired.

In order to encourage better business, more local involvement, and a renaissance in social responsibility in local hands, perhaps it is time to change how we look at leadership. Perhaps it is time to allow leadership to rise from the qualities of genuine optimism found in protecting consent at the most local level. We may not be able to break up and/or decentralize the military-industrial complex or the web of interlocking corporate directorships, or the many cartels that are too big to fail and too evil to expose, but we certainly can implement common consent in our community organizations and in our small businesses.

Consider that over a century ago we saw the birth of several service organizations like the Lions Club (1917), the Elks Lodge (1868), The United Way (1887) and Rotary (1905). Hundreds of organizations followed after these. After one hundred years, can we say any of these organizations are financially solvent? Or do they still depend on member dues? Even more striking is this: what level of dissent do they allow, and how is their leadership organized? Even when the Lions Club reached 1.4 million members, with so many people giving their annual dues and local fees, how much stays locally? What voice do they have as part of the whole? As reported by a family member who worked for the American Cancer Society, .60 of every dollar donated is spent on administration costs. What is most disturbing is the authority the ACS has over funding genuinely innovative treatments for cancer. We can only imagine the political gridlock in that organization.

Compare these service and non-profit organizations with the Mondragon Cooperative in the Basque region of Spain. Founded in 1956 by graduates of a local technical college, and with the inspiration of a young Catholic priest, by the end of 2014 the cooperative had grown to employ over 74,000 members with over 250 companies. They founded their own bank and their own university, and they offer several services to their members, including a retirement pension and an annual bonus. Every member employed by one of the businesses in the cooperative has a vote in selecting their immediate company leadership. When compared to stand-alone service organizations, the economics and the social impact favor the Mondragron Cooperative, and we should look to seeing more of this model in the future.

In another fifty years, where will the Mondragon Cooperative be? If it can fight off the typical centralization of control and protect the optimism of dissent, it might just surprise us all. A cooperative is built on each member having a real stake in the organization. What voice do we have with international organizations? The secret with the Mondragon cooperative is its natural small groups organized into businesses acting autonomously and yet part of the whole. Give people a greater stake with their labor and their volunteer efforts, and they'll naturally scale up to achieve great things. Service organizations and social clubs fail to give members a bigger stake, which is why they haven't scaled to a greater achievement even with a hundred years under their belt.

At city councils, school boards, county commissions, non-profit boards and even religious organizations, a small group serving a large population is typically put in power, either by appointment or by majority vote. Even local credit unions are run by a board, which selects a few candidates for the members to vote for. Regular members are almost never included in the selection process. This plays directly into the hands of political optimists and their insatiable desire for more centralized control. This does not say everyone serving on such a board is linear and political. It just says the process for electing them is controlled by power centers and not the wider appeal to a greater consent. Keep in mind that having a vote *without* a voice of consent is like having a police state without the consent of the people. It only takes just a few to sway a majority to believe in some new threat to justify centralizing more control. Even if currently run by a great leader, every organization run by this model will eventually collapse.

Increasing more consent in our communities and businesses means giving more room to applied belief, more recognition to active encouragement, and more voice to outspoken principle. We can only decentralize control if we demand the highest level of consent. It is the only way to include those who are non-political. Certainly we can all agree that we need less politics in the world.

While many people are looking for an awakening of humanity to combat rising global infighting and the sowing of discord within and between nations (most likely controlled by interlocking corporate interests), we need a solution with teeth rather than an indeterminate rising consciousness. Ideal consent in modular form in our communities is precisely that application: it's the purest form of social consciousness possible as well as the most efficient. It is the only way to bring the social subconscious together with social discourse.

It takes a community to absorb vital social responsibilities from outside political control, and it takes the consent of all in the community to secure individual voices. Today we lack community scale because we lack the voice of community consent.

For example, I found a young couple sleeping under cardboard boxes at the local library's basement entrance. The girl, about eighteen, was three months pregnant; the boy was also young, with no confidence and no employment prospects. He knocked on doors—including mine—late at night requesting a can opener. After he opened his can of tuna, I followed him to the library.

There at the bottom of the steps, his girlfriend peeked out from under the wet cardboard. It took me only a second to decide to bring them home; it was, after all, just before the Christmas holidays. They showered, ate, and slept on the corner sectional couch in the living room. The next day we made room in the camper trailer in the back yard for them to live in temporarily. Within a week, the young man was enrolled in college with financing, and he had a job. Within two more weeks, he destroyed the camper trailer and refused to follow up with the job and school. By the start of the third week, he was living in a tent near the river outside of town with his pregnant girlfriend. Survival to him was defiance against any threat of any social rejection or failure in life.

He was so afraid of life that he chose to live in a muddy patch of grass near the river instead of in a clean and comfortable space. Denial is so powerful that people actually choose to live like injured animals in the bush. Many homeless people live far off the grid, away from any real community reach. The only way communities can scale up to solve problems like this is to increase more consent in modular groups... and this includes the consent given to the homeless themselves.

When we hear stories like this from people on the front lines of serving in health, education, and welfare services, how do we determine what social responsibility is? Motivational speakers tell stories of someone accomplishing great things against great odds. Most of the time it is a story about someone lifting themselves—rather than someone helping another person. Political optimists emphasize the former and genuine optimists exhibit the latter. Most people prefer the first story of individual achievement because it gives a nice excuse to not respond to the second. We love the underdog who overcomes huge disadvantages with no help from anyone. It makes us feel good about ourselves. But is this optimistic? Obviously not.

It takes two to make a stand in order for one to overcome their challenges. If genuine optimists are the ones most willing to share applied belief, encourage action out of others, and express principle to help others in the community overcome, then there must be a way genuine optimists can take more social responsibility out of the control of political optimists who will not. Is this optimistic? Absolutely.

Iron Bubble

A private youth academy hired me to serve as president of the board. They were collapsing financially and near failure. Around the world we see the same problem repeatedly—a group effort is misunderstood as something we give to individuals to solve and not something we retain in common.

This problem surfaces on boards and committees that refuse to work under the optimism of ideal consent, preferring instead the constriction of central control. The minute we organize in common consent, we attract more genuine optimists and fewer political optimists. This is the greatest secret eluding us, something self-help and leadership publications don't discuss. The ideal of common consent attracts a broader and wider body of people, and it doesn't force a central figurehead on anyone. Our communities are being called upon to see the value of ideal common consent in a way not seen before.

With this youth academy, we performed an exercise during a meeting with parents and several board members. We printed words on circles and mixed them up.

On five large circles, we put the words, *vision, volunteerism, profit, management,* and *investment.* **See Figure 10-1.**

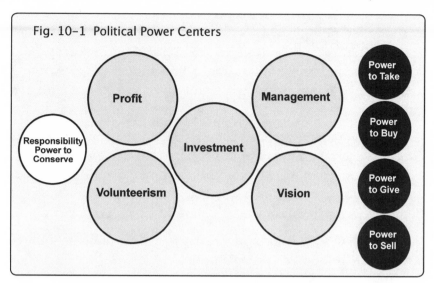

Fig. 10-1 Political Power Centers

On a medium-sized circle, we wrote *responsibility: the power to conserve,* and on four smaller circles we inscribed *power to take, power to sell, power to buy* and *power to give.*

About twenty people showed up for the meeting and we broke into four groups. We told all the groups to organize the circles in the best way to show what matters most and which powers should control other powers. Having some circles overlap into other circles helped to show this.

Some people put investors at center stage; others put vision as top dog; still others put the power to give in charge of everything else. In every situation, they designed their power structure in the typical way we diagram a business organizational chart. Some kind of power was always centralized and placed at the top. No one ever discussed the *process* used in assigning power.

From this experience, one thing became very clear. We get stuck in an iron bubble of central control without vision and without the consent of all members involved. This was the problem with that school. They wanted an authority to fix things rather than be inspired by vision and keep responsibility in their own hands and engage in honest debate.

An iron bubble is the political assumption that we need to centralize power in order to get something done. But every time we centralize control, we create something corrupt and void of vision, because our leadership model of networking through central power implies it. For a visionary mind, this is a poisonous idea.

Just imagine for a second if our leadership model was not a top-down structure but rather a bottom-up structure. What would it look like? How would it be organized? Better even, how can such a change help solve the problem of homelessness? Better even, how can such a model build a better company?

The worst periods in history are the result of control imposed by top-down leadership. From ancient Rome to Great Britain, and from China to Africa, at center stage we find political optimists pushing for more central control. At the same time, centralized leadership destroys volunteerism, personal initiative, and natural community enthusiasm. Political optimists seek greater central control because they believe consent from everyone isn't expedient. They argue that it takes more time and promotes too much disagreement.

Sadly, these are the very ingredients necessary to maintain a free society. A free society is necessary to promote great visionary solutions. Centrally controlled leadership is the most open to abuse. Political optimists call this expedient. Open discussion keeps a working culture from falling into darkness. Genuine optimists call *this* efficient.

Political optimists will always push for positions of power without discussion, without unanimous consent, and without the free exercise of dissent. We can see the effects when we look more closely at the least served in our communities.

No amount of work-for-food or proper documentation to prove need is enough to help someone living on the streets. It may be enough to give the homeless a bed for the night, or a vagrant food for the day, but this is as far as the political mind can visualize. Political optimists control what constitutes "need" for the sake of expediency. To them, need means serving an emergency only, and so they look to take care of the emergency and not the *real* need. On the other hand, the genuine optimist sees that the only way to change people to take on more responsibility (at least those able) is to create an environment where change can take place.

Even if it takes weeks to reach a consensus on one decision, that's far better than central control models that overrule dissenting minds. This is why political people never scale anything to greatness.

The Scale of No Return

In order for something to scale in growth properly, we need vision, architecture, and building. This seems obvious, but more often than not we neglect effective architecture. We think that all of the mechanics is in the building, and the visionary mind communicates directly to the builder in order to facilitate quick construction. What happens is the builder becomes political and seeks approval from the visionary, bypassing the need for proper architecture. The builder makes the mistake of doing things without a master plan.

All the mechanics are built into the architectural plan. The builder only knows how to perform the mechanics; he's not necessarily capable of designing the mechanics. The builder knows that he can build something. The visionary knows she *cannot* build it, and relies on the builder without any architecture in place. The visionary sees the workable end. The builder does not. If he can, he is also a visionary, but he cannot implement the project without the architectural plan.

Architecture—which includes engineering and mechanical design—is a mental process that records every action or mechanical process into a set of symbols. We manipulate the symbols to avoid waste. If the visionary says no, the architect can manipulate the plans very quickly without wasting valuable material or building costs.

The problem comes when either the visionary or the builder thinks they can be the architect. They can, if they can think through each of the mechanical processes. Impatience is the problem. We fail to think through the mechanics. The builder fails: if he just starts building from the vision, he might misinterpret. If the builder cannot draw up the mechanics in symbolic form for the visionary to approve, he will fail. If the visionary cannot draw up the plan using every mechanical step, the design will fail.

When individuals consent or dissent, they do so in agreement with, or objection to, the mechanics. If they object to the vision, then it's clear they cannot see, and should just walk away. If they object to the builder, they suffer a similar blind spot and should walk away. When one agrees with the vision but stands against the architecture, it must be around a specific point of engineering. Unanimous ruling consent weeds out fallacious objections. It allows for modification in the architecture until everyone agrees.

Business, government, and even local organizations think that a set of rules and policies is good architecture. Policies are not in the architecture; they are, rather, like speed bumps in a parking lot. In some instances they control, but in an emergency, they inhibit. Symbols and designs are better controls. How many businesses put up signs to designate entrances and exits, yet both work either way? Even symbols don't control; they simply encourage and often become discouraging—as do poor policies. The keenness of the architect knows how to implement better than those who make policy. This understanding comes through knowing the customer, the user, the member, or the citizen. The architect sees the psychology and convenience of the individual. If the visionary tries to control, he fails. If the builder controls, everything fails again. If the architect controls to please the visionary or the builder, she is not an honest architect.

The three must become one mind and the majority can never rule. This is the best and only policy because it protects the right to dissent and encourages the highest agreement. This is efficient.

Our modern email system is actually detrimental to the process of agreement. It is a limited two-way system between two parties. When three or more people are involved, a consensus is blocked. Between two parties, the receiver can object and offer a solution, but a third party has to object to both the sender and the receiver.

Architects have this problem when they fail to interpret the vision or fail to understand the builder's engineering. There should be more two-way communication between the visionary and the architect, and between the architect and the builder. If the visionary approves and understands the architecture, so will the builder—provided the mechanics are thought through in all particulars. This depends on how well the architect knows both the mind of the visionary and the engineering of the builder.

The architectural process examines every decision and every response. If not, the building will fail. This process is a process of interpretation. Some people have the gift of interpretation and the gift of asking questions. If either of these fail with the architecture, the whole will fail. Success is characterized by organized discussion. The typical meeting with a planned agenda always fails because one person is trying to govern the whole group. Each member should have an equal opportunity to present his or her concerns, and be able to vote on every proposal. Committees often don't allow votes. One member dismisses the comments of another, and the power center refuses questions, citing time expediency. Meetings crisscross between power centers and those individuals wanting to push their plan rather than learn something from others. It's all for the sake of expediency used to cover up efficiency, a great ploy of intimidating optimists.

Expediency implies that the public doesn't need to understand. All the thinking has already been done for them. Efficiency refers to a known principle—or an agreed-to process—that everyone understands. With expediency, a few decide. With efficiency, the path is decided by discussion and by open agreement. With efficiency, the individual is encouraged to understand, which is why efficiency is relational and expediency is linear. Linear thinkers who push for expediency don't promote understanding. Instead, they promote more worship for authority-knows-best.

Until we can work out the mechanics of conversation in our communities and in our businesses so everyone can see a better efficiency of things, we'll never scale responsibility to protect the right of dissent and the greater discipline of ideal consent.

Let's take a look at how this applies to the least-served in our communities, because serving the homeless is fundamental to scaling more responsibility into the entire community.

I recently took a late-night walk in the city park down the block from my home, and saw a man sleeping on a concrete bench. It was midnight and cold, and he was sitting hunched over, with his hands tucked deep into his coat pockets. I approached and he woke up with a spark of fear in his face. He responded to my greeting, but I could tell that he was really tired and scared that he might be talking to an officer in the dark. I asked if he needed anything and he said, "A few bucks would help." Wearing only sweatpants and indicating my empty pockets, I said, "I have no money on me, sorry." He told me that he was from Oregon and was in town because, as he said, "I have things lined up."

I went back home, made some peanut butter sandwiches, grabbed a few apples, and returned to the park bench. I woke him again to give him the bag of food and my business card and asked, "Are you interested in going to school?"

"No, I have something lined up," he said again, this time with some irritation at a stranger preaching to him. "Call my number if you're ever interested," I said. Every now and then I see him walking the streets with a heavy backpack and a large soda, obviously with nowhere to go.

Here's the problem. Very few people in the community know about this young man, and most of them have no relationship with the local homeless shelter where he gets his food. In fact, every night as I walk through the park, I see unopened cans of food given to homeless people. Like all political power over the community, central control in serving the homeless is the problem. It refuses to tap into the many community members with experience, direct contact, and concern for the homeless. The only real solution for the homeless is to increase greater personal responsibility across the board. It's not surprising how realistic this can be.

Rather than assign and appoint people to positions on boards, committees, and councils, why not open the doors wide for more people to get involved and increase the optimism of dissent. This means a different kind of scaling for community involvement. Think of Alcoholics Anonymous, where every person in the circle can challenge and question the other, and yet the circle is open to the public and there are many circles in the same community. If any circle gets too big, the circle naturally splits into two groups, like a hive splits when the bees get too cramped. We don't scale responsibility into small groups of common consent because we're too focused on the supposed expediency of central control run by majority rule over large bodies. Remember what central control over large groups creates: idolatry for authority, and no optimism of common consent.

If we don't allow more people to add value as visionaries, designers, and builders of solutions, then just about any instance of social responsibility will fail to scale properly to meet real needs. With so much history under our belts, we can't deny true understanding of efficiency, but instead we keep replacing it with expediency, which is a scale of no return. In other words, we too often scale in the direction of central power centers and never in the direction of responsibility held in common by the people. States or the federal government take control and appoint policies and agencies over the people with no public teeth to dissent. This is called social protectionism for those employed by this bureaucracy; in no way can we call this social *responsibility*.

If you were to get involved with your local homeless shelter, you would find that the shelter operates on an emergency status only; most shelters do. As long as they get enough food to support the needs of the hungry, and funding in donations or grants for their administration, they keep afloat.

In fact, just a few months ago a shelter in a nearby city was about to close down. A local businessperson jumped in and the shelter was given enough to stay afloat for the year—but not enough to stay alive with long-term solutions. Essentially, the businessperson took control of the board responsible for the homeless shelter. His invested capital justified this shift in control. The real value of personal responsibility cannot properly scale into more social responsibility with this kind of central control. It never works because it can never be sustainable.

If you want to be homeless in our community, great! We live in a beautiful community. We want you here. The one qualifier is that you have to be working toward receiving in full disclosure. If you have disabilities, we need to know. If our giving is not enough, we need to know. If you have skills, dreams, and the desire to work, we need to know. If you do not wish to work and take care of yourself, we need to know.

All this need-to-know information is derived from a more involved process of discussion designed to reach the greatest involved consent. If the homeless lie to get help, then what is given to them is done without informed consent.

When we look at the benefits of increasing common consent, we can easily see how it can scale from two people to the greater community with ease. Political minds do not want to see this happen.

What happens when everyone can voice their dissent to hold a small group up, or voice their approval to move the decision of a small group forward? We think this won't work because we are stuck in an iron bubble that idolizes authority and centralizes control. This just produces more linear thinking. Linear thinking assumes that we naturally advance the best innovations and the best ideas because we have leaders. This is not true. Leadership organized from the top down becomes a linear blind spot.

While vision comes from individuals, the advancement of a vision, its engineering and construction, does not. While groups can come together to flesh out a number of ideas to form a bigger and better vision, vision is the product of one person. And the only way for this one person to advance a vision without political controls getting in the way is through a body working in common consent, such as starting with a small group at the most local level. Remove central control and we give the genuine optimism of visionaries a better chance of promoting their belief, their encouragement and their principles.

As things stand now with our love affair with authority, visionary solutions are at a serious disadvantage. Ideal consent in modularized form is the only way to merge the social responsibility of a small collective with the personal responsibility of the individual. From here we scale to the community.

Take any issue, even abortion. A decision on abortion may scale to twenty people in full agreement or to many thousands. As long as the decision does not remove the twin powers of free agency held in every person, which is the foundation of a free society, and as long as the decision receives a full and complete consent, it continues to scale until dissent stops and the decision has found is natural geographic scale of no return.

Ideal consent is the social tool where genuine optimism flourishes and the political mind dies. If we think a new renaissance lies ahead, the key is common consent in graduated small groups. This alone protects the visionary who is often a dissenting voice.

The Collective and the Individual

Many great minds have wrestled with collectivism versus individualism. *Rugged individualists* emphasize the evils of collectivism; *collectivists* emphasize the evils of individualism.

Both are wrong in polarizing themselves as neither truly supports the social intelligence of common consent.

It's easy to see how we collectivize efforts to share schools, hospitals, roads, natural resources, and tax revenue to benefit the common needs of the community. The problem surfaces when we grant powers to write policy and decide how to manage these services without broader consent of individuals. Individualism in a collective organization is best realized when the individual retains two powers: the power of *dissent* to hold a small group up, and the power of *consent* to move a small group forward. Both powers, if retained in small groups, protect the independence and liberty of the individual because they conserve responsibility in the hands of the individual. Best of all, these two powers remove both idolatry for authority and the secrecy that tends to shift whole communities (and even countries) into the obscurity of central control.

With these powers properly understood, no school board, city council, or state or federal agency serving the people should be managed without protecting personal responsibility. This is why any effort to move the cause of liberty must protect the power to dissent in order to disagree as well as the power to consent to agree. When we reject individual free agency, corruption begins to fester like a cancer that eventually destroys the system. Surgery through revolution becomes inevitable, though preferably without spilling any blood. The best way to correct power is never from the top down: this way always produces war. We should start with a blank slate and organize ideal consent from the bottom up.

Imagine any American community, an inner-city community with a dense population several blocks in size, or a rural county with five thousand residents dispersed over many hundreds of square miles. Now imagine that local government services and all state and federal services of any kind are suddenly gone, along with any physical evidence that they ever existed. No library, no schools, no city council, no courts, no homeless shelter, no chamber of commerce, no animal control, no police, no planning and code enforcement, and no churches. All services that once applied to the entire community have disappeared, along with the tax revenue that supported them.

The only things left standing are the houses and the businesses, though they have no paved streets, no streetlights, no sewer system and no utilities of any kind to support them.

Here's the question: If you lived in this community, how would you organize it? How would you provide for the many needed services in common to all?

Keep in mind there are some power centers inside and outside the community with a lot to lose—and a lot to gain—with a newly organized government. Some will want the contract to build city buildings and install utilities. Others will want the contract to build schools and police stations, and still others want to control zoning to benefit land they own or businesses they have. Don't forget the many outside peddlers wanting to sell the newest police state technology or textbooks for schools. In other words, there are many power centers wanting to control a piece of the community action.

When we include the political optimists seeking control of these services for the honor it gives them, such as the position of mayor, a school board member, or council member, we must be aware of their tendency to create more central control without your powers of consent and without your will to dissent. So let's ask the question again: How would you organize this community?

Obviously people need many services, buildings, utilities, and resources in common in order to support their own needs. When we have a responsibility in common, every individual must retain the free agency to voice dissent in discussion to hold things up, and every individual must retain a willing approval to move things forward within a small group. If we cannot build community on this foundation, we will eventually fail.

We get this idea from John Locke and not from Thomas Hobbes. John Locke (1632-1704) believed that we are all born free. When two people come together to talk, and when they reach an agreement, Locke called this the state of nature, where all are created equal. The emphasis for Lock is on the willing consent of each member of a commonwealth, which he called a community. Thomas Hobbes (1588-1679) believed human beings were selfish and incapable of reaching organized and civil agreement, which is why Hobbes called for an authoritative centralized body over the people to keep them from destroying each other. He called this body a leviathan.

Disgusted with Hobbes' argument for a strong and domineering centralized authority, Locke promoted the famous division of powers, the legislative, executive and judicial branches of government. Locke divided the power of the state to break up Hobbes' centralized power grid. The problem is Locke gave up his precious *state of nature* held independently in every citizen in order to create his top down separation of powers without the ideal consent of all in a graduated body broken into smaller constituent parts. Sadly, the founding fathers took this model from Locke and ran with it, not realizing what real potential they had. The United States is now more like Hobbes than Locke's original principle that every human being is born good. Just read *The Federalist Papers* with James Madison, Alexander Hamilton and John Jay. It is filled with comments about the distrust toward humanity and the need for a strong, centralized government.

Central control models of leadership believe ideal consent is impossible over larger populations and so they redirect individual responsibility to controlling authorities for the sake of expediency. Corruption and cronyism flourish without discussion—and without involving any personal responsibilities. Think of it this way: if central control seems more expedient than the efficiency of ideal consent, why are we failing in education, healthcare, infrastructure improvements, business development, and general social progress? Why have we not done anything great as a people for so many years, even despite advances in technology? Why is war a constant threat? Why are we growing more and more polarized, divided, and separated? The answer is simple. Our worship of authority through a democratic majority breeds an ever-increasing division in the people.

A resource held in common can be anything. Most of the time a resource is another human. Think of it this way. Social responsibility is not something we take *from* the system; it's the personal responsibility we all give *to* the system—namely our consent. Allowing for open dissent without intimidation from controlling powers is equally important. Give everyone in every community the ability to keep things moving in a caucus-like structure, and we might be surprised at how this would promote visionary solutions rather than empower political controllers. The minute we design our societies and even our businesses around promoting ideas and not people, we increase more freedom for everyone. The public would become more knowledgeable of efficiency and less inclined to feel intimidated by expediency.

Does central control without personal responsibility promote genuine optimism? Gandhi, Martin Luther King, Christ, Socrates, George Washington, and many others did not take more power to themselves and limit access to others. Instead, they moved power *away* from themselves by believing in others, encouraging others, and standing for principles that others could not express.

When we centralize power, we don't promote genuine optimists—we promote people who are more political. We see this in both the social justice and the social contract models. Both are antagonistic to social responsibility organized by ideal consent.

Social Justice vs. Social Contract

A social contract is like a constitution or written law drafted by the people that equally applies to all the people. Social justice is a policy or law written that does not apply to all people, but instead is written for an oppressed group or an underserved minority.

If you look back in time, "social justice" *used* to mean "social contract." Then we changed "social contract" to mean "social justice." This happened when we shifted from the importance of a written document that protects the rights of every individual, regardless of class, to a politicized contract that advances an underclass. Social contract is an agreed constitution that applies equally to all. It's a living document that seems to fall short of being a living process in the people. It does not prevent political optimists who use social justice as a tool for elevating soldiers to generals and demoting generals to soldiers. If any social service satisfies only one segment of the population and not all equally, it is a political construction trying to force social responsibility. It ignores the value of ideal consent from the people themselves. More importantly, it rejects the notion that freedom works.

The people, in small groups, can more effectively solve problems and service needs. A social written contract cannot do this and social justice is far from ever solving the problem. Both a social contract and social justice are stagnant and only protect the rights of the abused, and sometimes not even the abused. They do not lift those in need. Personal responsibility scaled into the community can service the needs of the community best while a social contract protects the abuse of one's twin powers of agency. If social justice needs to bring up an issue, let it surface in a small group and rise naturally from the people and not be a political correction from the latest authoritarian social correction of the month.

Because our social contract does not necessarily create equality effectively, we force equality through social justice. The forced equality is a poor representation of social responsibility.

In fact, social justice is a polluted form of social contract; and a social contract, if you are willing to believe it, is less valuable than the social responsibility of reaching ideal consent.

In both social justice and a social contract, everyone is in fact not part of the process in taking responsibility, as the word "social" would imply. Just look at the political division in the United States. Democrats are largely responsible for the new progressive idea of social justice to secure more equality for various minorities identified as the neglected underclass. Conservatives are largely in favor of a social contract or rule of law to secure more rights for the individual despite their class. The only difference between the two is that Democrats fail to demonstrate personal responsibility while advocating for social justice (secured from the state), and conservatives fail to demonstrate social responsibility while advocating for a laissez-faire social contract (also from the same state).

Put another way, Democrats want the right to screw their rich neighbor through the state, and conservatives want the freedom to screw the state at the cost of more debt on their neighbors. Both groups manipulate the state for their gain. This obviously cannot define social responsibility where social justice and social contract are in perpetual opposition. Put them in a room with no authority and make them reach a full consensus: then we'll have social responsibility.

No matter where you go in the political world today, idolatry for the authority of power centers is the driving force in both the established power class and in the disenfranchisement of the newest underclass. If we were to force the underclass in power, would we suddenly flourish? This is what our modern idea of social justice implies. If all we do is rely on a social contract or a new document of rights to protect our freedom, then where is the process to take responsibility in order to maintain these same rights? In other words, where is the efficiency of an informed citizenry?

This is something conservatives, independents, and libertarians never think about when it comes to protecting their social contract. They seem to believe that if they maintain personal responsibility without securing the same for others, they are okay. They never consider that it takes social responsibility to protect personal responsibility, and it takes personal responsibility to keep all social responsibility in the same hands without any outside theft. In other words, they have never learned to scale their rugged individualism.

It seems that more and more of us are dislocated from the process, and fewer and fewer are actually involved.

Thomas Paine said, "Every generation is, and must be, competent to all the purposes which its occasions require."[2] This is what it means to have an "informed citizenry." If every generation is to be competent, then every individual must participate equally in the discussion. Like all great stands against political powers, a rising disobedience can take generations to foment until a time when, in the blink of an eye, the statement of *no* suddenly shifts the balance of power. Before that expression of dissent begins to surface in society, disciplined discussion by common consent in modular form becomes the key for lasting solutions.

At the start of a new paradigm shift, numbers always begin small. As the numbers of those involved grow, we fail to scale for proper consent, and the problem begins to morph into political corruption. Until we scale the vote to include everyone's consent, we will live through the same cycles of history.

How do we bring a small group of people together and keep them together without dissolving into a larger political whole run by controlling minds? Put another way, how can we scale the twin powers of personal responsibility (the power to say yes and the power to say no) into social responsibility in the community? If we can keep this fundamental question alive in open discussion where everyone has equal footing, there will be a shift of power back to the people. This is sure to end the repetition of historical cycles we have been subjected to for thousands of years. Before we can truly get off the rollercoaster of cycles and get back on the highway of genuine, long-term progress, we must truly explain the power of the open forum.[3]

For those with romantic tendencies, call it the round table. For others, call it the optimism of ideal consent, the only solution that truly motivates, inspires, and sustains humanity without any need to be political.

Community responsibility is the essence of social responsibility. There is no such a thing and national and international responsibility. It eventually ends bureaucratic control created by those in power to lobby for its own existence and not for the freedom of the individual. Excuses are given and political correctness is use to defend the existence of every bureaucracy. The idolatry for honor and power fuels it from the bottom. It is none other than that evil one saying, "Give me all the power, the honor, and the money, and I will see that not one soul shall be lost.

Social responsibility is not bureaucracy responsibility. It is individual participation with the right to say no to some one higher to have power when we can do it effectively on the local level. Of what value is money sent from the community to a bureaucracy who choses who by leverage and political control, who gets it back. There is more funds wasted on this foolishness of control, than the dishonest claims against the system. Efficiently is far more effective the more local the decisions are made. The reason we have central control is we thought some individual could fix things for us. We keep giving power to populist ideas and never assume the social responsibility that come natural to every community if we maintained common consent rather than majority rule.

11

The Optimism of Common Consent

> If Potter gets hold of this Building and Loan there'll never
> be another decent house built in this town.... Can't you
> understand what's happening here?.... Potter isn't selling.
> Potter's buying! And why? Because we're panicky and he's
> not.... Now, we can get through this thing all right. We've
> got to stick together, though. We've got to have faith in each
> other.
>
> *It's A Wonderful Life*

Sugar and Water

Not everything scales up. Some of the best ideas scale
down. When you preserve the liberty of each individual with
consent to move things forward, and when you give every
individual equal liberty to dissent to hold things up in a modular
group, both personal and social responsibility work together in
equilibrium. This means it's time we scale down power toward
the individual and then scale back to the community. Individual
and social responsibility mix naturally at the right proportions.

Imagine having a five-gallon bucket of sugar and one
tablespoon of water. If the sugar is personal responsibility and
the water is social responsibility, the two parts will not mix. This
is not how freedom works. Freedom requires the right amount
of social and personal responsibility to mix in proportion.

Remember when we talked about the conservation of
responsibility? Think of how centrally controlled institutions fall
into subjection by the drama of staged optimists, the intimidation
of power centers, and the irrational peddlers of magic. From
Citizen Cane to the blockbuster Hunger Games, central control
over vast numbers is the great antagonist to a free society.

Unfortunately, the hero never solves the problem by refusing to be king, as George Washington did. Instead, the hero is often a benevolent person who never really decentralizes control. Like Robin Hood, the new hero takes away control from the bad element, only to fall into the hands of a new controlling authority. Taking money from the rich and giving it to the poor is not sustainable by comparison. Theft is expedient—not efficient.

Compare Robin Hood to the legend of King Arthur and his knights of the round table. Imagine how radical it would have been for a king to give every man at the table an equal voice. Even if just a legend, the story of King Arthur is more optimistic than Robin Hood. With the Knights of the Round Table organized by common consent, personal responsibility scales naturally toward a brother-to-brother bond. Perhaps it is time to consider the potential for a genuine republic of common consent.

In a growing popular democracy, there's no real bond. There is no decentralization of power because we have no voice—and, the larger the democracy becomes, the more our votes diminish in value. In a modular republic of common consent (as opposed to a democratic republic of majority rule), groups split and divide at a certain number (I believe it to be 18) in order to maintain the proper scale needed to preserve consent in each group.

Again, social responsibility is about protecting the two powers of personal responsibility: consent and dissent. This means you can never value dissent only through a vote. You must value dissent with every individual's voice protected by common consent. Giving every person willing to engage in the process real teeth in common consent is the only way to preserve each person's voice. When there are too many people in the group, individual voices can't be heard. When there are too few people in the group, dominant personalities can pressure everybody's voice.

Here's our problem. The public has a hard time seeing the value of common consent in a segmental structure, and this leaves people stuck with the only alternative, the worship of authority propped up by majority-rule. The nature of social intelligence rising by common consent will slow things down, engage society in more discussion, eliminate political power centers and, most importantly, initiate greater local responsibility.

Many arguments using numbers, expediency, and pragmatism are made against common consent. The problem is that the political optimist uses these arguments with no real evidence that they solve a problem or that there is a problem. A political mind will always work against consensus by manufacturing a problem with their solution of executive control. In truth, the only challenge with common consent is the best way to scale it. For instance, the best way to scale common consent in a small business is different than for a university, which is different for a sovereign nation.

Until we give genuine optimists a fighting chance to rise in natural leadership organized by common consent, we'll never know what humanity can accomplish.

Most of us never think of leadership as the first voice of dissent. We think of leadership as the voice that rallies the troops and gets others behind them, or the first voice to amass power.

The problem is that we are always waiting for the right leader to come along, and in a head-to-head match with political optimists, the leadership of a genuine optimist has very little chance of prevailing. This is why we remember great leaders: they stand out in history. Yet history is riddled with more political minds than there are great leaders.

So what can we do to create an environment for more genuine optimists with belief, encouragement, and principle to surface naturally?

When a beehive grows too big and there's no room to propagate the colony in the space provided, the colony produces another queen and two-thirds leave with the new queen. This is when the hive swarms.

Much of the natural world is like this; nature has a way of creating room for all living creatures. We do not create a voice for all because we have not learned how to split, divide, and scale down into natural hives, packs, pods, and dens. In other words, we scale up into states, nations, and the globe and rarely down to state, county, community, neighborhood, tribe, clan and family.

Political optimists are all about scaling up to centralize more power; genuine optimists are all about scaling down to decentralize power. The first uses majority rule to scale up with more central control and more vertical power structures. The latter uses the common consent of the people and the two powers of freedom in each person to scale down all the way to family and then back to community through common consent.

How can scaling power up to the state or the nation really promote optimism in the people? It cannot. Power isn't something that should ever scale up. Instead, we should scale up principles that protect the liberty of every individual, like those found in the Bill of Rights, maybe the Beatitudes, the equality sought after by Martin Luther King, the independence promoted by Gandhi, and so on.

Ideas that apply to all people equally scale up naturally. Authority and power centers do not.

While political optimists thrive in big institutions with centralized power, genuine optimists die when they're forced to exist in political environments, especially principled optimists. If you want to know one reason for so much political leadership in the world today, you now see the answer. The best leaders are not included in the game: they're like small drops of water diluted in buckets of refined sugar.

The Insidious Whole of Big Institutions

If King Arthur invited Adolf Hitler to sit with his knights at the round table, what do you think Hitler's rhetoric would produce? Would he overpower the knights' motto "brother to brother, yours in life and death?" Do you think a back room sower of discord like Mao would convince one of the three musketeers to reject their famous, "all for one and one for all?" In truth, if managed by unanimous consent, they would have a very hard time obtaining their central control.

Political optimists see the power of social responsibility held in common, and they work to put that responsibility in their own hands. First they centralize all social services in the hands of the state (almost without a fight) and then they take away personal responsibility (the voice of dissent and consent).

An obvious example is Cambodia's Pol Pot. It's estimated that over one million people (out of a population of eight million) died during his four-year reign in Cambodia from executions, forced labor, malnutrition, and poor medical care. He died on the same day he was to be turned over to face a tribunal for genocide.

All you have to do to obtain centralized power is get people to worship you with the tools of political optimism. These tools include staged performances, intimidation of dissent, and spreading magic or a false promise. When all three are wrapped up in the same person we have a serious problem; people begin to lose their personal responsibility to say no!

It's easy to shut down opposing dissent. All it takes is central control in the name of some social good. From the Affordable Care Act to a local city council choosing to fine homelessness, social responsibility is imposed by authoritative rules without the consent of the community. Empowering benevolent authority in one person or in one agency is never a positive action. It leads to government control over personal responsibility and the impossibility of scaling widened democratic consent at any level.

When a majority rule governs society, people are naturally forced to adopt more idolatry for authority in order to properly align with the most promising power center. The justification for this insidious direction to control is to say it's for your own good. If power centers directly attacked your personal responsibility, you'd see it coming, but when they *take* your social responsibility away with the use of majority rule, you lose all responsibility at the same time. In other words, you would have no voice.

Look at the U.S.'s Environmental Protection Agency. When beekeepers started losing 40 to 90 percent of their hives, they started to share their findings in conferences and in group meetings across the country and around the world. Many theories surfaced and eventually they called the problem Colony Collapse Disorder (CCD). This is when entire hives suddenly die off. The commercial beekeepers then found a link between systemic pesticides called neonicotinoids and CCD.

Smaller governments in other countries employed cautionary practices to halt the use of harmful pesticides in the environment. In the United States, it doesn't work this way: we halt nothing. Even with hundreds of beekeepers speaking out, and with hundreds of millions lost in revenue, it wasn't enough to move forward with caution and halt (not ban) the use of systemic pesticides on crops. This is because the EPA is an intensely centralized power center far removed from public dissent in exercising timely and effective responsibility. Even with a massive body of beekeepers rising in direct disagreement with the agency, they did nothing. Organized by an executive order by President Nixon and then later ratified in the Senate and House in the early seventies, the EPA was created by Congress with no checks and balances against its eventual rule over the environment. Both policy and enforcement, when put in the same hands, fail to offer real immediate help.

For instance, in the midst of a crisis of beekeepers losing their hives to CCD, the EPA required more science to prove a direct cause; especially since the disorder didn't show up for several months after farmers applied the pesticides. Congress then introduced the Save America's Pollinators Act OF 2013 (H.R. 2692). Designed "to direct the Administrator for the Environmental Protection Agency to take certain actions related to pesticides that may affect pollinators...," the act had over 45 cosponsors, and when referred to a committee on July 16, 2013, it died. This is the result of the insidious whole, where all central control commands over honest dissent.

The problem gets worse when discussion includes real dissent. For instance, when you hear the voice of organic beekeepers, you learn about the hardship commercial beekeepers impose on their bees, such as the stress of moving them across the country and making them pollinate a single crop with no real diversity in their diet. Organic beekeepers argue that commercial beekeepers are starving their bees to death in addition to subjecting them to poisons.

If the legislative powers set up the EPA as an impartial research body, and had the states retained the enforcement of environmental protections, the power to halt serious environmental threats would become more efficient. As it stands, we promote more central control without any requirement for consent.

Think of the insidious whole as a growing control grid of adulation engineering and propped up by performance art. This is where whole groups governed by majority rule—and even bureaucracies—work together against productive ideas to obtain more honors that they award to themselves. We call this authoritarianism. All totalitarian models grow in power when people worship authority. Just about any tool of political optimism can cause people to worship staged performances, the intimidation of potential naysayers, and the persuasion of deluded magic. However, upon close inspection, the root cause is the centralization of both powers of personal and social responsibility.

When individuals no longer have the freedom to dissent and the right to consent in modular form, and when both these powers of personal responsibility are put in the hands of a very small body far removed from the people, corruption ensues and the cycles of history continue to repeat themselves.

Think of knots on a yo-yo string. As a culture begins to spin downward to keep its own energy alive, the knot of authority halfway down jerks people into an unnatural wobble out of control. As the people try to rise back up, a wobbling motion inflicted by the same knot makes it twice as difficult to move freedom back in the palm of each person's hand. When people release more of their freedom in exchange for some protection, security, or benefits from the public treasury, that same knot of authoritarianism gets bigger. We see the same problem with corporations and religious institutions all the time. Authoritarians tie people up with knots by destroying personal responsibility in the palm of each person's hand.

Take the will to consent and the will to dissent. When centralized in one place outside of the individual, people are unable to participate in social responsibility. When this happens, we've created a political world by pushing genuine optimists to the side and more often out the door. Absolutely nothing optimistic comes from this political process.

Restoring Natural Leadership

In many leadership and motivation books, the emphasis is either on inspiring the individual to achieve greatness, or inspiring the individual to foster greatness in others. When we talk about motivation and leadership, genuine optimists are already there. They already bring out the best in themselves, they encourage the best out of others, and they stand for the best ideas. They are the first to volunteer, the first to take charge, and the first to take responsibility. So why are there so many books on motivation and leadership when genuine optimists are already willing to lead and serve?

The problem is that the political world doesn't favor genuine optimists—because believing, encouraging, and standing for principle demands complete freedom. In other words, genuine optimists require complete control over their agency. Until we change our paradigm and organize ourselves as a people without the idolatry of authority over us, we will suffer the loss of our real power.

In a political rather than a free world, we focus on the greatness of individual achievement rather than the powers of personal responsibility to secure freedom in each individual. This is why we prop up individual achievement and create idolatry for kings, CEOs, presidents, and authority of all kinds. Supporting the two powers of personal responsibility is a better approach for each individual to give to the whole without the whole becoming insidious to each individual. There is no better approach to restoring natural leadership than through supporting models of unanimous consent.

Social responsibilities in health, education, welfare and even responsibilities in business and government will naturally mature and serve many until ideal consent reaches its scale of no return. The payoff of this approach is that we get hundreds and thousands of incubator communities across the country and even micro groups in a business all working with the autonomy given to solve the same problems. This is superior to one nation under an appointed czar or bureaucrat who cripples the country with endless regulations void of any real wide-body consent.

In order to restore natural leadership in the hands of each individual, we need to stop idolizing the individual as authority over others and instead start promoting our natural state of humanity. This is far more revolutionary than all combined books on motivation and leadership because the focus is not on power centers but the freedom at hand for all.

You can take two people such as a husband and a wife. If one spouse does not try to control or manipulate the other through guilt; and when both offer their best direction to take, they listen to each other, modify their thinking, and they come to a consensus. However, when a couple engages in argument, they do not teach or educate each other. Rarely does one add new information in an argument or realize more about the situation from the other. Their fear overrides; they pass guilt and never ask questions of the other in order to learn more. This does not mean argument is bad. It just means if consent is overruled, argument is futile.

In a group, the process of asking questions shimmies the mind like a brick on wet mortar. Given enough time to think, we become enlightened. If we continue our attempts to control and avoid questioning, we remove the spirit of love, joy and peace—the dynamics of shimming the mind. When we lay bricks and fail to shimmy each brick into place, the seal is not strong enough to hold. Therefore, when we limit discussion and when we shut down asking questions for expediency, we raise a political structure that will eventually fall. For the sake of the truth and not expediency, we must separate into smaller modular groups according to their locality. Let members in each group ask questions during the same time as other groups and more questions can transpire in the same time. Once each smaller group reaches a consensus, let a representative attend a higher group in order to shimmy the entire structure. When we shimmy each brick just the right amount, we strengthen the entire wall.

Round Tables, Long Halls, and Open Forums

There's no evidence that King Arthur's knights of the round table ever existed. This doesn't matter: we have the ideal etched into our minds. The model of a round table encourages something powerful. It puts everything into the open with no figurehead in control.

This open round table concept only works when everyone is sitting at the round table—and not working behind the scenes in factions and parties. The only way to shut down manipulation behind the scenes is to abolish the majority rule that strengthens power centers. Once everyone is sitting at the table, two features need to come into effect to make wide-body horizontal freedom the standard.

First, both powers of personal responsibility must be fully welcome at the table. Second, the only way to protect these powers is to govern by unanimous consent. If we fall to a majority rule, we put in place the hidden intentions of secrecy that grow unchecked.

Imagine two nonprofit organizations, each with a board of directors. One board makes decisions by a two-thirds majority vote and the other requires 100 percent unanimous consent. Which board would you rather sit on? If you say the former, you're a political optimist—you seek power and you align with power centers. If you say the latter, you're a genuine optimist— you seek freedom and you require equal power to protect it.

The power to consent, to move things forward, and the power to dissent, to hold things up, come from the freedom of individual responsibility. Each person on a board must retain both powers in order to suppress the political optimist from centralizing control. Unanimous common consent is the only way to protect the two powers of freedom in personal responsibility. *This is* both efficient and ideal.

If you don't believe that such a practice can work, look at one of the least-known inspirations for the bicameral legislative body in the United States Constitution, the Five Nation Iroquois Confederacy, which protects the two powers of personal responsibility better than any known document of its kind.

The word Iroquois (French for *people of the long house*) refers to a band of five tribes or nations, the Mohawk, Oneida, Onondaga, Cayuga and Seneca nations. A sixth nation, the Tuscarora, joined the confederacy later.

The most striking quality of the Iroquois nation is its ability to reach common consent. The lords gather in a long house and the individual councils from each nation gather separately in the same. Here is a small section of the Five Nations Confederate Council:

> All the business of the Five Nations Confederate Council shall be conducted by the two combined bodies of Confederate Lords. First, the question shall be passed

upon by the Mohawk and Seneca Lords, then it shall be discussed and passed by the Oneida and Cayuga Lords. Their decisions shall be referred to the Onondaga Lords, (fire Keepers) for final judgment.

The same process shall obtain when a question is brought before the council by an individual or a War Chief.

In all cases the procedure must be as follows: when the Mohawk and Seneca Lords have unanimously agreed upon a question, they shall report their decision to the Cayuga and Oneida Lords who shall deliberate upon the question and report a unanimous decision to the Mohawk Lords. The Mohawk Lords will then report the standing of the case to the Fire Keepers, who shall render a decision as they see fit in case of a disagreement by the two bodies, or confirm the decisions of the two bodies if they are identical. The Fire Keepers shall then report their decision to the Mohawk Lords who shall announce it to the open council.

If though any misunderstanding of obstinacy on the part of the Fire Keepers, they render a decision at variance with that of the Two Sides, the Two Sides shall reconsider the matter and if their decisions are jointly the same as before they shall report to the Fire Keepers who are then compelled to confirm their joint decision.[1]

Even when moving a subject along through each council in the long house, the demand of common consent maintains social responsibility. There's no popular majority vote at any level because it would nullify discussion and circumvent dissent. If such a culture can master this for many generations, all we have to do is scale it for our time. If there is one thing we can do with modern technology, we can learn to scale just about anything.

Our backward approach, allowing for constant division and party factions, actual*ly thrives on majority rule.* This is foreign to both *the Iroquois Nation and* the genuine optimist. Providing a confederate council with no parties, no platforms, and a constant changing of speaker, protects the two powers of personal responsibility.

Because genuine optimists aren't afraid to speak and act independently, their natural ability to voice dissent perseveres when given the equal footing of common consent. However, stick a central authority over the group, something that believing, encouraging, and principled people despise, and you'll see parties and factions divide apart from the group and separate from any possible consensus.

It's now clear why optimism is an organizational problem and not an attitude problem in each person. In fact, attitude has never been a problem for genuine optimists, at least not when they organize into common consent. This is because dissenting voices appear disruptive, but we must understand that disruptive dissent in the mere expression of an idea in the open forum where all ideas have equal voice is genuine optimism.

The key is to dissent against a specific proposal. Disruption *for its own sake that is* not tied to a specific proposal, it is simply antagonistic to civil discourse. Eventually the disruptor will feel isolated and incapable of manipulating the group. A change in their approach is eminent or the disruptor leaves on their own.

Think of the kind of person who always asks questions, slows you down, keeps the discussion from ending, and takes almost forever to make a decision. This person could have an agenda to frustrate the group or perhaps this person wants to know the truth. How do you tell the difference? The only way is through more open discussion driven by unanimous consent.

The challenge is to keep driving through the process until you know the truth.

If such a person were in your group, would you push toward majority rule in order to shut this person out and stop them from their disruptions? If yes, then you are a political optimist.

Until we start to protect the dissenting voice, even when they aggravate us with questions and comments, we can never become a people of enlightenment. Does this mean we have to feel stuck and incapable of forward movement? No: this is where technology and better organizational structures come into play. Yes, we can scale it!

One of the secrets to making common consent work is to focus on proposed ideas and to encourage progress toward consent. One person presents an idea, it then goes around for a vote. If everyone doesn't agree, members in the group may leave a brief comment explaining why. The idea, proposal, or nomination returns to the originator and they decide to revise, discard, or start a new proposal or nomination. This process removes all posturing for importance. There's no authority to worship, and no central control to pander to. In our digital world, this will take supportive technology. For more information, follow us at www.localcommonwealth.org or listen in at www. thegenuineoptimist.com. With technology, we can achieve consent more efficiently. First, we need to get the discussion going.

The Restoration of Common Consent

Contrary to what movies and fairytales tell you, worshipping a king who rules with assumed goodness and wisdom is humanity's central failure. The more we idolize authority, the more self-destructive we become.

Just compare North Korea with Switzerland. In Switzerland, a seven-member federal council operates as a combined cabinet and collective presidency: together they hold executive power. Their chancellor, a ceremonial president, holds that position for only one year. Compare that to North Korea's president, who holds all power over the state for life. In fact, North Korea changed their constitution in 2009 to call their president "Supreme Leader." They say a picture is worth a thousand words. If so, **Figure 11-1** summarizes humanity's central problem.

Every unstable country or organization with excessive power centralized in the hands of a few promotes combinations of power that collaborate in secret by using the tools of political optimism. What follows later is more political optimism—and,

Fig. 11–1

eventually, dictatorial rule. We romanticize the knights of the round table because the king was willing to give more freedom to others. What we don't realize is that this same power rests in our hands.

It is clear that freedom in the United States is under massive assault with no apparent opportunity to correct things. Freedom is a rare gift that suffers every time we allow a single person, party, or small central body to exercise pressure against disagreement. When a corporation commands excessive central control and refuses to trust in the agency of its workforce, we call the company corrupt. Why do we not say the same about social responsibilities when the state and federal governments, and even when religious organizations, centralize power into the hands of a few?

People find themselves withdrawing from any connection to their community because there is no real means to connect with their consent. For instance, a former student sent the following email:

> I'll admit, politics frustrate me more than anything. Although I'm sure that makes me no different than anyone else. Actually, I can't even say so much that it's politics per

se, as it is ignorance and the refusal of a great deal of people to question what they are being told.

I used to spend a great deal of time writing blogs and attempting (that is the key word) to encourage people to understand that not everything we are told by the media (or politicians for that matter) is fact. I quit because it only resulted in the comments section being flooded with nastiness....

Honey Rollins

What's the solution to prevent personal responsibility from reaching a point of total dilution? How much longer can we stand to see all social responsibilities taken over by political optimists?

Let's consider five solutions we can begin to apply in our businesses, our communities, and eventually our states and our nations:

1. Stop using majority rule.

When administering boards, foundations, nonprofits and even corporations, use more *common* consent of those who are close to the needs and problems and who can effect change without political optimists gaining control.

2. Increase board or council membership to at least nine but never more than eighteen members before needing to split.

Allow these boards, committees, and councils to split with nine members in each once you reach a total of eighteen. Two independent boards is not a bad idea. Each quorum can then handle the issues independently by segregating inappropriate power centers and liberating the natural dissent for good that vision demands. The larger the organization, the more this should be considered. Having three to five forums at the top completely limits political opportunists. If all forums can agree unanimously, you know the result is a constructive one. A developing concept www.localcommonwealth.org will become a model to experiment with.

3. **To advance ideas, allow a brief declaration, and then let everyone vote for or against the declaration, and allow for comments to justify the negative vote.**

What we need is a media with a longer life cycle. A media where there are no central controls. A media with every member of the community acts as editor and publisher in common, and a media that moves through several layers of thoughtful consideration. Such a media is about ideas and not the news of the day. It is about people and not editorial panels. At Local Common Wealth, our mission is to give more voiced dissent in order to liberate better solutions.

4. **Increase access to all.**

For businesses, include the employee as much as you can. Look to the successful cooperative business models called COOPs or ESOPS (Employee Stock Ownership Plans), or intelligently crafted operating agreements or the newly spawned movement of holacracy that gives more autonomy to teams and individuals. They have the lowest turnover rate and often the greatest productivity from their employees. For example, replace your chief operating officer with a chief operating council to become more headless as an organization. Consider exiting your company to a COOP or an ESOP, and not to private investors.

5. **Protect dissent to promote honesty.**

Majority rule spawns polarization. This causes many to remain unsatisfied and with less productivity. Therefore, dissent is the only real check against dishonesty, which thrives on polarization and majority rule.

When we begin to apply these basic principles, more discussion will follow, with the intention of reaching consent. Political individuals will hold out if they think they can get a majority. If a unanimous vote is required, they become more rational and practical. Dissent must be protected until everyone agrees. Any open disagreement will stay with the genuinely honest who hold to principle, but be warned that honesty diminishes when majority rule is imposed. Allow for members to revise or modify their view for the sake of adaptive progress. Small things will pass easily, but more difficult issues will take time in order to reach agreement. The use of common consent in modular and graduated form is better because it avoids drastic changes that do not have the backing of those who are in the trenches.

Looking at the Numbers Realistically

As of 2012, the United States census gave California a population of roughly 38,000,000 residents. If you subtract those under the age of eighteen, you're left with roughly 34,000,000 residents. While many people talk of direct democracy as the essence of a truly free society, this isn't true because each citizen isn't given power to dissent or consent. The intimacy and direct discourse required in a direct republic is never promoted.

This means we could easily dissect California into its constituent parts, such as neighborhoods, cities, counties, and perhaps regions, maybe even split the state into two states. Since secession from the federal government is on the minds of Texans, certainly division is more appropriate: it's where we could reinvent our legislative system to accommodate more common consent. Can you imagine the secession of a state into a central control grid run by majority rule? The vipers and political opportunists would be out in droves.

Using a populous state like California as an example and building from the bottom up with eighteen members in each group, the numbers could begin with the following. See **Figure 11.2**.

Fig. 11-1 A California Republic		
1st	1,889,568 Groups	X 18 = 34,012,224 total members
2nd	104,976 Groups	X 18 = 1,889,568 total members
3rd	5,832 Groups	X 18 = 104,976 total members
4th	324 Groups	X 18 = 5,832 total members
5th	18 Groups	X 18 = 324 total members

Starting with the most local level in one's own neighborhood, everyone can take part in this process. The numbers show that the ideal of common consent scales better than majority rule. You can improve common consent substantially by limiting one member per household. This would inspire the lowest level to incorporate a household discussion. Households are easier to track and tabulate. It also avoids packing discussion groups with an agenda.

At the start, a direct republic of common consent may look fat and wide with a vast horizontal reach of many groups, but it does scale up. California currently has roughly forty members in the state senate and about eighty members in the state assembly, for a total of one hundred twenty members. Even if structured to reflect the same one hundred and twenty eight state representatives, a direct republic of common consent shows there is no better way to remove political agendas from the voice of the people.

If you multiply five levels by eighteen, this comes to ninety members between you and the highest legislative body in the state. You could add one last legislative body of eighteen members at the top, but why narrow consent this much? Eighteen groups with eighteen members in each (or a bicameral legislature with two houses) satisfy nicely as the highest legislative body in the state. Is there historical evidence that common consent with such large numbers can work? Yes!

The Third Estate in France in 1789 drafted their Tennis Court Oath with an almost perfect consensus of 576 in favor and just 1 against. Did the revolution turn bloody after that? It sure did, mostly due to a few in the media who continued with, "Take off their heads." The point is, they stopped reaching consent after their Tennis Court Oath. Had the people properly scaled the voice of consent into the new model in order to avoid power centers from influencing the majority and fomenting so much internal strife, they would not have endured such a bloody revolution. Certainly 324 representatives in California can reach a unanimous consent on the very best ideas without shedding blood. And because those who reach the top are not necessarily party favored or party approved, we can return our humanity back to the natural free state of the individual without the baggage of political division and separation.

Imagine the total rejection of lobbying, corporate favoritism, and imagine how much greater access the people would have to their government? More importantly, imagine the potential for the very best ideas and principles to rise to the top. It may take those ideas a long time to rise to the state and even the nation, but this is preferred over the state incrementally taking more power in the name of expediency.

Imagine having only ninety people between you and the highest legislative body in a very populous state like California? You can even modify the top level just a little and create five major councils, a structure similar to that of the Iroquois Confederacy. All proposals then must pass through all councils at the top with a unanimous consent. A direct democracy could never give this much voice to each individual, and political optimists could never gain a majority with so much access for everyone in a direct republic of common consent.

People argue against common consent because they see it as impossible: "it's too slow," "we don't have enough time," "some groups will never come to full consensus," "people naturally don't agree," and "there are too many differences of opinion."

Oddly enough, these are the same arguments used for promoting more central control and more idolatry toward leaders. In all centrally controlled structures, people are perceived as selfish.

Always remember, genuine optimists do not see humanity as selfish and so they would never impose controls like political optimists do. They see people as born free and good. It is a far better approach to organizing humanity. By limiting access only to the most politically skilled people, however, society is easily controlled but never progressive in the purest sense of the word.

In common consent, humanity changes in the same way a teenage gang member changes when suddenly put in a college literature class where everyone is sharing ideas about romantic poetry. Environment affects us, and our humanity adjusts to the environment. So why not create an environment that promotes the highest and best that humanity has to offer?

Consider when seven racially prejudiced jurors are forced to confront five jurors not racially prejudiced. Because a jury is strictly organized by unanimous consent, the racially biased majority cannot overrun the minority. Both minority and majority are protected equally. Is this not a better form of social justice than to take a side and assume you speak for the disadvantages of a marginalized minority?

If juries can decide complex cases every day, who is to say that we cannot scale unanimous consent in modular form out to the larger community? Put the state and the nation aside for now. At least we can begin to experience in our communities, private organizations, and businesses the vast possibilities of common consent. As long as we continue believing that reaching common ground is impossible, we give up the imaginative solutions yet to be discovered and we empower the idolatry of more political control.

The Ideal of Common Consent

Common consent begins with a discussion between two people. A third, fourth, and fifth person joins until seventeen is reached. As long as any forum reaches full agreement as touching one thing, they have reached the ideal of common consent.

When any forum reaches eighteen members, the group splits evenly into two autonomous groups of nine. Every new forum splits the same way at eighteen members.

Eventually when five forums are reached, each group elects a representative to the next higher level and all base levels below must agree unanimously to pass an issue above that will affect all. Until then, each group decides their own issues under current law. Only those who believe that our natural state is good actually believe in this model. They are genuine optimists. However, political optimists disagree and will even fight against it. A social revolution of ideas is looming.

How forums are divided and at what exact number may be debated. It should be warned, though, that if the group gets too big, it becomes too difficult to hear the voice of dissent and the drum beat of majority rule begins to set in; and if the group is too small, members too easily succumb to a power center not willing to stand for greater consent. It is easy to see why most of human history has been dominated by the divine right of kings, tyrants, executive power centers and the narrowing access granted only to bureaucrats. A majority will always default to more centralized control. Does this mean that humanity is weak? No! It means that in order to prove the natural state of each individual is free and good, the widest body of consent possible is required.

A ruling majority, either fifty-one percent or a super majority of seventy five percent, argue that humanity is inherently selfish and evil. A majority can prove this because it naturally promotes political power centers that sow discord in the direction of social self-destruction. This self-destruction of humanity guarantees the secured position of political optimists. The consequences that follow mean more central control. Oddly, when pockets of unanimous common consent rule humanity, this will prove that we are inherently free and good.

Imagine thirty years from today. A global, interlocking corporate power structure has moved humanity much closer to a uni-polar world government. From our point of view today, the world will be unrecognizable in thirty years, just as the world today is completely unrecognizable to the past. The push for more central control under the banner of progressivism, social justice, or any new turn of phrase, is the tool used by many misguided idealists. Their idealism is founded on the idea that humanity is inherently selfish and that it needs to be managed at a distance and by a central authority in order to avoid our own self-destruction. Rather than begin with the genuine nature of ideal consent, political opportunists pushing for more central control actually sponsor the injustice they create.

Just look at the G7, the G20, The Transpacific Partnership (TPP) signed in secrete, the United Nations, non-government organizations, and the many summits, both private and public, such as the Council on Foreign Relations and many similar organizations. They all advocate for more central control. Not one of them will admit the value of scaling power back to the people. It is not in their interest and it is not in their business plans.

Just within the past few days before publishing this book, a State of California Senate Committee on Education voted in favor of forced vaccinations for students statewide. They did this even despite the overwhelming voice of dissent from hundreds of parents who showed up in opposition to the policy, all expressing their personal concerns over the negative effects of vaccinations. When you have several hundred show up in opposition and just nine members on the committee with seven voting in favor of forced vaccinations, there is nothing ideal about this. It is the very model that proves we are selfish and in need of an authority over us.

Widen the reach of consent with no political bottleneck and a better humanity will surface with no *separation, no duality, and no* polarity. We will get back to our natural opposition and work things out.

In the same week before publishing this book, news resurfaced about Vermont's Act 120, the first act by a state requiring the labeling of genetically modified organisms (GMO). Large multinational corporations and lobbying groups have already combined in power to fight the act through legal means. When you read the act, it is like reading the Declaration of Independence where a list of grievances is given to justify the act. Here are three of them:

(B) Under its regulatory framework, the FDA does not independently test the safety of genetically engineered foods.

Instead, manufactures submit safety research and studies, the majority of which the manufacturers finance or conduct. The FDA reviews the manufacturers' research and reports through a voluntary safety consultation, and issues a letter to the manufacturer acknowledging the manufacturer's conclusion regarding the safety of the genetically engineered food product being tested.

(C) The FDA does not use meta-studies or other forms of statistical analysis to verify that the studies it reviews are not biased by financial or professional conflicts of interest.

(D) There is a lack of consensus regarding the validity of the research and science surrounding the safety of genetically engineered foods, as indicated by the fact that there are peer-reviewed studies published in international scientific literature showing negative, neutral, and positive health results. [2]

The point to note is that the constriction of consent into a narrow authority, and with no teeth in having a dissenting voice, and with power centralized at a great distance, this is the enemy of freedom.

While many will continue with a popular vote as the idea of democracy, they will never come close to the ideal of common consent. When we start to associate democracy with the later, we start on a path for a better tomorrow, a day when we relate with one another as individuals and not as camps, parties, causes, and factions. The first is relational and the second is linear.

Last Word

Being political comes from the idea of standing to one side without any relational thinking. We are stubbornly blind and fanatically in denial. Our only way out is to participate in long discussions that edify and do not polarize. This means stepping to the side at times to ask important questions rather than keeping our political posture for the honor and acceptance we hope to gain by worshiping a certain authority.

Beware of standing your ground unless it's a fundamental principle based on a true harmonic of love, faith in others, and patience toward open discussion. Laws have to be simple and just. A consensus is the only guarantee (as illustrated by the sixteenth-century Iroquois Indians and the original intent of an American republic). John Locke as illustrated earlier was right, all men and women are created equal, we all have the same twin powers of yes and no. The mistake John Locke made in his two *Treatise on Government* was in creating the division of powers in the form of a legislative, executive and judicial. Each one of these now operates by centrally controlled nominations or popular vote. The highest level of consent derived from the free voice of each person was never considered. There is a better division of power that needs to begin at the community.

It's time for a change. Implementing this change privately in families, communities, churches, local service organizations, and cooperative business enterprises is the beginning of a great open-source project. It's a project destined to shift the balance of power back to the side of genuine.

When we stand on a single point, or embrace a duality of good and evil, we do not seek relational facts and we fall into linear thinking and political posturing. This method will drive whole nations into destruction and the world into darkness.

It doesn't matter whether you're a progressive liberal or a canonical conservative: duality doesn't let the genuine optimist scale personal responsibility into the community. National conservative laws are better if local methods are retained to exercise understanding through more liberal attitudes.

Forcing liberal attitudes on a grand scale (as suggested by Plato) makes a nation irresponsible because it lacks individual conservative thinking on the local plane. The canonical conservative wants conservative laws but takes no responsibility for anything social. The progressive wants liberal laws with no community responsibility—the state becomes the community, and they take no personal responsibility in expressing a voice of dissent.

This dichotomy is destroying America and all nations, because we're not trying to reach a consensus on one point at a time and from the most local source first. We group things into massive concepts to intimidate everyone into more central control and the worship of authority. The libertarian is no different where everything is about protecting individual liberty that fails to scale into social responsibility.

The United States Constitution didn't rise out of tradition. It rose out of an open dialogue and out of the freedom of discussion. It was necessary to suffer tyranny before they could understand what new direction was becoming available. In our time, we should be prepared to suffer the tyranny of our own idolatry for authority before we can see the wisdom to prepare for change.

To look into the future is to understand that an effective revolution doesn't overthrow oppressive controlling power; rather, it separates us from the tyranny inherent with centralized control.

From the beginning of the American republic, politicians with good intentions have missed the mark on legislating equity because they've failed to apply the conservation of responsibility at the most local level possible. Those who polarize the issue into globalism (the new statism) on the one side, and rugged individualism (a defenseless patriotic liberty) on the other side, do not address the conservation of responsibility within the community. As long as we have a two-headed party with one side fighting for the welfare state and another side arguing for the warfare state, we'll continue down a path of prophesied destruction, because no matter how precious the rights of each human being are, central planning run by a majority always wins over the visionary gumption found in individuals.

It takes local people to rise in consent around a vision from their own ranks to solve the most complex problems created by the posturing of supposed optimism. If libertarians could understand this, they could change the world. Looking to take over a conservative party with the intent to return to a constitutional social contract is not good enough.

Our time in history lacks insight. We are forever split into the motives behind leadership fueled by the same fight for personal rights versus state responsibility. The more we allow for this division of personal responsibility from federally assumed control for all public services, the greater the separation of power from the people, and the greater the separation of the people into survivalist individualism on the one side, and state-mandated idealism on the other.

Many people hide behind freedom-loving patriotism that ignores local responsibility for the health, education, and welfare of others. They will remain in battle forever against the newest progressive central-planning idea. While some people advocate for individualism through inalienable rights, others advocate for collectivism through state control for our good.

Neither is responsible.

When we demand responsibility at the most local level, those people calling themselves leaders for good in our communities are seen for what *they* are—political optimists. The majority cannot see the motive of those who advocate the divine right of kings. From the one who would be king to the freedom fighter who wants to eliminate the king and replace him with personal liberty, the battle has destroyed the good that people in communities are destined to accomplish.

The conservation of responsibility must be taken back and secured by the voice of local consent held in common. When the state, or any central authority at a distance, assumes our voice as a people and not our vote as individuals, in time we'll lose both. We are now faced with more and more centralized power in business, in government, and in religion. We must invest in a wider and graduated voice of consent in our communities, in business, and in governments and take back the optimism of dissent protected by the social intelligence of common consent. It is the only way to combat the monstrous leviathan we call majority rule.

Let's come together at www.localcommonwealth.org.

Let us not seek the Republican answer or the Democratic answer, but the right answer. Let us not seek to fix the blame for the past. Let us accept our own responsibility for the future.

John F. Kennedy

The Staged Optimist

1 Orson Welles on Acting.
https://www.youtube.com/
watch?v=m1CS_LRfwd4.
Also quoted in: http://a-bit-
tersweet-life.tumblr.com/
post/49785836946/i-think-acting-
is-like-sculpture-in-other-words.

2 John Stewart Mill. *On Liberty.*
Chapter II Of the Liberty of
Thought and Discussion.

3 http://www.telegraph.co.uk/news/
earth/energy/6491195/Al-Gore-
could-become-worlds-first-car-
bon-billionaire.html. Accessed
January 26, 2015.

4 http://www.washingtonexaminer.
com/obama-the-repeal-debate-
is-and-should-be-over/arti-
cle/2547402. Accessed January
24, 2014.

5 Samuel Louis Dael *The Platonic
Idiom*. Vision Impact Publishing
2007

6 Marcus Aurelius *Meditations* Book
II

Intimidating Optimist

1 http://www.presidentialrhetoric.
com/speeches/02.04.05.html.
Accessed January 26, 2015.

2 Scott, Susan. Fierce Conversations. 2002

3 John F Kennedy. "President
and the Press." Address before the American Newspaper
Publishers Association. April
27, 1961. http://www.jfklibrary.
org/Research/Research-Aids/
JFK-Speeches/American-News-
paper-Publishers-Associa-
tion_19610427.aspx

4 Thomas Paine. The Rights of
Man.1779.

5 https://www.youtube.com/
watch?v=GiPe1OiKQuk. Ac-
cessed on January 28, 2015

6 https://www.youtube.com/
watch?v=k3bbqlif_eQ. Accessed
on January 28, 2015

7 http://en.wikipedia.org/wiki/Mari-
nus_van_der_Lubbe. Accessed
on January 28, 2015

8 A slogan popularized by Karl Marx
in his 1875 Critique of the Gotha
Program.

9 R.J Rummel. Statistics of Democide: Genocide and Mass Murer
Since 1900. Center for National
Security Law. www.mega.nu/
ampp/rummel/note5.htm

10 R.J Rummel. Freedom, Democracy, Peace: Power, Democide
and War. Introduction. http://
www.hawaii.edu/powerkills/

Irrational Optimist

1 Byrne, Rhonda. *The Secret*. 2006.

Responsible Faith

1 Drew Barrymore. "Here's Looking
at Drew." Ladies' Home Journal,
February 2009. By Marisa Fox.

2 Becker, Ernest. The Denial of
Death. The Free Press, 1973.

Encouraging Optimist

1   Colonial Origins of the American Constitution. Edited by Donald S Lutz. 1998.

2   http://www.jfklibrary.org/Research/ Research-Aids/JFK-Speeches/ American-Newspaper-Publish- ers-Association_19610427.aspx, Accessed on March 3, 2015.

Principled Optimist

1   John Taylor Gatto. Weapons of Mass Instruction: A Schoolteach- er's Journey Through the Dark World of Compulsory Schooling.

2   Ted talk by Eduardo Briceno at Ted Manhattan Beach. Accessed on February 24, 2015. https:// mail.google.com/mail/u/0/#- search/dean.g.boren%40gmail. com/14bafae70830a01d?pro- jector=1

3   Carol Dweck PhD. *Mindset: The New Psychology of Success.* 2007.

Personal Responsibility

1   Chang, Jung, and Halliday, John. The Unknown Story of MOA. 2005. Pages 13-15.

2   Paine, Thomas. The Rights of Man. 1892. Page 13.

3   Luke 1:17. King James Version of the Bible.

4   http://press-pubs.uchicago.edu/ founders/documents/v1ch3s6. html. Accessed on March 3, 2015.

5   http://www.ownershipassociates. com/pdf/brief1.3.pdf. Accessed on March 4, 2015.

6   http://www.ownershipassociates. com/pdf/brief1.3.pdf. Accessed on March 4, 2015.

7   http://www.esop.org/. Accessed on March 4, 2015

8   http://www.usnews.com/opinion/ blogs/peter-roff/2010/03/09/ pelosi-pass-health-reform-so- you-can-find-out-whats-in-it. Accessed on March 11, 2015.

9   Personal email reply from Samuel Louis Dael, dated March 09, 2015.

10 Chang, Jung. Wild Swans: Three Daughters of China. 1991.

Social Responsibility

1   Thomas Carlyle. *Past and Present.* Chapter 2

2   Thomas Pain *Rights of Man* Part 1

3   Samuel Louis Dael. *The Christian Folly*

Restoration of Common Consent

1   Constitution of the Iroquois Na- tions: The Great Binding Law, Gayanashagowa. www.constitu- ion.org/cons/iroquois-p.html

2   http://www.leg.state.vt.us/ docs/2014/Acts/ACT120.pdf. Access on April 21, 2015.

A

actions, right, 101, 102, 126, 128

B

believing optimists, 6, 122, 124, 125, 126-33, 135, 137, 138, 139, 141, 165, 167

C

CCD (Colony Collapse Disorder), 235
Colony Collapse Disorder (CCD), 235
common consent
  direct republic of, 164, 248, 249
  optimism of, 230, 231, 233, 235, 237, 239, 241, 243, 245, 247, 249, 251, 253, 255, 257
  practice of, 103, 175, 205
  principle of, 3, 173, 174, 177
  reaching, 61, 143
  republic of, 186, 202
  social intelligence of, 222, 257
  true republic of, 182, 201
common dissent, 68, 175, 187
community discussion, 150
community responsibility, 229, 255
community service, 175, 207, 208
Conceptual minds, 104, 105, 106, 107
consent
  local, 45, 46, 179, 182, 256
  unanimous, 143, 149, 167, 168, 183, 184, 190, 191, 234, 238, 240, 242, 248, 249, 250
conservatives, 45, 46, 227
control
  central, 46, 47, 82, 136, 155, 178, 179, 184, 185, 186, 198, 214, 219, 234, 251-52
  collective, 48
controlling authority, 47, 50, 68, 224

D

death, 17-18, 21-25, 29, 47, 53, 55, 108, 121, 123, 125, 134, 136, 139, 234, 236

fear of, 121, 122
deflection, 6, 39-42, 44, 51, 53, 89, 148
democracy, 9, 16, 45, 66, 68, 83, 84, 104, 156, 163, 194, 197, 202, 253, 258
denial, 23, 24, 25, 88-90, 95-96, 100, 101, 108, 109-10, 114, 115, 118, 121, 122, 134
denial of responsibility, 86, 93, 108, 109
discord, 7, 24, 160, 161, 162, 168, 202, 205, 210, 234
discourse, social, 39, 66-67, 148, 151, 210
dissent
 down, 40, 41, 49
 open, 8, 52, 93, 198, 225
dissenting voices, 40, 41, 64, 72, 81, 187, 191, 221, 242, 253
diversity, 45, 49, 50, 119-22
division, 71, 105, 166, 167-69, 171, 191, 202, 247, 256

E

enjambment, 6, 64, 65, 66, 67, 69, 78
enlightenment, 91, 93, 95, 117, 119, 120, 130, 242
enthusiasm, 6, 13, 96-97, 99, 174
ESOPs (employee Stock Ownership Plans), 184, 246

F

faith, 57, 66, 87, 95-96, 100, 101-3, 115, 118, 119, 121-23, 129, 142, 150, 164, 173
family, 4, 8, 37, 61, 69, 87, 109, 110, 116, 128, 129-30, 159, 165, 206, 233
fear, 19, 20-25, 53, 79, 90, 91, 94, 95-96, 101, 110, 111, 115, 117-19, 122, 144
 denial of, 6, 11, 12, 13, 15, 17, 19, 21, 23, 25, 27, 29, 114, 118, 121
 human, 16, 18, 104, 109

G

genuine optimism, qualities of, 201, 202, 205, 208
genuine optimists, 112-14, 120, 124-26, 128-30, 135-38, 151, 154, 162, 172-74, 187, 211-12, 232, 233, 237-38, 241
guilt, 46, 56, 59, 91, 111, 114, 116, 238

H

Hamlet, 18, 134, 135, 137
harmony, 160, 161, 162, 163, 164
hierarchies, 6, 80, 81-83
humanitarian aid, 193
humanity, 107, 139, 140, 204, 210, 224, 232, 238, 243, 249-51

I

ideal consent, optimism of, 212, 228
idolatry, political, 7, 180, 195, 197
Intimidating Optimist, 56, 57, 59, 61, 63, 65, 67, 69, 71, 73, 75, 77, 81, 82, 83
intimidating optimists, 59, 67, 68, 69, 80, 84, 105, 198, 217
intimidator optimists, 56, 58, 59, 60, 64, 85
intimidators, 54, 56, 61, 64, 65, 67-68, 70, 83, 84, 85, 86, 89, 96, 138, 148
irrationalism, 89, 93, 95, 99
irrational optimist, 6, 85-93, 95, 96, 97, 98-103, 105, 106, 107, 109, 111, 164, 167, 175, 198

L

linear minds, 9, 15, 16, 36, 37, 39, 46, 104, 108, 134, 135, 136, 137
linear thinking, 21, 23, 24, 43, 45, 107, 136, 193, 220, 254

M

majority rule, 66, 67, 185, 187, 191, 194, 196, 197, 235, 236, 239-42, 245, 246, 247, 248
management, 13, 212-13
motives, 38, 39, 42, 65, 68, 96, 100, 115, 116, 118, 120, 122, 148, 192-93, 256

N

natural opposition, 150, 167, 169, 170, 171, 175, 252

O

optimism
  irrational, 87, 88, 89, 94, 103
  real, 16, 32, 82, 84, 135
optimism of dissent, 209, 219, 257

optimist
  encouraging, 138, 140, 141, 142, 143, 145, 147, 148, 149, 150, 151,
    153, 154, 155, 156-57
  principled, 7, 138, 151, 157-59, 161, 163, 164, 165, 167, 169, 171,
    173, 175, 177, 233

P

Pack rats, political, 10, 11, 32
Pareto Principle, 197-98
personal responsibility, 7, 46, 179, 180-83, 191, 192-99, 201, 205, 219,
    220, 221, 225, 227, 230, 234-35
  powers of, 231, 237, 238, 240, 241
  twin powers of, 182, 185, 196, 200, 228
political control, 78, 112, 159, 178, 208, 210, 229, 250
political control model, 151
political optimists, 8-9, 15-17, 25, 26, 44, 117, 148, 149, 172, 173-75,
    185, 187, 198, 200, 203-4
popular democracy, 71, 186, 192, 195, 196, 199
positive thinking, 12, 57, 86, 101, 177
progress of freedom, 171

R

republic, 191, 194, 195
responsibility
  conservation of, 7, 173, 175, 230, 255, 256
  individual, 96, 98, 119, 162, 192, 194, 224, 240
  real, 23, 24
  taking, 23, 24, 45, 89, 100, 102, 121, 174, 175, 226
responsible action, 52, 57, 64, 85, 87-88, 91, 94, 95, 100, 101, 102, 103,
    109, 121, 122
responsible faith, 6, 68, 100, 113, 114, 115, 117, 119, 121, 122-23, 258
responsible meaning, 51, 52, 108, 109

S

scale, 169, 174, 175, 177, 182, 184-85, 215, 219, 220, 221, 228, 230,
    232, 233, 241
scale responsibility, 218, 219
scaling, 179, 182, 218, 219, 233, 234
self, faith in, 129
Shakespeare, 19, 53, 105, 107
small groups, 50, 52, 182, 183, 187, 196, 197, 198, 219, 220, 221, 222,

223, 226, 228
social contract, 7, 225-27
social justice, 7, 45, 84, 225-27, 250, 251
social responsibility, 45, 46, 71, 99, 100, 179, 205-13, 219, 220, 221,
    225, 226-31, 234, 235, 236
Socratic, 114, 150, 151, 166, 168, 169
staged optimists, 30-31, 33, 34, 35, 37, 38-45, 47, 49, 51, 53, 68, 96,
    127, 128, 130
state control, 151, 256
success, 8, 15, 18, 25, 29, 118, 121, 125, 141, 154, 176, 177, 189, 217,
    259
symbols, 21-22, 25, 215, 216

T

table, round, 168, 228, 231, 234, 239, 244
teacher, 103, 109, 121, 169, 176
traits of genuine optimists, 44
Tree of life, 7, 166-67, 170, 171
truth, faith in, 164

V

value dissent, 231
vision, 63, 64, 154, 155, 162, 163, 164, 167, 172, 177, 188, 189, 204-5,
    212-17, 221
visionary, 154, 205, 215-17, 219, 221

W

worlds, possible, 14, 112, 136, 178